LEADERS ON
LEADERSHIP

THE LEADING EDGE SERIES

LEADERS ON LEADERSHIP

JACK HAYFORD

C. PETER WAGNER

LEIGHTON FORD

J. ROBERT CLINTON

ELMER L. TOWNS

GENE GETZ

H.B. LONDON JR.

DOUG MURREN

RICHARD CLINTON

KENNETH GANGEL

TOM PHILLIPS

HANS FINZEL

WALLACE ERICKSON

JIM VAN YPEREN

WISDOM, ADVICE
AND ENCOURAGEMENT
ON THE ART OF
LEADING GOD'S PEOPLE

GEORGE BARNA

CONTRIBUTOR AND GENERAL EDITOR

Regal

From Gospel Light
Ventura, California, U.S.A.

PUBLISHED BY REGAL BOOKS
FROM GOSPEL LIGHT
VENTURA, CALIFORNIA, U.S.A.
PRINTED IN THE U.S.A.

Regal Books is a ministry of Gospel Light, a Christian publisher dedicated to serving the local church. We believe God's vision for Gospel Light is to provide church leaders with biblical, user-friendly materials that will help them evangelize, disciple and minister to children, youth and families.

It is our prayer that this Regal book will help you discover biblical truth for your own life and help you meet the needs of others. May God richly bless you.

For a free catalog of resources from Regal Books/Gospel Light, please call your Christian supplier or contact us at 1-800-4-GOSPEL *or* www.regalbooks.com.

Library of Congress Cataloging-in-Publication Data
Barna, George.
      Leaders on leadership / George Barna.
          p. cm.
      Includes bibliographical references.
      ISBN 0-8307-1862-1 (trade paper)
      1. Christian leadership. 2. Leadership—Religious aspects—Christianity. I. Title.
      BV652.1.B36 1997   96-52238
      253—dc21   CIP

  16 17 18 19 20 21 22 23 24 25 26 27 / 16 15 14 13 12 11 10 09 08 07

Rights for publishing this book in other languages are contracted by Gospel Light Worldwide, the international nonprofit ministry of Gospel Light. Gospel Light Worldwide also provides publishing and technical assistance to international publishers dedicated to producing Sunday School and Vacation Bible School curricula and books in the languages of the world. For additional information, visit www.gospellightworldwide.org; write to Gospel Light Worldwide, P.O. Box 3875, Ventura, CA 93006; or send an e-mail to info@gospellightworldwide.org.

CONTENTS

ACKNOWLEDGMENTS

Allow me to express my sincere gratitude to the people who have made this book possible.

Fifteen people have contributed chapters to this book. I believe that the cumulative efforts of this team have demonstrated the meaning of synergy. My thanks goes to each man who shares his knowledge, wisdom, experience, time and heart with us through his contribution to this book.

My friends at Regal Books have been supportive partners in ministry for many years. I count them as friends, colleagues in ministry and respected professionals in publishing. They deserve our appreciation for sharing the vision for this book and exhibiting great patience in waiting for it to come together.

My family probably makes the greatest sacrifice of all each time I create a book. My tendency is to devote myself fully to completing a book project, emerging from my room for meals and to tuck the girls in at night. My wife, Nancy, becomes the true leader of the family in my absence during such periods of literary hibernation. My daughters, Samantha and Corban, probably wonder what happens to Daddy during these periods.

Although I tried to keep our family time sacred during the days when I worked on this book, I know all three girls gave up some of the time and interaction that we cherish. Nancy, in particular, worked hard to protect my time and facilitate a reasonable level of uninterrupted concentration. In the equation of eternal value, I pray that the trade-offs made during this project are justifiable before God. I love Nancy, Samantha and Corban and pray that this book will help to raise up the kind of leaders who will enhance their lives.

In the final analysis, however, this is a vain exercise in chasing the wind if it does not produce that which brings greater glory and honor to God. Like every true Christian leader, my desire is that this effort is one that will enable many more people to know, love and serve Him with all their hearts, minds, souls and strength. For that is the chief end of humankind. It has been my privilege to know Him and to offer this project as a means of being a blessing to Him and His people.

PREFACE

When I was young, sports were the center of my world. I was especially interested in major-league baseball. Besides spending most of my waking hours playing baseball, watching baseball, thinking about baseball or talking about baseball, I also played a board game called "Challenge the Yankees." Back in the early sixties, the New York Yankees were a perennial powerhouse, always a good bet to win the American League pennant. The point of the game was to create a mythical all-star team that would play against the Yankees to see if the Bronx Bombers could be beaten.

I was born in New York City and was an avid Yankee fan during my formative years, so I spent hundreds and hundreds of hours playing that game. (An inveterate statistician, even by age six, I developed notebook after notebook of hand-tabulated statistics based on the pretend battles these fantasy teams waged. Sometimes it is easy to foresee what a child will do with his life when he is grown.) One of the most enjoyable aspects of the game was dreaming up a killer lineup of opposing players to take on the champs. (It was the modern-day equivalent of the "Dream Team" concept popularized by America's Olympic basketball teams.)

That was a couple of decades ago; but the same sense of joy and wonder was rekindled in creating this book about leadership. As the one who conceived the project, I began with a blank slate, starting with the topics I thought should be included in a handbook about leadership aspects. I then had the privilege of asking a veritable all-star team of leaders and leader developers to join me in creating this volume.

The substance of this book comes from a team of experts that is as awesome as any you can imagine assembling from within the Christian community. Much like an all-star team, each of the participants is "playing his own position"—that is, writing about the topic or subject he has studied, experienced, mastered and mentored about for years. It is exciting to provide for you the words of wisdom from men who have an intense passion for the topic about which they have written.

A long time ago, I discovered that there are two kinds of people: those who try to cut costs by accepting inferior products that will enable them to "get by," and those who pay more to get the best products that, hopefully, last longer and provide superior performance. This book reflects the latter strategy: get the best "talent" available and benefit from their experiences and insights. This lineup of talent parallels that of the 1961 Yankees:

- **Jack Hayford**, "the pastor's pastor," instructing us about the *character* of a leader;
- **Leighton Ford** describing what it takes to *develop* a person who has potential into a transforming leader;
- **Peter Wagner** focusing on the significance of *prayer* in leading people;
- **Bobby** and **Richard Clinton** outlining the *phases* and *cycles* that naturally occur in the life of a leader;
- **Gene Getz** exegeting *Scripture* to remind us of what God looks for in a true leader;
- **Elmer Towns** unraveling his years of experience to divulge how *change* and *innovation* define a leader;
- **Kenneth Gangel** providing an overview of *what leaders do* that make them leaders;
- **H. B. London Jr.** revealing how a leader can maintain the paradoxical balance between being *tough and tender*;
- **Doug Murren** sharing his experience and education regarding what it takes to be a *change agent*;
- **Tom Phillips** explaining the process of *building a team* that gets the job done;
- **Hans Finzel** awakening us to the importance of *organizational culture*, and how to develop a culture that facilitates influence;
- **Wally Erickson** giving insight into the process of preparing for and implementing *transition*—passing the torch;
- **Jim Van Yperen** guiding us through the methods of per-

ceiving, acknowledging and *resolving conflict*—the situations that often make or break the leader.

Now the confession. The only way I could get named to this team was to create it! So part of the fun for me in this process was appointing myself to the team—the advantage of owning the ball required to play the game.

I trust this book will open your mind and your heart to new truths, principles and possibilities you may not have considered. My horizons have been expanded by the wisdom and perspective so generously offered by this team of leader-servants.

One last baseball analogy. A fascinating aspect of the Yankees was that the team played well together even though they came from a variety of backgrounds and had diverse lifestyles. The team ranged from the hard-drinking, rowdy party boys such as Mickey Mantle, Jim Bouton and Whitey Ford to the clean-cut, Christ-honoring Bobby Richardson. Long before tolerance, pluralism and diversity were social fads, the Yankees were exemplifying a form of harmonious diversity.

Well, this book contains some diversity, too. If I were to write each of these chapters, I would have presented a different perspective from what some of the present authors have provided. Remember this: *Leadership is an art*, not a science. If you wish to lead God's people, you must fashion your own philosophy of leadership that is consistent with His principles of personal righteousness and biblical leadership, find your own voice and style as a leader and demonstrate internal consistency in how you lead. The ideas in this book are just that: *ideas* for your consideration. If you agree with everything in this book, you have not been reading carefully or reflectively. You *must* disagree with some of the content. That is healthy. Leaders are independent thinkers—strategic in their independence, but thoughtful enough to know when to agree and when to disagree with ideas to which they are exposed.

ABOUT THE TEAM

Before we get into it, let's take a moment to consider the influence agents contained in these pages. You may not be familiar with all the players, so let me provide a few words of introduction.

George Barna: As president of the Barna Research Group, Ltd. in Oxnard, California, he has served clients ranging from Fortune 500 companies to churches and parachurch ministries across the nation. He has written more than 20 books, including *The Frog in the Kettle, The Power of Vision, Turning Vision into Action,* and publishes a bimonthly newsletter, *The Barna Report.* A former pastor, and seminary and university professor, he is also executive director of the American Perspectives Institute.

Richard Clinton: Currently leading a new church focused on reaching young adults, Richard has taught courses about leadership at Fuller Seminary and is involved in leadership development activities around the world. He also helps to lead Barnabas Resources, a channel for the leadership materials developed with Bobby Clinton. He lives in Southern California.

J. Robert Clinton: Professor of Leadership at Fuller Seminary, Bobby has devoted his life to challenging, motivating and enabling leaders through teaching, modeling, mentoring and providing leadership resources. In addition to founding Barnabas Resources, he has written *The Making of a Leader* and has coauthored *Connecting.* He also serves as a consultant to many ministries regarding leadership development, and works with thousands of Christian leaders toward facilitating their gifts and abilities.

Wallace Erickson: After serving as senior pastor of four churches, Wally went to South Korea as field director for Compassion International. He later initiated field operations for Compassion in Central and South America, and became the ministry's president in 1975. During his term of leadership, Compassion's annual gross revenues went from $3 million to more than $50 million; the number of sponsored children jumped from 25,000 to more than 180,000. An Eagle Scout and member of several boards of directors, he lives in Phoenix.

Hans Finzel: Executive Director of CB International, the missionary sending and training agency of the Conservative Baptist Association, located in Wheaton, Illinois. After spending ten years in Vienna, training Eastern European pastors in biblical education, he returned to the United States to help lead CBI. Among his books is *The Top Ten Mistakes Leaders Make.*

Leighton Ford: Known to many as an evangelist, he spent many years working with the Billy Graham Evangelistic Association as an associate evangelist and vice president of that ministry. He is the Honorary Life Chairman of the Lausanne Committee for World Evangelization. He currently focuses upon developing young evangelistic leaders through his ministry's Arrow Leadership program. His ten books include *The Power of Story* and *Transforming Leadership*. He lives in Charlotte, North Carolina.

Kenneth Gangel: Vice president of Academic Affairs and academic dean at Dallas Theological Seminary, where he also is a professor of Christian education. He has served in pastoral ministry in several churches. Kenn has written more than 20 books, including *Leading and Feeding, Competent to Lead* and *Leadership for Church Education*. He has also written more than 1,000 articles for periodicals, and has authored the Personal Growth Bible Studies and the Accent on Bible Truth Study Series.

Gene Getz: A former Bible college and seminary professor, Gene is best known as a Bible teacher and church planter. He planted and is currently the senior pastor of Fellowship Bible Church North near Dallas. He has written more than 30 books, including *The Measure of a Man, A Biblical Theology of Material Possessions* and *Sharpening the Focus of the Church*. He directs the Center for Church Renewal and is also the featured presenter on the daily radio broadcast "Renewal."

Jack Hayford: Since arriving as senior pastor of The Church On The Way in Van Nuys, California, in 1969, the church has grown from 18 people to 8,000-plus members today. He can be heard on a daily radio broadcast and a weekly television broadcast, and serves as editorial advisor to *Ministries Today* magazine. He has written more than 20 books, including *Restoring Fallen Leaders* and *Worship His Majesty*, and was general editor of the *Spirit-Filled Life Bible*. A prolific song writer, he has composed nearly 500 songs and hymns, including "Majesty."

H. B. London Jr.: After pastoring for 31 years, including the 3,200-member Pasadena First Church of the Nazarene, H. B. is presently vice president of Ministry Outreach/Pastoral

Ministries for Focus on the Family. For 20 years he hosted a daily radio program; currently hosts a monthly audiotape series, "Pastor to Pastor"; and communicates each week with pastors and church leaders through "The Pastor's Weekly Briefing" fax-letter. His coauthored books include *The Heart of a Great Pastor* and *Pastors at Risk.*

Doug Murren: As senior pastor of Eastside Foursquare Church near Seattle for 15 years, Doug led that congregation to grow to more than 4,000 weekly participants, using innovative methods and programs. He is also responsible for planting more than 60 churches. Currently he is involved in radio ministry, evangelistic campaigns and worship development. He is a monthly columnist in several Christian magazines and has written several worship songs. His books include *The Baby Boomerang* and *Leadershift.*

Tom Phillips: Formerly a pastor and for many years the International Director of Counseling and Follow-Up for the Billy Graham Evangelistic Association. Tom now serves as the president of International Students, Inc., an evangelistic ministry to foreign students enrolled in American universities. He has written the book *Revival Signs* and is a frequent speaker at leadership conferences and a guest preacher in churches around the world. He lives in Colorado Springs.

Elmer Towns: Dean of the School of Religion at Liberty University in Lynchburg, Virginia, he has also served as president of a Bible college and a seminary professor. He cofounded Liberty University with Jerry Falwell. More than 2,000 articles of his have been published, and he has written more than 50 books. Among those books are *The Names of the Holy Spirit, 10 of Today's Most Innovative Churches* and *Evangelism and Church Growth: A Practical Encyclopedia.*

Jim Van Yperen: A marketing strategist and creative communications consultant, Jim has worked with a wide variety of churches, parachurch ministries and nonprofit organizations in the areas of vision development, strategic planning, communications, resource development and conflict resolution. Among his most recent efforts have been serving several churches as Intentional Interim Pastor.

C. Peter Wagner: Longtime professor of Church Growth at

Fuller Theological Seminary, Peter has been a leader in the global prayer movement, through the A.D. 2000 ministry, Global Harvest Ministries (over which he presides) and as one of the founders of the World Prayer Center in Colorado Springs. He has written and edited more than 30 books, including *Leading Your Church to Growth*, *Strategies for Church Growth* and *The Prayer Warrior Series*. A former missionary to Bolivia, he now resides in Colorado Springs.

WARNING: BAD LANGUAGE USED

One of the tragedies of communicating in the English language is its inability to smoothly convey certain concepts. An example of that limitation relates to the use of pronouns. Neither I nor the contributing authors believe that only one gender can lead people; we emphatically insist that both men and women may provide leadership in various situations and through different styles of leadership. Unfortunately, our language does not have an inclusive pronoun, one that means "he or she." Consequently, we are left with several inadequate choices in sentence construction. The constant use of "he or she" is structurally cumbersome and often undermines the flow of the content. To insert "their" is grammatically improper.

Thus, throughout the book I have utilized "he" as the primary pronoun related to the leader, solely to facilitate a smoother flow. Forgive me if you find this offensive or uncomfortable: I experienced considerable anguish in seeking a viable alternative. I was unsuccessful in that quest. I pray that it will not prevent you from absorbing the intended meaning of the words, which has nothing to do with gender and everything to do with leadership in the service of a God who loves all His people.

ONE

NOTHING IS MORE IMPORTANT THAN LEADERSHIP

GEORGE BARNA

I have spent the last fifteen years researching all facets of American life. Using nationwide surveys among representative samples of large numbers of Americans, I have studied people's values, beliefs, lifestyles, attitudes, opinions, relationships, aspirations and demographics. I have examined the expectations, goals, strategies, strengths and weaknesses of businesses, ranging from Fortune 500 corporations to one-man consulting enterprises. I have devoted thousands of hours to getting inside the world of Christian churches and parachurch ministries, exploring the belief systems, training practices, educational procedures, worship experiences, fund-raising adventures, community-building endeavors, organizational structures and staff procedures of those entities.

For context, I have spent many weeks overseas, gaining exposure to various cultures, perspectives and styles of activity. I have spent many hours praying for wisdom, discernment and insight. I have sought the counsel of others who are older, wiser, more experienced, brighter and better read than I am.

Some have said I am obsessive about having information before making a judgment. Granted, I like to do my homework before drawing a conclusion. The more important the conclusion, the more convinced I need to be that I have covered all the bases and have astutely analyzed and interpreted the data. Now, after fifteen years of diligent digging into the world around me, I have reached several conclusions regarding the future of the Christian Church in America.[1]

The central conclusion is that the American church is dying due to a lack of strong leadership. In this time of unprecedented opportunity and plentiful resources, the church is actually losing influence. The primary reason is the lack of leadership.

Nothing is more important than leadership.

Now, the theologically minded will immediately attack this statement and say that the most important thing is "holiness" or "righteousness" or "commitment to Christ" or "radical obedience to God." On a theological level, I wholeheartedly agree. Unfortunately, most Americans do not live on a theological level. The reality is that for any of us to become holy, righteous, committed to Christ or radically obedient to God, we need leaders who will do whatever it takes to facilitate such qualities in us sinful, selfish, misguided mortals.

God has provided us with leaders year after year to attempt to guide His people forward spiritually. If leaders were not required for us to progress in spiritual depth and Christian formation, He would not have sent them. He would not continue to send them. We do not serve a God who tinkers or fools around with our lives out of curiosity or idleness. He could, of course, but He doesn't. Therefore, leaders must be necessary.

If leaders were not necessary, He would not have included leadership among the spiritual gifts; the Bible would not provide so many incredible principles of leadership; and the Holy Spirit would not have inspired the authors of the Bible to incorporate so many examples of strong leadership. For instance, Jethro would not have rescued Moses from the burden of administration. Jesus would not have trained the apostles. Paul would not have mentored Timothy, and so on.

CHURCHES MUST BE LED BY LEADERS

I have witnessed pastor after pastor, extensively trained to exegete the Scriptures, and gifted to communicate God's truth, undeniably fail when it comes to guiding the Body of believers. They have failed in mobilizing the people for action, holding them accountable for their behavior, motivating them to sustain a spiritual revolution and attracting the resources necessary to do the work modeled by Christ.

I have discovered through our research that even in evangelism, we place our emphasis on preaching, when, in fact, the greatest evangelistic effect comes from relationships between believers and nonbelievers.[2] That is a matter of strategy—a leadership issue.

Most recently, I have discovered that the current exodus from the Church is partially attributable to the flight of the laity who possess leadership abilities, gifts and experience. These individuals, whom the Church so desperately needs, are leaving the Church because they can no longer stomach being part of an alleged movement that lacks strong, visionary leadership. These are people of capacity, people who can make things happen. I have watched with sorrow as they have tried to penetrate the culture of the Church and offer the benefit of their gifts. They have been unable to contribute because their churches are neither led by leaders nor by those who understand leadership. Yes, thousands of ministries possess good leadership, but in the larger scope of American ministry, those churches and parachurch ministries are the exception to the rule.

I have studied modern history to comprehend the dynamics of revolutions, people movements, societal systems and national fortunes. The result is the conviction that there have not been—and are not likely to be—any significant and successful movements, revolutions or other systems in which strong, visionary leaders were not at the forefront of those groups, leading the way for change in thought, word and deed.

I believe in preaching the Word of God, worshiping our Lord, confessing our sins before one another, celebrating the miraculous works of the Holy Spirit, returning at least a tenth of our resources to God's work, the power of prayer and salvation by grace alone through the atoning blood of Christ: I believe all this and much more. I also believe that in America today, fewer and fewer people will embrace these things unless the Church can raise up strong servant-leaders who will commit their lives to using their natural abilities, marketplace experiences, education, training and spiritual gifts to maximize their call to lead God's people forward.

I am *not* saying that leadership is more important on a spiritual or eternal level than our theology and spiritual commitments. I *am* saying that without effective, godly, Christ-honoring leadership, most people in America seem destined to a life in which Jesus Christ is little more than an expression uttered in times of frustration, or an ancient and personally irrelevant teacher of nice principles and antiquated religious practices.

That realization wounds me deep in my spirit. I want my non-Christian neighbors and my Christ-rejecting family members to know Him, love Him and serve Him as I do. I have come to discover, however, that unless we can develop effective leadership within the Church, we are not doing all we have been called by God to do to effectively and obediently serve Him.

That is why I believe nothing is more important for the future of the Christian Church in America than leadership.

LOOKING AT THE HEART OF LEADERS

In this book you will read about the heart, the mind and the practices of leaders. You will learn about ways of developing your potential if you have been called by God to lead. You will discover some of the trials that great men of God have experienced in their own journeys of leadership within the Church.

Most importantly, be affirmed in this: If God has called you to lead, let nothing stand in the way of the privilege you have to serve Him and to serve His people through applying the gift, the resources and the opportunity He has provided to you. You are among a special group of people who have been identified by Him for a challenging but rewarding task: leading His people to victory. In His eyes you are no better than anyone else by virtue of that call or that gift, but you are undeniably special as you pursue that calling. Keep Paul's words foremost in your mind: Run the race in such a way as to be holy and pleasing before God, so that one day you will hear those cherished words—"well done, good and faithful servant" (Matt. 25:21).

DEFINING LEADERSHIP

What exactly are we speaking of when we throw about this word "leadership"? Indeed, if we are going to spend the next 300-plus pages together considering this crucial subject, let's at least be clear about our focus.

Unfortunately, there is no universally accepted definition of leadership. Ask ten leadership analysts to define their discipline and they will probably provide a dozen or more definitions. How is this possible? Because leadership is not a science; it is an art. Art, by its very nature, virtually defies definition. Even the most brilliant team of people would see different elements and nuances in a Picasso or Rembrandt— as they do when asked to specify the essence of leadership.

Nevertheless, some very smart and experienced people have tendered some descriptions of leadership that merit our consideration. I have narrowed the list from more than 20 fascinating definitions down to the half dozen in the following list. They are listed in alphabetical order by author. I believe that these, for the most part, represent the heart of the variety that exists in recent popular literature about leadership.[3] Read them. Think critically about them. Then I will add my two cents.

Warren Bennis and Burt Nanus
"Leadership is...doing the right things."

James McGregor Burns
"Leadership is when persons with certain motives and purposes mobilize, in competition or conflict with others, institutional, political, psychological and other resources so as to arouse, engage and satisfy the motives of followers."

Vance Packard
"Leadership is getting others to want to do something that you are convinced should be done."

Tom Peters
"Leadership is mastering paradoxes and what they stand for."

J. Oswald Sanders
"Leadership is influence."

Garry Wills
"Leadership is mobilizing others toward a goal shared by the leader and followers."

Each of these briefs adds a nice touch to our comprehension of leadership. I believe, however, most of them are not completely adequate. Bennis and Nanus, for instance, have turned a nice phrase, but their definition is too broad. In the course of daily activity we do many things that are "right," but are not destined to draw followers to us—hence, they are not acts of leadership. For instance, when I put my daughters to bed at night and turn out the bedroom lights so they can sleep better, I have done the right thing, but this is not an act of leadership. Granted, leaders do the right thing, but they do much more than that, too.

Incidentally, as savory as it is, the definition by Tom Peters suffers from the same fault: it is simply too broad. The definition by Sanders fails the test for the same reason. His words suggest that any time you affect someone, you are exerting leadership. Again, consider an example to demonstrate my point. I attended a sociology class in which the professor persuaded me that household income is closely tied to educational achievement. His teaching has forever influenced my thinking. However, I am not his follower. He affected my thinking, but the mere act of informing me or even changing my notion of household economics is not to be confused with providing leadership.

The definition by Mr. Burns fails the test in that it is eminently possible to "arouse, engage and satisfy" my motives, yet I may not be a follower of the one who instigated such a personal response. The music of Billy Joel accomplishes the aforementioned trio of verbs, but I am not a follower of Mr. Joel. When I finish reading a novel by John Grisham, I have been aroused, engaged and satisfied, but he has not provided me with leadership, only diversion.

The Packard definition speaks more of manipulation than of true leadership. I believe people can be led without being hoodwinked into doing that which they ordinarily would disdain.

I am most comfortable with the definition offered by Garry Wills. Although it leaves out many of the specific attributes that must be involved in leading, his is a simple definition that does not preclude the elements I would incorporate (e.g., communicating vision, inspiring, directing and empowering people), yet does preclude the kinds of routine daily behaviors that the less careful definitions failed to screen out.

> ## "LEADERSHIP IS MOBILIZING OTHERS TOWARD A GOAL SHARED BY THE LEADER AND FOLLOWERS."
> **GARRY WILLS**

So the preferred definition—and one that will serve us well in this book—includes five key attributes. A leader is one who **mobilizes**; one whose focus is influencing **people**; a person who is **goal driven**; someone who has an orientation **in common** with those who rely upon him for leadership; and someone who has people willing to **follow** them.

THE CHRISTLIKE CHARACTER OF A LEADER

- a servant's heart
- honesty
- loyalty
- perseverance
- trustworthiness
- courage
- humility
- sensitivity
- teachability
- values driven
- optimistic

- even tempered
- joyful
- gentle
- consistent
- spiritual depth
- forgiving
- compassionate
- energetic
- faithful
- self-controlled

- loving
- wise
- discerning
- encouraging
- passionate
- fair
- patient
- kind
- merciful
- reliable

THE COMPETENCIES OF A CHRISTIAN LEADER

- effective communication
- identifying, articulating, casting vision
- motivating people
- coaching and developing people
- synthesizing information
- persuading people
- initiating strategic action
- engaging in strategic thinking
- resolving conflict
- developing resources
- delegating authority and responsibility
- reinforcing commitment
- celebrating successes
- decision making
- team building
- instigating evaluation

(continued➜)

> - creating a viable corporate culture
> - maintaining focus and priorities
> - upholding accountability
> - identifying opportunities for influence
> - relating everything back to God's plans and principles
> - modeling the spiritual disciplines
> - managing other key leaders

WHAT MAKES A LEADER A LEADER

In subsequent chapters you will discover in greater detail what leaders do. Give me a moment to identify what makes a leader someone we identify as a leader.

All the Christian leaders I have studied—in Scripture, in person, in history books—possess three distinct but related qualities. The combination of these qualities is what enables them to do what leaders do. Remove any one of these qualities, and the person would be a valued member of a group, but not a leader.

First, a Christian leader is **called by God**. He is called to servanthood, but a unique brand of servanthood. This is one who serves by leading. The vast majority of God's human creation are followers. Those who have been anointed by Him to lead are most valuable to the Body of believers—in functional terms—by their willingness to follow their call and do that which followers so desperately need.

Second, a Christian leader is a person of **Christlike character**. Because the central function of a leader is to enable people to know, love and serve God with their entire hearts, minds, souls and strength, the leader must himself possess the kind of personal attributes—characteristics of the heart, manifested through speech and behavior—that reflect the nature of our God.

Third, a Christian leader possesses **functional competencies** that allow him to perform tasks and guide people toward accomplishing the ends of God's servants. These are the abilities that receive prolific attention: inspiring people, directing their energy and resources, casting vision, building teams, celebrating victories, delegating authority, making decisions, developing strategy, accepting responsibility for outcomes and so on.

In Christian circles, we often think of this package of elements as "the spiritual gift of leadership." The gift involves receiving from God all of the necessary "stuff" to be a great leader for God's purposes. (A believer, incidentally, may be given that gift and choose not to use it—which represents a loss to both the Church and to the leader personally.)

The literature about leadership focuses almost exclusively on functional competencies. Those abilities are important, to be sure, but a leader who has great technical abilities and skills, but lacks God's call, is merely following his personal inclinations. One who lacks the personal attributes that model Christian principles will be an ineffective leader, unable to maintain followers. Of course, one who desires to lead people but does not have the competencies to get the job done will never build the track record necessary to attract followers.

> A CHRISTIAN LEADER IS SOMEONE WHO
> IS CALLED BY GOD TO LEAD; LEADS WITH
> AND THROUGH CHRISTLIKE CHARACTER;
> AND DEMONSTRATES THE FUNCTIONAL
> COMPETENCIES THAT PERMIT EFFECTIVE
> LEADERSHIP TO TAKE PLACE.

Notice, of course, that the first element necessary is God's call to lead. If you have not been chosen by Him to lead His people, it does not matter how wonderful your character or how well skilled you are for the task, you will never become a great Christian leader. You may lead, of course—our political system, educational institutions and corporations are packed with people who are leading in spite of not being called by God to be spiritual leaders. The difference is that we are not talking about leading God's people to higher profitability, or to greater efficiency, but to superior godliness and to spiritual truth. Further, we are not talking about meddling in human affairs to make incremental gains for worldly purposes, but about investing in people such that they recognize and maximize the ways God has called, gifted and seeks to refine them.

THE CALL TO LEAD

How do you know if you have been called by God to be a spiritual leader of people? This is another of those items, as is the definition of leadership, that generates substantial controversy. Let me throw my fuel on the fire by suggesting some elements to look for as you try to discern whether or not you have that calling.

The following eight signs indicate that you have likely been called to be a Christian leader. In my experience, those whom God has tapped to lead possess all eight of these traits.

Sensing the call. If you truly have been called, you will have a sense of divine selection for the task. You will have an inner conviction that, as amazing as it may seem, God wants you to lead people for Him and to Him. You have a real sense of God's Spirit confirming within you the fact that you are among the relative handful of people whom He wants to use to influence followers to live for a different purpose, in different ways. Josiah, the boy-king of Judah, revolutionized his father's kingdom, based upon the certainty within that he was raised up by God for that time, in that place, for that purpose. Sometimes, incidentally, a leader will fight or deny this call. The Holy Spirit is persistent, however, and as the evidence mounts, we cannot resist—unless we are comfortable engaging in willful disobedience.

Undeniable inclination. True leaders are naturally inclined to lead. Sometimes they assume a position of leadership reluctantly, as in the case of Timothy or Nehemiah. Other people, such as Bill Hybels, Pat Robertson or the apostle Paul, are eager to lead because they simply cannot help it: it is who they are. A person may either be drawn into leadership or have a natural enthusiasm and enjoyment for leadership. Ultimately, though, the urge or felt need to serve as a leader is undeniable.

Mind of a leader. A leader perceives and thinks differently from others. Leaders, by definition being people of vision, are focused on the future. They think about the long-term implications of today's opportunities and choices. They are mindful of the big picture, not satisfied with focusing only on the micro-level events of the day. They harbor a streak of idealism that is sometimes expressed in revolutionary thinking. They are excited by change and want to shape it. They work hard, but more importantly, they work smart: they are strategic thinkers.

Discernible influence. A true leader is one whose life bears the fruit of effective leadership. If you have been called by God, He will manifest that call by giving you tangible evidence of a special gift to lead. The accumulation of evidence that you have the ability to change the way individuals or groups think, speak and live is one of God's means of convicting you of the call and encouraging you to persist in spite of hardships.

The company of leaders. People are most comfortable around others who are like themselves. I have found that most leaders like to hang out with other leaders. There is a natural camaraderie among them. They speak the same language. They resonate with the same issues and struggles. Being in the presence of other leaders defines the comfort zone of one called to lead.

External encouragement. One way of knowing if you are called to be a leader of God's people is whether you receive affirmation from other people. Such affirmation is most noteworthy when it comes from other true leaders. Leaders know their own kind: they know what it takes and what it looks like. If they sense the call in you, listen to their words. Timothy received such exhortations from his mentor, Paul.

Internal strength. Surprisingly few people have the internal strength to stand up for what is right. We call this courage. God's leaders are always people of great courage. If you are comfortable taking reasonable risks, traversing uncharted territory, and do not flinch at the prospect of taking the heat for the decisions you have made, you may well have the inner stuff God provides to those who are called to lead His people. There is no better example of these qualities than Jesus Himself.

Loving it. Leading people is rarely a joyride. God's leaders—yes, even those called by Him—endure incredible amounts of heartache, controversy and animosity. The end product—the outcomes of leadership—is what makes it worthwhile for leaders. If you have received that warm, tingling feeling of victory, a sense that all the hardships were worth the outcome, you know what a called leader experiences in the trenches of the spiritual battle.

TRUE IDENTIFICATION

Before the adjoining chapters move us into the nuts and bolts of character and function, let's be clear about one more thing. Leading is different from managing, teaching, counseling and helping. I have seen many ministries undermined by people who serve in positions of leadership, but are incapable of leading.

The most common design is for a church to expect leadership from the senior pastor. He tries to provide it, but most pastors are, by their own reckoning, trained and gifted as teachers. They try to lead by using their teaching gifts and abilities. Teaching can influence people, but as I noted in reference to the Sanders definition of leadership, leading takes more than just influence.

Eventually—almost inevitably—the pastor-teacher fails as a leader, the church becomes disgruntled and havoc results. The same happens when people who are gifted as administrators (i.e., managers) or counselors or helpers attempt to provide primary leadership. They become frustrated, their people become frustrated, and the ministry is harmed. Because they are not leaders—and because they refuse to team up with people who can complement what they bring to the table by providing the necessary degree of leadership—they do not attract followers, and the entire ministry enterprise is undermined.[4]

Again, please do not take this out of context. I believe that people who have the teaching gift are greatly needed in the Church today. They need to use that gift to challenge, instruct, inspire and enlighten God's people. Teaching, however, is not synonymous with leading. Yes, some people who teach well are also gifted leaders. We cannot assume, though, that because a person has an advanced degree and aspires to the senior pastorate (or a similar position in a parachurch ministry) he is a leader.

The Bible is rather clear in demonstrating that leadership happens best when it occurs in the context of a gifted team of people supporting a leader who has been called and gifted by God for the purpose of leading. Moses had Joshua, Aaron and Hur. Jesus had Peter, James and John. Paul had Timothy, Tychicus, Luke and Titus. As Paul wrote in 1 Corinthians 12:7, each believer is given a gift to be used "for the common good" (NIV). As such, it is not meant to be exhaustive, but complementary. No gift (or individual possessing a gift) is better than any other.

As a leader, I need great teachers, administrators, counselors and people of other gifts to help me lead. As a teacher, I would want great leaders, managers and other helpers pulling their weight alongside of me. God created us to be in community; we need each other for the Body to function properly. Creating a framework in which such synergy can occur is one of the great challenges to a leader.

Make no mistake about it: management is not leadership. Teaching is not leadership. Counseling is not leadership. These other disciplines are no less valuable than leadership, but they must not be confused with or substituted for leadership.

MAKE HIM PROUD

The Church in America is in a crisis time. We have a crisis of faith: Tens of millions of Americans are searching for something to believe in. We have a crisis of spiritual depth: Millions of born-again believers have little or no spiritual depth. They are ineffective servants of God because they do not know what they believe, or how to use their faith to change their lives, much less the world. We also have a crisis of innovation: The Church seems afraid to invest in new modes of being the Church, breaking free from antiquated models and irrelevant traditions toward living the gospel in a twenty-first-century context.

Most of all, we have a crisis of Christian leadership. I contend that all these other crises would not be crises but simply opportunities for radical transformation—if we had true leaders leading the Church. Leaders would inspire widespread, genuine interest in Christianity through the strategies and structures they would facilitate for the faith to become real in people's lives. People would become intensely Christian, committed to knowing, living and sharing their faith if they had leaders who modeled that faith in action and who empowered them to do the same. The Church would infiltrate American society to its very core if we had leaders in charge, people who experiment, take risks and create new possibilities through casting God's vision. Leaders are the missing link to the health of the Church.

If He has called you to lead, lead. It is your privilege, your responsibility and your joy. Praise Him for the opportunity to experience the life He has given you to its fullest through the exercise of your call, your gift and your abilities. Lead God's people in such a way as to make Him proud.

Notes

1. To examine some of the data that have brought me to my conclusion, you may wish to explore *The Index of Leading Spiritual Indicators,* George Barna (Dallas: Word Publishing, 1996). That book provides a compilation of data related to the spiritual condition of our nation drawn from nationwide studies I have conducted from 1982 through 1996.

2. The data for this may be found in "Reaching Without Preaching," an article that appeared in our bimonthly newsletter, *The Barna Report,* in the March-

April 1996 issue. Additional data backing up this discovery is found in *Evangelism That Works*, George Barna (Ventura, Calif.: Regal Books, 1995); and "Casting the Net," a report published by the Barna Research Group, 2487 Ivory Way, Oxnard, CA 93030, in 1995.

3. To do these authors justice, let me identify the places from which their remarks are drawn. Bennis and Nanus wrote this famous phrase—which, in full, says "managers do things right...leaders do the right things"—in their terrifically readable book *Leaders*, published by HarperCollins in 1985. Burns wrote a book simply entitled *Leadership*, published in 1978. Packard wrote *The Pyramid Climbers* in 1962. The book by Tom Peters, *Thriving on Chaos*, was released in 1987 by Knopf. Sanders is the author of *Spiritual Leadership*, produced by Moody Press in 1976. A book often overlooked by students of leadership, but that has been particularly valuable to me, is Garry Wills's *Certain Trumpets: The Call of Leaders*, from Simon & Schuster (1994).

4. I have discussed this situation at greater length in various prior publications, including *Today's Pastors* (Ventura, Calif.: Regal Books, 1993).

TWO

WHAT LEADERS DO

KENNETH O. GANGEL

Churches, mission boards, colleges and seminaries, parachurch organizations and scores of other Christian organizations suffer in these crisis times because of misleadership. Not because of bad people. Not because of laziness. Not because of insufficient funding. Not because their contribution to the Kingdom is not needed. They suffer because of ineffective leadership.

Like its companions, this chapter takes a narrow focus clearly identified in its title. After thirty-seven years in academic life, however, I balk at moving any farther without sharing the definition of leadership that has shaped my thinking and the content of this chapter. I consider leadership to be the exercise of one's spiritual gifts under the call of God to serve a certain group of people in achieving the goals God has given them toward the end of glorifying Christ.

Now let's get specific. What do leaders do? I believe the tasks leaders fulfill come in six primary areas of activity: relating, organizing, achieving, thinking, envisioning and enduring.

LEADERS RELATE

I intend no order of priority in offering the units of this chapter; *all leaders do all these things all the time.* I must begin, though, with the behavior that distinguishes *leadership* from *management* or *administration.* The latter two terms, most will agree, are synonymous, describing how to handle resources and procedures within an organization in a manner designed to reach its goals.

Recently I crossed the border into Canada to teach at a graduate institution there for one week. For the better part of an hour, I was detained in the immigration shack, filling out paperwork required by NAFTA and paying the fee that would allow me to function for one week as a guest lecturer.

By God's grace, the line was short. The two clerks gave their attention to me and after endless computer entries, paperwork, stamping proper seals and approvals, I was on my way into the province of British Columbia. Those clerks were doing what they had been told and my presence seemed irrelevant to the task. They were "managing," but they were not "leading." They were guarding resources, laws, procedures and guidelines.

Most Christian leaders have such responsibilities *all the time*. Put another way, most Christian leaders are required to be good managers (administrators), as well. *But leadership focuses on human resources*. It has to do with the way we treat people, develop people and relate to people.

Visibility

Leaders cannot escape visibility. They stand up front at meetings (or sit on the platform at church services) and they meet with boards and executive committees regularly. We must also acknowledge a certain "image leadership" conveyed to large groups of people at a distance. Millions of people who have never met Billy Graham personally would not hesitate a moment to affirm his leadership. In the trenches, in the day-by-day functioning of a Christian organization, however, a leader achieves goals and accomplishes tasks through relationships.

John Maxwell talks about a developmental sequence for leadership potential based on a long-term process of working with a group of people who genuinely desire to grow. That model consists of five progressive components.

    I MODEL—I do it.
    I MENTOR—I do it and you watch me.
    I MONITOR—you do it and I watch you.
    I MOTIVATE—you do it.
    WE MULTIPLY—you do it and train someone else.[1]

Expectations

People joining Christian organizations often expect utopia. Believers, however, do not check their old natures at the door when signing contracts or taking positions in a "ministry." Constantly on guard for their own behavior and alert to the attacks of Satan in a secular organization, they let down that guard in a church or parachurch ministry. An unspoken, unseen motto seems to say, "Our people are Christians; therefore they will automatically be better workers, higher achievers and kind to everyone." Then the sin nature asserts itself, people act upset and hurt and we start wondering where the Bible went wrong in its explanations of *koinonia*.

Of course, this is a leadership problem. Leaders have a clear-cut responsibility to protect the absolute centrality of relationships within the organization. CEOs, vice presidents and managers explain what we can become through God's grace as we learn about the process of Christian leadership. Make no mistake about it—*leadership is learned behavior.*

Style

Part of effective leadership relates to understanding people. In a helpful article in the *Harvard Business Review*, Judy Rosener explains how women differ from men in how they lead. According to Rosener, women focus on "interactive leadership," encouraging participation, sharing power and information, enhancing the self-worth of others and energizing others.

Rosener calls on organizations to encourage leaders to lead in their own styles and strengths and says, "Then the newly recognized interactive leadership style can be valued and rewarded as highly as the command-and-control style has been for decades. By valuing a diversity of leadership styles, organizations will find the strength and flexibility to survive in a highly competitive, increasingly diverse economic environment."[2]

Some would call this "transactional leadership." Recent research argues that followers form leaders as much as leaders form followers and that transactional leadership (Rosener's "interactive") has the best chance of becoming "transformational."

In their famous book *Leaders: The Strategy for Taking Charge*, Warren Bennis and Burt Nanus view institutional vision as coming from the top down, shaped, articulated and communicated by the leader.[3] Then the followers appropriate it as their own. As significant and valuable as that book is, it allows little room for team leadership except at the level of middle management and below. Perhaps the bias of the book results naturally from the research methodology, "a study of 90 *individual* leaders."

Leaders relate to people. Though secular leadership literature talks a good bit about relationships and many of its concepts are of inestimable value, Christians ultimately come to the New Testament for the truth about this subject. Look at the church participants throughout the book of Acts. Watch them select a replacement for Judas in chapter one. See them in action electing leaders to serve the widows in chapter six. Carefully observe them sending out the first missionaries in chapter 13. The team model dominates everything. Amazing, isn't it? The more Christian leaders decentralize programs, deliberately and intentionally pushing authority down the ranks, the more biblically they function.

The Bible mandates that spiritual leaders possess and display the fruit of the Spirit (see Gal. 5:22) and a loving, caring, burden-bearing attitude toward others (see Phil. 2:1-4). Then their capacity for leadership relations is God given and Spirit empowered. What stands in the way is our inadequate knowledge of how to make it work in a realistic, carefully designed pattern down in the trenches on the front lines.

LEADERS ORGANIZE

In their most helpful book *Credibility*, James Kouzes and Barry Posner describe the differences they discovered in their survey of leaders between 1987 (for the publication of their outstanding book *The Leadership Challenge*) and 1993 (for the publication of *Credibility*). According to their report, *honesty, vision* and *inspiration* all ranked higher in 1993 than they did six years earlier. Of the factors that made the top-ten list in 1987, only *competence* and *intelligence* dropped in perceived importance.

May God deliver us in Christian organizations from managerial superiority without biblical compassion and Spirit-filled behavior. *May He also deliver us from thinking that Bible knowledge and spiritual lifestyle somehow substitute for competence in leading a Christian organization.*

Administration
The New Testament could not be more clear about the gift of adminis-

tration. The word *kubernesis* appears in Acts 27:11 and Revelation 18:17 where the context demands its literal meaning of "helmsman" or "shipmaster." In 1 Corinthians 12:28, though, Paul uses the word metaphorically to describe "organizers," people who carry out administrative leadership in the Church.

> You are Christ's body–that's who you are! You must never forget this. Only as you accept your part of that body does your "part" mean anything. You're familiar with some of the parts that God has formed in his church, which is his "body": apostles, prophets, teachers, miracle workers, healers, helpers, organizers, those who pray in tongues (1 Cor. 12:27-28, *The Message*).

Sadly, the lack of interest in organizing as a core leadership behavior betrays some carelessness among Christian leaders in this postmodern era. I chose to discuss the relational component of leadership first because leaders must communicate with people. If I were creating a stair-step chart of what leaders do, however, organizing would be my first step, for without it one can only expect to stumble on the rest. In the following quote from Peter Drucker, simply substitute the word "organizing" for "management" and you have the essence of the idea.

> Pastors need management [organizing] not because they should manage, but because it is the only way to get the time, thought, and freedom for the real job. It is their tool for making sure all the other things that have to be done get done and yet do not eat them alive in the process.
> Management is not the answer to all the problems of ministry. Yet management is a tool all of you need. You must learn to get the other things done by managing yourself, your parish, and your job. You must learn to set objectives for yourself and for the various major tasks you think you should be doing. That's the hardest thing to do: to think through what you are to accomplish.[4]

Job Descriptions

Because the "organizing" menu is so vast, let's punch up one basic dimension for closer observation: creating job descriptions. Job control is essential to any adequate leadership, but job control will never be yours until you know what the job is. As you read these words, someone somewhere faces evaluation according to a set of imaginary perceptions rather than on the basis of clearly defined tasks and achievable objectives. In short, he has been working without a job description and stands organizationally defenseless before any superiors who "feel" or "think" that person's leadership performance has been inadequate.

Of course, job descriptions can be misused. People who should know better and whose boundaries of innovative leadership should reflect greater maturity will say on occasion, "I won't do that; it's not in my job description." That no more argues against adequate job descriptions than somebody's divorce papers condemn marriage and family life.

Robert Welch warns, "In a recent informal survey of ministry personnel in a major evangelical denomination, nearly a third of the pastors and more than half of the non-pastoring staff began their positions without job descriptions. In another informal survey, nearly two-thirds of support personnel either had no written job description or felt the ones they had didn't accurately describe what they were doing."[5]

Welch goes on to give us a clear-cut definition:

> A job description is a written instrument that portrays in a systematic, concise, and logical fashion what is expected of an individual who fills a certain position. Job descriptions should be created for all ministry positions: for professional ministry staff, support staff, even unpaid, designated lay leadership positions. A job description should contain five elements: (1) a title, (2) a statement of principal function, (3) a description of how the person fits into the organization, (4) a statement of qualifications for the position, and (5) a listing of task duties.[6]

Organizational Charts

Developing and using an organizational chart is every bit as important as a job description. An accurate chart offers two pieces of information without which no leader can adequately function: *lines of authority and span of control*. I have talked about these at great length in *Feeding and Leading* and more recently in *Team Leadership for Christian Ministry*, so there is no need to expand them here.[7] Suffice it to say, organization depends upon one's ability to know where he serves in the organization, where and how others function and how the myriad interrelationships come together to create that leadership team.

LEADERS ACHIEVE

Larry Bird, the basketball great, once explained why he was so dependable in the clutch. He told reporters that lots of players want to be the hero and take the last shot when the score is tied or the team is ahead. Only a handful, however, want the ball when their team is down a point; that's the mark of a champion.

If we can distinguish leaders from managers by their commitments to people relationships (and we can), they are further marked by their focus on goal achievement rather than time spent in the office. Someone once suggested that leaders face four tasks: to fulfill the goals of the organization, to provide for innovation, to involve other people and to sustain personnel morale. In my view, if the first of those goes awry, the rest do not matter.

Specification

We hardly have space here to make fine-line distinctions between *mission, goals, objectives* and *action steps*. Most readers will recognize that those terms represent a precise and definable increasing of specificity. What must all leaders know about objectives? It is useful to know what objectives do for us. They make possible the concentration of resources and efforts. To do that, they must be capable of conversion into specific targets and assignments. The objectives of an organization, at least in general, must be known and understood by all employees, especially the members of the leadership team. People in our organizations must "claim" objectives, recognize them as their own and work at them with collective enthusiasm.

All this, of course, stems from the mission statement—our reason for being—the boundaries that wrap the ministry like an attractive Christmas present.

Small Wins

Remember, too, that we manage the pace of organizational change and goal achievement by what Thomas Gilmore calls "small wins and large gains."[8] Picture a pastor who agrees to serve a struggling rural church. Attendance slides on a slow decline, offerings do not meet the budget, few lay leaders want training and it looks as though some minor miracles may be necessary. Not so. Setting clear-cut goals can create a scenario for small wins—that is, implemented outcomes of moderate importance that give hope to supporters, attract people's attention and lay a groundwork of encouragement that future good things may be on the way!

Unachieved Goals

Of crucial importance here is the willingness not to be deterred or discouraged by a few unachieved goals. A leader who has not followed the process of goal setting may set a list of ten goals for his organization during a given year. Let's assume only seven are achieved satisfactorily. Actually, that is an outstanding record, well above any batting average or field goal shooting percentage a professional athlete might achieve. Two things surface here: First, those seven achieved goals probably represent several more than one would achieve without the process described here. Second, the remaining three, if they have been prioritized correctly, may either be dropped (because they are no longer necessary), restructured or moved higher in the priority list for the next year.

All Christian leaders—young and old, veterans and rookies, serving huge organizations or tiny ministries—should be able to say to their superiors, "Don't judge me by the time I spend in my office; judge the effectiveness of my leadership by how well this leadership team achieves the goals we have mutually agreed upon month by month, year by year and over the long haul."

LEADERS THINK

Surely one major flaw connected with much Christian leadership in our day is that too many leaders have too little time to think. It seems typical of autocratic leaders to make "knee-jerk" decisions based on "gut-level" feelings about how certain things should be done. Sometimes these decisions result from past experience with similar problems, and other times they are the result of watching other leaders function in a similar way. To the uninitiated, such quick decision making looks like strong leadership: the ability to respond immediately by telling us "what we should do."

More likely, such behavior results from a lack of training in decision-making process, problem-solving techniques and the general discipline of thinking. To be sure, not every decision a leader faces allows for full problem-solving process. But many do, and once decisions have been submitted to that kind of procedure, future decisions will be facilitated and improved. Better thinking comes through intelligent practice. Good leaders cultivate the skills of observation, fact gathering, reflection, reasoning and judgment to arrive at a solution that advances the cause of the organizations they serve.

In many ways, to think is to learn. We all have mental pockets in which debris of old, unresolved problems lies rotting by the stream of thought. Serious mental exercise of decision making can clean out those pockets and make room for fresh and creative ideas.

Ineffective Decision Making

What causes ineffective decision making? I have already hinted at the inability to handle the processes involved, but at least four other things jump to the front of the line here.

1. *Lack of clear-cut objectives.* Leaders without clear-cut objectives for their own ministries or who serve organizations without clear-cut objectives based on the mission will struggle to make wise decisions.

2. *Insecurity of position or authority.* If you are not sure you have the jurisdiction to make the decision, that doubt will often obscure the decision itself. For example, a college president must know exactly what can be decided by him and his cabinet and what has to go to the board of trustees. Make no mistake about it, that delineation process works both ways. He must not allow the board to make decisions that govern administrative details any more than he can allow the cabinet to set policy for the institution.

3. *Lack of information.* Critical thinking/decision making is a great deal like research. One goes through procedures, and the old adage certainly applies—"garbage in, garbage out." A major decision affecting the future of your organization could work against you very quickly if you lack a crucial piece of information.

4.   *Fear.* Good decisions are often hindered by fear: fear of
change, fear of making the wrong decision, fear of the
consequences that might ensue, maybe even a fear of
the decision-making process itself. This alone has para-
lyzed many and driven them out of ministry leadership
positions. In an information age that both complicates
and facilitates critical thinking and decision making, the
late twentieth-century leader throws out old boundaries
and approaches problems, programs and organizations
with new paradigms, constantly asking questions that
penetrate the root of the problem and give impetus for
truly unique solutions.

Critical Thinking

How do we define this method of approaching the world and its problems afresh? As Stephen Brookfield notes, "Central to critical thinking
is the capacity to imagine and explore alternatives to existing ways of
thinking and living....Critical thinkers are continually exploring new
ways of thinking about aspects of their lives." He expands on the definition: "Critical thinking is complex and frequently perplexing, since
it requires the suspension of belief and the jettisoning of assumptions
previously accepted without question."[9]

Brookfield's definition leads to an interesting line of thought for
Christians who ground the security of their faith in the inerrancy of
Scripture. How far can we go in mental processes without moving into
the shifting sand of relativism? The answer, of course, is that everything
we do in leadership is tempered by our loyalty to Scripture. Christian
leaders hold a mandate to bring people to maturity, to genuine adulthood, to a place where they are no longer tossed about nor indecisive
about the foundations of their faith (see Eph. 4). We must ask what
Christian maturity looks like, and how and where do critical thinking
skills fit into that maturity. Only mature leaders make mature decisions.

Cooperation

Team decision making or "partnering" implies an intense willingness
to dispense with authoritarian rule so the team can function freely.
Cooperation, not competition, becomes the key word. A cooperative
environment designs ways the whole Body can move forward, not
ways one part can shine at the expense of another. Wise leaders "do

not listen to the advice of others and then make their own decisions." Such outdated "process" may adequately describe Eisenhower determining when to invade Normandy, but it has no place in a Christian leadership team.

V. A. Howard and J. H. Barton describe a good meeting as one in which the participants engage effectively in rational discussion, "doing good thinking together with others and helping them do good thinking with each other, engaging in a process of inquiry, presenting and defending and challenging your own opinions and those of others through a dialogue of discovery."[10]

Good critical thinking/decision-making meetings take place when participants understand the purpose of the meeting, enjoy freedom to express their viewpoints without reprisal, do a reasonable amount of preparation for the meeting and willingly abide by the team's conclusions.

LEADERS ENVISION

Some recent management literature, including from the pens of those who should know better, has commonly confused mission and vision. Mission is that simple and terse statement that identifies why an organization exists and what it expects to do on earth. *Vision then describes how that organization will design its future to achieve its mission.* Vision grows out of mission, but they are hardly identical concepts. In one important way, however, vision and mission are alike—they are both unique to the individual organization.

Uniqueness
To be sure, mission statements sound a great deal more generic than vision descriptions, but the mission and vision of any organization dare not be based on what other churches or similar organizations have achieved. Herein, in my opinion, lies the weakness of much ministry strategy. Describing successes and categorizing their similarities tends to press us all into seeking to be like somebody else rather than asking in simple purity and expectation, "Why has God raised up this ministry in this place at this time and what does He want from us?"

Focus
Vision brings many good things to an organization, not the least of

which is encouragement and the anticipation that "we are going some-where." Even more than encouragement, though, perhaps is focus. Too many leaders (and hence too many ministry organizations) remain unfocused. They carry out their day-by-day activities in something of a survival mode rather than lifting their eyes to the whitened fields. As Barna put it, "For the vision to be effective...it must be simple enough to be remembered and specific enough to give direction."[11]

Obviously, envisioning requires thinking time in even greater amounts than does decision making. One of the great virtues of dele-gation is to free up leaders to think about the future. My friend Leith Anderson reminds us:

> It takes years to reach a point of both trust and time, but the pastor who works toward that sweet spot begins to spend more time on future possibilities than on current programs. Time is found to dream about such activities as starting a daughter church, providing a Saturday-night service, expand-ing staff, or spearheading new missions projects. At a mature stage of a pastorate, these are fitting tasks, but they typically remain unreachable in a pastor's early days at a church. Pastors need to look out the window, but in the early years particularly, they are better off preparing for that responsibili-ty by spending plenty of time at the desk.[12]

So both reputation and credibility loom essential for the visionary. Anderson is right: Young, immature, inexperienced leaders need to spend time at the desk, perhaps quietly anticipating what can later be developed with others as a collective ministry vision for the future of that work.

LEADERS ENDURE

Surveying 2,218 pastors, and receiving a response from 758, John LaRue describes a "Profile of Today's Pastor: Transitions."[13] He dis-covered a typical tenure of 4.9 years for a pastor of forty-six (the mean age in the study). In ministry for eighteen years, he has changed churches three times and has only neared the midterm of his career. In fact, claims LaRue, since the mid-1970s, tenure has declined from an average of seven years per church to less than five.

Why do they leave? LaRue's respondents offer four reasons:

1.   The pastor acquired a new vision or sensed a call to a new place (responsible for 37 percent of the departures);
2.   The pastor achieved a sense of resolution: the ministry was complete or could go no farther under his leadership (26 percent);
3.   The pastor was given an opportunity to do something greater elsewhere (i.e., occupational advancement or promotion [23 percent]);
4.   Unresolved or ongoing tension or trouble within a church or ministry (18 percent).

For all Christian leaders, the ability to endure is crucial.

Holding On to the Ball
To what familiar metaphor can we compare leadership longevity? Permit me a parochial choice whose cultural and geographical boundaries the reader will immediately see. In the early '90s, the Dallas Cowboys consistently fielded a losing football team. One year they posted a 3–13 record and allowed their rookie quarterback, Troy Aikman, to be battered all season long. Just a few years later they won two Super Bowls. What made the difference? Some will argue the coaching of Jimmy Johnson. Others will suggest the acquisition of running back Emmitt Smith or wide receiver Michael Irvin.

Football experts, however, have long agreed that Troy Aikman exhibits a quality of leadership uncommon even among professional quarterbacks—the ability to stay in the pocket as long as possible. He cannot outthrow Dan Marino, and he certainly cannot outrun Steve Young. But knowing he will be bruised and battered, he advances the team by holding on to the ball until the last possible second.

Too often Christian leaders throw the ball too soon. Maybe they will throw it to spare themselves a nasty hit or to avoid losing yardage. Perhaps they fumble or, in a panic, throw an interception that results in a touchdown. But I stand in danger of pushing the metaphor too far. The point is obvious: Effective leaders stay in a ministry as long as necessary to get the job done. The ability to plan, to make decisions and to envision a ministry's future requires a willingness to see yourself in the scenario for a long time. If followers see you as "interim," short-term, or even a career climber who considers a present post only temporary, they will defer their interest in following and shy away from involvement in team leadership.

Failure Breeds Success

Take a look around. The effective corporations as well as the effective churches in North America are usually headed by people who have "stayed with the stuff" over the long haul. They have seen good times and they have seen bad. They have faced both and many have had to deal with downsizing. They have all learned that the old axiom "success breeds success" is inadequate. Under the right conditions, and with the right kind of leadership, failure, too, may breed success. What initially appears to be a failure experience may simply be the means through which a person develops maturity, credibility and the right to be called "leader."

LEADERS MAKE GOOD THINGS HAPPEN

What do leaders do? They do precisely what God has called them to do, and they recognize that the calling to lead springs from His grace. Some have learned through years of training and mentoring by a godly example. Others have learned from watching failure. General Norman Schwarzkopf once said:

> Some of the best leadership lessons I learned as a young officer were from terrible officers. I mean, absolutely morally bankrupt officers who had no redeeming qualities. People followed them out of sheer wonder for what they would do next. You learn far more from negative leadership than from positive leadership. Because you learn how not to do it. And, therefore, you learn how to do it.[14]

What do leaders do? They relate, organize, achieve, think, envision and endure. Perhaps most important, though, is that they do none of these things alone. The ancient concept of the leader as Mosaic prophet or monarchical ruler speaking alone with God and then coming down to tell ordinary people what He said will not stand up to the powerful thrust of team leadership in the New Testament. The apostle Paul and his missionary team involved themselves in the lives of people around the Mediterranean world, and churches were born or grew and developed. The apostle takes pain in his letters to explain that he did not move into town as a thunderous and dynamic personality, but boasted in only two qualities he could truly call his own: weakness and suffering (see 2 Cor. 11:16—12:10).

Modern transactional leaders develop ministry teams by "joining" the troops as servants. The joiner then becomes the affirming leader because affirmation is a servant's way of securing the importance of other people and their ministries. Forget how *you* played. Did the team win?

Ken Callahan included a wonderful sentence in an article about leadership. "All the while the manager is preoccupied with policies, the boss with power, the enabler with process, and the charismatic inspirer with the next apocalyptic event, the leader is 'preoccupied' with helping the group toward fulfillment of the foundational life searches."[15]

Notes
1. John C. Maxwell, "Practices of Leadership in the Context of Pastoral Leadership," *Christian Education Journal* (Autumn 1991): 57.
2. Judy B. Rosener, "Ways Women Lead," *Harvard Business Review* (November/December 1990): 125.
3. Warren Bennis and Bert Nanus, *Leaders* (New York: HarperCollins Publishers, 1985).
4. Peter F. Drucker, "Time Management," *Leadership Handbooks of Practical Theology*, Vol. III, James D. Berkley, ed. (Grand Rapids: Baker Books, 1994), p. 80.
5. Robert H. Welch, "Job Descriptions That Work," *Your Church* (May/June 1995): 46.
6. Ibid.: 48.
7. Kenneth O. Gangel, *Feeding and Leading* (Wheaton, Ill.: Victor Books, 1989).
8. Thomas N. Gilmore, *Making a Leadership Change* (San Francisco: Jossey Bass, 1988), p. 243.
9. Stephen D. Brookfield, *Developing Critical Thinkers* (San Francisco: Jossey Bass, 1987), pp. 8-10.
10. V. A. Howard, and J. H. Barton, *Thinking Together: Making Meetings Work* (New York: William Morrow and Company, Inc., 1992), p. 13.
11. George Barna, *The Power of Vision* (Ventura, Calif.: Regal Books, 1992), p. 19.
12. Leith Anderson, "Setting the Vision," *Leadership Handbooks of Practical Theology*, Vol. III, James D. Berkley, ed. (Grand Rapids: Baker Books, 1994), p. 158.

13. John C. LaRue Jr., "Profile of Today's Pastor: Transitions," *Your Church* (May/June 1995): 56.
14. Norman Schwarzkopf, "Points to Ponder," *Reader's Digest* (May 1993): 211.
15. Kennon Callahan, "The Key to Effective Church Leadership: Moving from Professional Ministry to Missionary Pastor," *Pulpit Digest* (March/April 1990): 83.

THREE

THE VISION THING

GEORGE BARNA

Let's get one thing straight from the start. If you want to be a leader, vision is not an option; it is part of the standard equipment of a real leader. By definition, a leader has vision: What else would a leader lead people toward, if not to fulfill that vision? Understand that to be a *Christian* leader, the vision toward which you lead people must not be a vision of your own making, but a vision God gives to you.

So what is vision? It is a clear mental portrait of a preferable future, communicated by God to His chosen servant-leaders, based upon an accurate understanding of God, self and circumstances. Granted, definitions are dry as sawdust—this one is no exception—but they are vitally important for the purposes of clarification, insight and for framing one's understanding. Take a moment to ponder each of the characteristics embedded in this definition.

VISION IS A CLEAR MENTAL PORTRAIT OF THE FUTURE

Vision is "clear," suggesting that the leader who possesses such vision knows exactly what he wants to achieve and what the end product will look like. This clarity permits a leader to be confident and decisive.

Vision comes in the form of a "mental portrait," indicating this is a picture that exists in the mind's eye of the leader. To some, the very concept of vision may seem mystical and "out there," but to those who possess it, vision is as tangible as your tax bill. Vision focuses on what does not yet exist, but should—a "preferable future."

The term "preferable" is key, because it mandates change. Vision is about creating something new, not in disdain for the past, but built upon the foundation of the past and the present, emerging with a reality that is better than that which is currently available. When fully enacted, vision brings us closer to our ideals.

VISION COMES FROM GOD

True vision comes from God. When we personally conjure up a vision of the future, it is fallible, flawed and limited; God's vision is perfect in every way. Only He knows what is best for us; only He cares enough about us to call leaders to the fore and instill His vision within them, for the benefit of all. Notice that the vision originates with God, and He presents it to "chosen" people. In other words, His vision is a gift, and it is given when He is ready to give it, to whom He wishes to give it. His choice of recipients are "servant-leaders": those He has called to be leaders of people, but who maintain hearts and demeanors of servants.

Servant-leaders are not doormats, but those who serve constituencies by providing godly, effective leadership. Their leadership is their service, in the same way auto mechanics may serve by repairing the broken down cars of single mothers.

The definition also informs us that the vision God provides will always be consistent with the context of the leader, hence its relationship to "an accurate understanding of God, self and circumstances."

Vision, then, is a view of the kind of world God wants us to live within, a world He can create through us if all those He has called as leaders would lead according to the guidance provided by His Spirit. Once you grasp the vision, you will never be the same. If you are a true leader and truly Christian, the world will never be the same either, because you will be totally sold out to that perspective of what the world could, should and will be as a result of that vision.

Leaders, contrary to popular thought, are actually a rare commodity in America. My research suggests that fewer than one out of every five people is a leader by nature; perhaps one out of ten adults is a leader by calling and spiritual gifting. Most people want to be led, but they will not voluntarily follow someone they deem unworthy of their support. In essence, they will refuse to place their trust and future in the hands of an alleged leader who does not possess vision. After all, vision is a clear and compelling picture of a better tomorrow that inspires people to change, to get involved, to care and to do things that contribute to the common good. Who wouldn't want to be part of such a movement of humanity and Spirit? Or, to look at it from the other side of the coin, who wants to be devoted to a leader who is pursuing something less than the ideal?

Solomon gave us a precise understanding of the importance of vision: "Where there is no vision, the people perish" (Prov. 29:18, *KJV*). The *NIV* rendering is even more telling: "Where there is no revelation, the people cast off restraint." In other words, unless the people have a definite sense of purpose, direction and parameters, they live according to their own choices and will—much to their own detriment.

LESSONS FROM POLITICS

The centrality of vision permeates leadership in every dimension of life, whether we discuss leadership within the family, within the Church, within public education or any other field. Because national politics touches each of our lives and because the media applies such detailed and unceasing scrutiny to those involved in the political arena, the world of politics provides the most accessible window through which we regularly see the importance of vision in leadership.

In seeking reelection in 1992, George Bush ridiculed the media's constant quizzing about his vision for the nation's future, sarcastically noting he'd had enough harping about "the vision thing." He was defeated by an unknown challenger who appeared to provide such a vision—although it was at odds with the ideological preferences of the nation. People are attracted to those who have vision—even when that vision is not entirely consistent with their own inclinations.

The importance of vision is underscored by the change in Bill Clinton's own fortunes as the nation's political leader. As I write this chapter, we are entering the final few weeks of the 1996 presidential election. Clinton has had a huge lead over his Republican challenger, Bob Dole, ever since Dole became his party's nominee.

By all measures, Clinton should be an overwhelming favorite. During his first term in office, the national deficit has been reduced by 60 percent. Interest rates are low. Capital spending and economic investment are up. Unemployment is low, thanks to the creation of 10 million new jobs since Clinton entered the White House. The "misery index"—a joint measure of inflation and unemployment—is at its lowest level in three decades. A majority of Americans say the president has done a good job with the economy. Forty-three percent say they are better off today than when he took office. Although Mr. Clinton's personal life and morals have been widely chastised, our surveys suggest that his morality is less important to the average voter than what the president will do for household finances and crime reduction: Remember, he "feels our pain."

Yet, regardless of the election's outcome, Americans are suffering from acute political malaise. Mr. Clinton is but one of many political leaders holding office today who have helped to create such universal disenchantment. Using the president as a means of explaining this sense of despair, Mortimer Zuckerman of *U.S. News & World Report* offered some insight.

> The reason is that he [Clinton] does not seem to project a positive vision of where he wants to lead the country. He has defined himself more by what he is against than by what he is for. His wanderings from one side of the political spectrum to the other have created a sense of uncertainty about who he is and what he stands for.[1]

That analysis contains several insights: the need to constantly convey vision to followers; the necessity of providing a vision that relates to positive change; the need to remain ideologically (or, theologically) consistent; the importance of using vision to facilitate confidence among followers; the role of vision in defining what you, as a leader, represent.

Being a Real Leader

Perhaps the most significant insight this critique brings to mind is this: The only justifiable reason to accept the privilege and responsibility of leadership is to help people accomplish the fruition of a vision from God. Those who wish to lead because they are gifted, because they are experienced, because they enjoy the power, because they have innovative ideas, because they love the attention, because they have been groomed for such service—these are dangerous people. Their motivations are inappropriate. Because a leader is a servant, and the leader's primary task is to provide the guidance people need to become more Christlike, those who seek positions of leadership for reasons other than fulfilling a God-given vision are not truly leaders.

Look again at Zuckerman's analysis of Mr. Clinton. At the risk of offending some readers—and I do not intend to do so—we must ask ourselves how many people in positions of ministry leadership the Zuckerman critique fits. We all know ministry figures who are superb at bemoaning the deterioration of cultural mores and personal values, the collapse of the family or the decline of biblical knowledge and lifestyles.

How many of these figures offer practical and intelligent alternative courses of action for us to follow? How many of them place those concerns into the "big picture" of today's conditions and opportunities, inspiring us to rise above mediocrity and comfort to do that which is morally and ethically right, regardless of the cost? How many challenge us to evaluate our potential responses to circumstances by considering God's Word? How many refuse to play the victim of changing realities, but instead reflect a comfort about taking us to a better reality, no matter how difficult some of the steps toward that superior outcome might be?

Real leaders do more than simply point out problems; they articulate and involve people in real solutions. Those solutions, however, are indefensible unless they are based on true vision. Solutions that are not based on vision tend to be remedial in nature, akin to placing a bandage on a gunshot wound. True vision leads to holistic, consistent and transforming action. It results in neither temporary nor disjointed solutions. Vision brings victory.

The presence of vision is one of the most accurate means of determining if a person is a leader or merely filling a position of leadership. The equation is quite simple: no vision = no leadership. Many people dress like leaders, speak like leaders and have titles that suggest they are leaders. There is one inerrant measure of Christian leadership, however: does the person possess God's vision for the people he has been called to lead. Vision is a necessary (though by itself incomplete) requirement for authentic leadership.

GOD'S TRACK RECORD

As I was doing research for my book *Turning Vision into Action*, I had the opportunity to dissect the biblical accounts of the leadership provided by several dozen people. In examining the lives of people such as Joshua, Josiah, Nehemiah, Peter, Paul and Jesus, it became abundantly clear that each of them had a clear sense of vision they had gained from God. If you evaluate their stories closely, it is possible to describe the unique vision God gave to each of them.[2]

My exploration into the world of biblical visionaries also uncovered eighteen lessons about vision.[3] This is not the place to reiterate those insights, except to suggest that if you are called by God to be a leader, an incredible track record has been accumulated for us by our predecessors in the Kingdom. By carefully studying how they identified the vision and how it affected their leadership, you can grow in some profound ways. One of the hallmarks of God is that when He calls someone to lead people, He always provides that person with all the tools and resources necessary to be a great leader. Vision is one of those tools.

Among the insights I gleaned from an earlier book I had written concerning vision is that four primary factors are involved in discerning God's vision for your life and ministry.[4] Briefly, those four aspects are:

- *Knowing yourself:* God cannot trust you with the leadership of His most beloved creation, nor with the wise use of His precious vision, unless you understand yourself inside out. Great leaders know who they are at the most intimate levels of self-knowledge. Anything less would render them dangerous.
- *Knowing God:* You are most useful in the unfolding of His kingdom when you are willing to be used for His purposes, in His timing, in His manner, to His glory. He will open your eyes to a captivating version of a future reality, one you may play a significant role in bringing to fruition, when you have gained intense intimacy with Him. You do this through prayer, through meditation, through fasting and through reading the Scriptures—especially those passages that model His relationship with historical visionary leaders.
- *Knowing your context:* God works through us within the context of human reality. If you are to be useful in shaping the future, you must understand the past and the present. This means getting a good grip on the commu-

nity you have been called to lead within; the people who will be touched by, and taking part in the ministry endeavor you will lead; other Christian leaders God has also called to minister in your midst, albeit in different ways and with different (but invariably complementary and connected) visions; and your worldly competitors, who work on the basis of human vision and seek to distract people from the things of God.

- *Knowing good advice:* One of the benefits of working with others is that they may see things we cannot because we are too close to a situation. When it comes to the prolonged process of determining God's vision for our lives and ministries, it is easy to lose ourselves or our grip on reality in the process. Often, one of the most valuable assets on the vision-determination trail is to seek the counsel of a handful of people who intimately know you, God and your ministry context. As iron sharpens iron, they may well provide you with keen insight you are incapable of mustering in the midst of your vision quest.

Let me offer a few more bits of insight that might help you as you work through the vision development process. A hard pill for some followers to swallow is that God conveys His vision to leaders without asking His followers for their input! As a leader, you may wish to ask for people's input; but remember that the ultimate definition of the vision is from God, not your peers. They may play a role in helping to shape your thinking or perhaps the way you ultimately articulate or position the vision. Vision, however, is not determined by a two-thirds vote; it is not the result of consensus among a group of interested parties; and vision is not identified through a committee-based process.

If God has called you to lead, perhaps the most vital and significant function you will fill is that of being the projector and the protector of the vision. The goal is not to become the people's most popular leader, but to become God's most trustworthy leader. Leadership is not easy; it involves taking a lot of unfair, unnecessary and unfathomable hits. Sometimes you won't be able to tell your backers from your detractors (even with a scorecard!). In the end, although leaders receive a lot of applause and are frequently in the public eye, leadership is a lonely business. It is a wearing task. Gaining God's vision for the future is exhilarating. Putting it into practice in this fallen world is punishing. If you want to be a visionary leader, gird up for the battle.

THE NINE ACTS OF
VISIONARY LEADERSHIP

If you want to be a visionary leader—which, incidentally, is a redundant expression because you cannot be a leader unless you have vision, and God will not give you His vision unless you are going to lead—nine sequential steps are related to maximizing your visionary leadership.

Understand the Concept

You won't get very far if you take the George Bush approach—pooh-poohing the significance of vision without really comprehending its centrality and its power. You must understand the purpose of vision, its importance and impact, and its potential applications.

Vision exists to provide a link between mission and action. Contrary to a widely held misconception, vision and mission are not synonymous. Mission is a broad-based description of why you exist—your purpose for being. It defines the outer parameters of acceptable activity. Vision is much more specific; it details the particular direction you will pursue within the broad framework of your mission. Vision provides focus. To use a sports analogy, mission is the stadium in which you will play; vision identifies the sport to be played within the stadium. Vision, then, is a specific, detailed, customized, distinctive and unique notion of what you are seeking to do to create a particular outcome.

Vision is important because it provides guidance that makes you effective as a leader and influential as a team of people. I have discovered that the primary benefits of operating in concert with God's vision are that vision provides continuity with the past while building a superior future; it empowers people to do the work of God; it heightens people's commitments to their faith, their community of faith and their own sense of calling and self-worth; and it brings unity to God's people.

Vision is an indispensable tool as a leader begins building momentum for positive, life-transforming change. Vision becomes the core from which strategy and tactics are developed, culminating in a plan of action that people can implement and evaluate. A leader who has God's vision will use it in conversation, in conceptualization, in evaluation, in resource development—well, in just about every dimension of leadership activity. God's vision motivates people to get excited and to get involved. Obviously, vision is the kind of tool no leader can afford to be without!

Understand the Content

A person who attempts to lead others without vision is simply playing a dangerous, arrogant game. Anyone who is called by God to be a leader must devote serious time, energy, study and spiritual commitment to discerning God's vision for ministry. The elements described in the previous section outline how to go about identifying the vision.

Let me add an important caveat. Gaining the vision is simple, but it is not quick. I have worked with many great Christian leaders across America who spent months or years (literally) interacting with God to gain access to the vision. The amount of time invested in discerning the vision is not related to the person's experience, godliness or natural abilities. It is simply part of God's refining process for you. I firmly believe that God takes greater pleasure in the process of working with us to get the vision than He takes in us finally attaining it. Most visionaries admit that the process of seeking the vision brought them closer to God than they had ever been before. The process is every bit as important as the product; do not rush it.

Own the Vision

God has developed the vision for you, specifically. It fits your abilities, your context and your opportunities. He does not carelessly provide generic visions: each one is tailor-made to fit you, and you alone. That vision will empower you to accomplish great—sometimes miraculous— things for Him. But you have to own the vision completely. It must be a perception of a coming reality to which you are totally committed.

Martin Luther King Jr. described it this way: "If a man hasn't discovered something he is willing to die for, he isn't fit to live." Ultimately, of course, you and I must be willing to die to self and to die for Christ. How do we objectively do that? By committing our lives to Him, giving Him full power and authority over our lives. This relates to our trust in Him, and Him alone by His grace, for our spiritual salvation. For those of us called to be leaders, it means that we put ourselves on the line, every day, to see His vision for His people come to life through us.

Are you willing to die for the vision God has entrusted to you?

Make It Real

Vision is not an ethereal, mystical concept; it is a practical tool. You must make the vision real. Because the purpose of vision is to help you lead people, this intimates that you must make the vision tangible and compelling not only to yourself, but also particularly to others.

The key to this process is creating a vision statement. This is a brief and memorable (but not trite) description of the vision. Choose the language carefully. Keep it to no more than two sentences, probably no more than twenty words: people won't remember more than that. Avoid technical or ecclesiastical terminology. Memorize it so that it not only flavors your thinking, but also is always at your fingertips should it be a useful addition to a conversation or other communication.

The following examples of mission and vision statements are provided to give you a feel for what we are talking about.

> Ministry: Barna Research Group
> Mission: To serve the Church through marketing research while remaining profitable. (NOTE: Barna Research is a for-profit corporation.)
> Vision: To provide current, accurate and reliable information, in bite-size pieces, at reasonable prices, so ministries can make better strategic decisions for ministry.

> Ministry: Oakdale Community Church
> Mission: To exalt God; edify the saints; equip believers to serve; evangelize the community; extend God's love to the believers.
> Vision: To provide a safe and loving place where emotional healing occurs, culminating in an extensive network of affirming relationships.

Pass It Around

For a leader to be effective, he must influence people. For that influence to happen, the leader must motivate people to act. It is the vision that will inspire them to sacrifice who they are, and to accomplish something that is not purely selfish. For this to occur, then, you must articulate the vision.

When should the vision be communicated to people? At every

opportunity. For instance, senior pastors might relate the central message or theme of their sermons to the vision; include applications of the vision in their letters to congregants or articles they write for the church newsletter; raise the vision as an idea generator at planning meetings; evaluate the ministry in comparison to the vision; inspire visitors to the church with a motivating presentation of the vision as the heart of the ministry; prepare the budget in relation to the applications of the vision; and so forth.

How should it be articulated? By expressing enthusiasm, relevance and confidence. Whenever you have a chance to influence someone with the vision, exploit the opportunity. Realize that vision is most effectively caught not by mass presentations, but by example and through relationships. Sermons and other mass-event presentations can certainly raise people's awareness of the vision and perhaps intrigue them. My experience in studying the transfer of vision from the visionary to his followers, however, is that people are most likely to buy the vision when they have an intimate meeting with the visionary, or someone else who has wholeheartedly embraced the vision and has become an evangelist for it.

In mass presentations, interest may be raised, but so are many unanswered questions. In a one-to-one discussion about the vision, those questions are put to rest and the vision can be more easily personalized. What makes a vision most attractive is fervor. When someone finds someone else of like mind who is passionate about a cause, the person wants to know more about it—in much the same manner non-Christians are most often attracted to Christ when they have observed a believer who is ardently in love with Christ and has committed his or her life to serving Him.

Sell It

It is one thing to be passionate and genuine in your vision. It is another thing altogether to invite others to embrace the vision with the same zeal you possess. Visionary leaders are, to some extent, salesmen: their abilities to lead depends in part on their abilities to attract people who will invest in the ministry, and that decision hinges on people's desires to see the vision be fulfilled. No matter how appealing the vision may be, it will take some degree of salesmanship to attract people to get on board.

Perhaps this seems crass; or maybe you have a distaste for selling. It may be you do not believe that a great idea—God's idea, no less—

should require any kind of human promotion. If so, I have two thoughts for you to consider.

First, realize you are interacting with fallen people, in a competitive marketplace. Truth does not always win over people's hearts—although all truth is God's truth. When truth has an effective champion, however, people's eyes can be opened and their hearts won by what is right. Vision is no different. When God's vision has a die-hard proponent who can effectively and persistently communicate that vision to people who are searching for a compelling cause and a can't-miss proposition, you are not so much selling as you are counseling people.

Second, if you get to the point where God entrusts His vision to you, selling won't seem like such a big deal. Your focus shifts from self-centeredness ("what if they reject me," "what if I feel uncomfortable," "what if I don't do an effective presentation") to God-centeredness ("I can't let God down," "what a blessing to be able to serve Him this way," "His people will want to get in on this").

Put It into Action

If your vision remains just a compelling idea or an alluring dream, you have failed. Vision is about creating a preferable future. Part of your responsibility as a leader is not only to identify, articulate and sell the vision, but also to ensure that it becomes a reality.

Implementing the vision calls for several things. You must have a team that is energetically behind the vision. You must amass the resources required for implementation. You need a plan, complete with goals, strategies and tactics, to move forward effectively and efficiently. You need to create processes to introduce the vision into ministry in practical ways. You must have evaluative tools prepared so you can assess how well you are doing along the way, fine-tuning your implementation efforts as you go along.

Please make an important distinction here. Your salvation is not affected by how well you champion the vision. Your eternal place in His presence rests solely on your response to Christ's death for you on the cross. Your response to your call to lead, your involvement in using your leadership gift and talents, and your success in making the vision a reality are elements of your obedience—demonstrations of your willingness to serve. Put the vision into action for the right reason—not to gain jewels in your crown, but to know the joy of making a positive difference in the world by pouring yourself into serving Christ.

Refine the Vision

In the course of time, things change: demographics, your ministry team, your opportunities and so on. On the one hand, I discovered that the vision usually outlives the visionary (which, incidentally, makes a strong case for not only passing the vision on to the next generation, but also for developing an emerging generation of leaders who can carry on the vision with your passion and knowledge). On the other hand, during your pursuit of its fulfillment, you will probably have to "touch up" the peripheral contours of the vision. Understand that the core elements—the heart—of the vision will not change. What may shift somewhat are some of the less central elements of the focus.

Reinforce the Vision

Naturally, when people get involved in a cause that is countercultural (and what ministry isn't?), which demands considerable personal sacrifice, and is in competition with a plethora of other alternatives for people's attention, involvement and resources, an effective leader is one who will reinforce people's decisions to choose the vision as their focus. This, of course, is a basic tenet of good marketing: Always reinforce the buyer's decision. It is also a fundamental principle of great leadership: Always encourage your people, for without their hard work and continuing passion you are no longer leading.

You reinforce the decision in the following ways:

- By expressing appreciation for their involvement.
- By celebrating their successes.
- By constantly recommunicating the vision in new ways, in unique but relevant contexts.
- By providing them with insight into progress made.
- By describing the growth of the movement or the effect of the cause.
- By letting them observe, in unguarded moments, your genuine and unbridled enthusiasm for the vision, the people who have caught and nurtured it and the forward movement that is evident.
- By finding new ways to motivate people who are on the verge of burnout or loss of perspective.

As I have studied visionary leaders break through barriers that nobody but the visionary's own people believed could be overcome, these nine steps have been the consistent path to such overachievement. These have been beneficial, along with a constant diet of spiritual discipline: prayer, meditation, fasting, devouring Scripture, praise, worship, communion among the brethren and confession.

GET VISION!

A phrase from Proverbs that is used repeatedly sticks in my mind: "Get wisdom!" As we consider what it means and what it takes to be a leader, we can modify that phrase slightly to underscore one of the fundamental needs of a godly leader: "Get vision!"

Realize that a leader is called to a higher standard of performance than are followers. The means to pleasing God in leadership is through radical obedience to His will for our leadership. Vision represents a succinct description of what we are striving to accomplish through the act of leading God's people. Vision is the starting point of effective leadership. It is also the end point because all our efforts are ultimately measured in terms of the progress we made toward fully and faithfully implementing the vision.

So what is God's vision for the people He has called you to lead? Until that vision is crystal clear to you, you will not be God's leader for the time and space in which you operate. Honor God and His people by discovering that vision and committing your life to it.

Notes
1. Mortimer Zuckerman, "Does He Still Feel Your Pain?" *U.S. News & World Report* (September 2, 1996): 64.
2. I did include what I thought might be a paraphrase of the vision of eight of the biblical leaders I described in the book, as well as the verses that seem to crystalize their vision. This information is located in chapter 3 of *Turning Vision into Action* (Ventura, Calif.: Regal Books, 1996).
3. These eighteen lessons are located in chapter 4 of *Turning Vision into Action.*
4. A much more extensive discussion of the process of gaining God's vision is contained in chapter 6 of my book *The Power of Vision* (Ventura, Calif.: Regal Books, 1992).

FOUR

THE CHARACTER OF A LEADER

JACK W. HAYFORD

The words have echoed in my mind ever since I first read them years ago in a book by Adela Rogers St. Johns, *Tell No Man.* They are not put in the mouth of one of her characters, but they recur again and again as something of an antiphonal reflection on the repetitive flow of human responses to life from era to era:

> Everything's different but nothing's changed, and everything's changed but nothing's different.

Having recently concluded the final year of my fourth decade in public ministry, those words resounded again. They are neither a cynical statement born of weariness or boredom, nor are they spoken from a presumptuous platform of pretentious snobbishness. As with all of life, however, customs and technologies, structures and fashions change, there is still "nothing new under the sun" (Eccles. 1:9).

The constant that makes this true is human nature—nothing changes. In reference to the matter of leadership, after the swelling of a wave of insight and information about systems analysis and management technique the past ten to fifteen years have given us, the maxim still applies. As far as leaders go, *"Everything's different"* (e.g., many aspects of perspective on style) *"but nothing's changed"* (regarding the presuppositions that undergird most leadership thought). To this day, the notion that skill and strength, talent and tenacity are the source of effective leadership is as common as ever, including in Christian circles. The prevailing mind-set is that leaders "win" by applying smarts and style.

Of course, few venture an outright statement to this effect. If pressed to the wall, not a thoughtful leader around would disagree that the real "stuff" of a leader goes deeper than his gifts. We all know the right answers: Substance before style; what you are is more important than what you do. Without the slightest slur intended, and without any measure of sneering disapproval, however, I know that most of us who lead are tempted and pressed to find the "tricks of the trade," to learn how to "work the angles" or to seek to "position myself for the 'breaks' when 'opportunity knocks.'"

It is more than likely I bump into these temptations a little more frequently than do some pastor-leaders. The fact that God's sovereign grace and providence has situated me in a setting usually described as "megachurch," puts people like me on the spot in at least two ways. First, outsiders presume we have learned some secrets—that we have some transferable methods or "godly gimmicks," if you please. Second, inside we feel periodic pressure to answer questions about church growth, fruit or "success," in terms that seem sufficiently intelligent (i.e., in touch and familiar with the cutting-edge lingo of the current executive/managerial theory).

I find these matters tough to talk about—maybe "delicate" is a better term. If there is anything I do not want to do, it is to sound like some "old dude" who has gone sour on whatever is new or progressive. Even more, I never want to come across sounding self-righteous or "above all that." I wrestle with the demands of leadership as much as anybody, including the requirement that we keep in touch with methods, systems, technologies and so on. Still, the things that never change (even though "everything's different") keep staring us in the face:

- Possession of godly character, alone, assures true fruit, lasting influence and durable leadership. No amount of "fancy footwork" or "bells and whistles" ever produce a genuine, godly leader.
- Our human disposition finds it easier to spend time

"tweaking systems" than prioritizing honest-to-God introspection and constant availability to transformation.

A HUMBLING PHONE CALL

This chapter is the result of a phone call: "Jack, would you write about a leader's character?" When I asked "Why me?" I was looking for help about direction in the article, but the answer went something more like this: "You are so frequently mentioned as a trusted leader, one whose leadership is based on elements of character that get us closer to Jesus more than on the prevailing 'hot leadership ideas.'" The words were humbling to me. "Lord," I prayed, "I hope in Your eyes this is true, and not simply an impression or conclusion mistakenly drawn by undiscerning souls."

However imprecise anyone's opinions about me might be, I knew that at least those words express the central value of my own approach to leadership. Although I have no suspicion or criticism to make of any zealous leader's efforts to seek help from leadership methods or systems, true leadership ultimately is found only *at Jesus' feet* and is shaped and kept only *in the heart.*

So I knew I had found a viable approach to handling the subject matter of this chapter: I would simply relate the way character in leadership most frequently surfaces in my own life.

A RECURRING SCENARIO

It seems like a scenario I have lived out a hundred times.

We are approaching the conclusion of a leader's conference. I have been speaking to gifted church leaders for several sessions—sometimes for two or three days. We have had some interchange before this, but now the floor is open. It is the listeners turn to talk about anything that is on their minds.

The theme or focus of the conference usually makes no difference once we reach this point. The subject of my messages or seminar sessions may range from vision casting, worship leadership, staff management, sermon preparation or spiritual gifts to finances in the church, eschatology, men's ministry, family life or whatever else. Irrespective of the subject, once the floor is open for questions, it seems inevitable that something like what follows will take place.

Question: "Pastor Jack, how many hours do you spend in study each week?" or (and often joined to those words) "How much time do you spend in prayer, say, weekly or on an average each day?"

My reply: "Thank you. It's a worthy, indeed, a greatly discerning question. But with all due respect, let me ask you for two things. First, your forgiveness, because I would rather not answer that question. Second, I want to ask for your patience, because I'd like to discuss the subject I believe is behind such a perceptive question."

Of course, in responding within these Q and A sessions I have always clearly affirmed the fundamental importance of steadfast prayer as a discipline and of systematic study as an essential discipline for a pastor-teacher. I would not be embarrassed to describe the pattern I employ in each of those two pursuits nor the amount of time involved. My primary reason for not answering the question is because it overlooks the "heart" of the leader. Even the disciplines of devotion and scholarship are capable of being employed with such systematic style and skillful pursuit that a person could easily remain self-dependent or unwittingly carnal.

SETTING THE AGENDA

Keeping this in mind, then, let me set forth my agenda for this chapter. Without intending to mock the value of practical methodology, or to minimize the importance of such basics as prayer and study, I want to focus on what I view to be the key to true leadership: the leader's "heart." Even if you are not involved in any role of church leadership, join me in targeting the central issue of how a leader's character is cut. Although the lessons and illustrations I share are taken from my journey as a pastor-teacher, I think the underlying principles and life applications will be equally and fully applicable to anyone:

To the pastor, or leader, or churchman;
Or the businessman, or foreman, or clerk;
Or the politician, or attorney, physician;

Or the wife, or husband, or technician;
Or the manager, or homemaker, or teacher.

The principles and patterns discussed here apply to every *person* who leads—and leading is something we *all* do. Every one of us has *some* kind of leadership role, although the scope of influence and the number of observer followers varies widely. None of us ought to ever consider ourselves insulated from the responsibility to cultivate principles that will assure the daily pursuit of Christlike character marks our leadership. In my view, nothing is more essential to this than a distinct stance of the soul—a "heart quest" that transcends even one's disciplines of devotion or diligence in duty.

A CLUSTER OF THREE

It is hard to say exactly when it began, for in moments even in my youth God was doing preliminary work in these regards. My parents and my church upbringing unquestionably factor into the equation, but the watershed point took place shortly after I came to my present pastorate.

It was twenty-seven years ago, after thirteen years of already-fulfilling-and-fruitful ministry. My earlier years had been so blessed that I was fully ready to launch my new assignment with the same zeal and leadership style I had practiced for more than a decade. A cluster of three things had happened in the preceding few years and months, however, all of which seemed to converge one day and bring me to a point of reconsideration.

The first was, even then, rather distant in time. I had experienced a "near-fall," a time when God delivered me from a potentially adulterous relationship. The experience broke the back of an unperceived self-righteousness within me. That rescue-by-grace also taught me how deceptive "success in man's eyes" can be, for my near disaster had occurred in the midst of a season of great blessing on my ministry.

A TIMELESS PARADIGM

The second was more recent: only months before I had been greatly stirred by the Holy Spirit at a conference on evangelism. The profound awakening I experienced was not to a zeal for winning souls—I already felt that. I was shaken to the roots of my spiritual thought and perspective about ministry by a new revelation to me in the Scriptures: Worship is the Church's first ministry, and when biblically pursued it will become the fountainhead of evangelism! Given my prior orientation, this insight was thoroughly "off the wall." I was geared to promotionalism, to "dynamic, contemporary communication and outreach" and the like. Suddenly, however, I was confronted with the one timeless paradigm for leadership.

This unplanned soul-shaping encounter showed me a timeless paradigm for effective leadership *and evangelism* that is woven throughout God's Word. Consider:

- Abraham, leaving a trail of altars (and thereby becoming the father of nations);
- Moses, barefoot before the burning bush (and thereby becoming the deliverer of a nation);
- David, worshiping as a youthful shepherd (and finding the way to victory over enemies ranging from lions to Goliath);
- Daniel, kneeling before God in prayer (and rising to become an influence in the courts of kings);
- The one hundred and twenty saints tarrying in the presence of God for Spirit-fullness (and finding the Church's age-long harvest born from their praise); and
- The Antioch elders "ministering to the Lord and fasting" (and discovering the Holy Spirit's plan for world evangelism).

Through the stirring of the Spirit I was introduced to a radically different perspective about leadership and profoundly influenced for the rest of my life. The whole notion of leading on God's terms called me to a new mind-set—one quite different from my inclination to rely upon promotional techniques and ministry style. It was not as though I had never included prayer on my agenda, nor had I previously been so arrogant as to presume "the arm of flesh" as my strength. I hadn't! I still had been far more shaped by the "externals" of leadership enterprise, however, than by the "internals" of my heart's "touch" with God.

A PRECIPITATING MOMENT

The third event was the realization that whatever gift of "leadership" any man or woman has, it is never a gift to be held in our own hands. I was stunned by the realization that the finest gifts I may have received from God Himself might be exercised apart from His Spirit's control. It occurred to me that those gifts might be idolatrously cherished as though they were my own, a selfishly treasured possession.

Suddenly I saw that my leadership is a day-to-day gift, something only to be stewarded from out of the hand of the Father. I saw how Jesus Himself led and ministered only on a moment-to-moment basis: "I did not speak of my own accord, but the Father who sent me com manded me what to say and how to say it....So whatever I say is just what the Father has told me to say" (John 12:49,50, *NIV*).

EMBRACING A CONCEPT

This "cluster of three" set the stage in my own soul for pursuing my leadership far more simply and, by every apparent gauge, far more effectively.

I was melted with a sense of my own perpetual vulnerability to evil, and my own perpetual capacity for self-deception. I was awakened to my own need for regular breaking before the altar of private worship, and to my call to steadfastly lead people to the same stance of soul before our Creator-Redeemer. Indeed, these three lessons convicted me of the need to never presume I know anything about leading—today or any other day—and to learn to exercise my leadership in dependency upon the grace and wisdom of God day to day, moment by moment. This marked the end of my unconscious habit of depending upon my own experience, acquired skills, learning or expertise.

Gradually, I came to embrace this concept I believe constitutes the key to becoming a leader. I believe it enables one to become a leader who is truly *effective* (irrespective of how "efficient" he may be); who builds *trust* (and thereby never needs to "demand loyalty"); and who realizes long-term *durability* (which is born of abiding substance that outlasts transient "styles").

Best of all, such a leader realizes fruitful leadership—defined not as the ability to "produce results," but as the capacity to bring those I lead to their deepest enrichment and highest fulfillment. Fruitful leadership is not getting others to fulfill my goals (or even my God-given vision for our collective enterprise and good), but helping others realize

God's creative intent for their lives—personally, domestically, vocationally and eternally.

To become such a leader, I believe the central challenge we each face is to learn to tend to our primary challenge: *to keep my heart as a leader.*

CUTTING TO THE CORE

It is popular these days to announce one's "core values." Nothing is more *chic* in management circles than formulating a mission/vision statement. Companion to this is a set of "core values"—a list of basic emphases intended to declare the controlling principles seen as essential to fulfilling the mission and vision.

In applying such a procedure, we learn how the goals of a company or enterprise not only may be declared, but also how its character will be determined. In essence, its character will be decided by the leadership's commitment to the core values established as the set of controlling principles expected to effect success.

It is possible that this practice could serve to direct the efforts of a person in much the same way, except for one critical reality. There is a radical difference between managing and measuring a secular business's success and evaluating the true fruit of a spiritual leader. Everything about a company relates to the market: The corporation operates in a public, rather than a private venue. Further, business or corporate enterprise is motivated and measured by external evidences of having succeeded (e.g., by an economic or material goal, by awards or recognition), all of which is measured on a scale framed by human criteria.

The depth and height of success in the personal life of a leader, however, centers in a private venue: the heart. The true measure of a leader is in diametric opposition to his being controlled by techniques or methods, by slogans or statements, or by visible evidences of success, acceptance or recognition. Further, the criterion of a leader's ultimate measurement comes from a plane higher than human origin. The character of a true leader requires an answer to a call that sounds from the *highest* source and shapes him in the *deepest*, most personal corners of his soul. "Success" at these levels—at the highest and deepest—will only be realized as a leader commits to an inner accountability to faithfully, constantly and honestly answer one question: *Am I maintaining "integrity of heart"?*

INTEGRITY OF HEART

Years before I discovered this theme in the Bible, I had begun learning the "daily, mid-course corrections" way of living. Two experiences ten years apart are fixed in my memory.

The first relates to my mother's practice of teaching her children to keep an accountable "heart" toward God. I can remember her saying, "Son, I want to ask you a question but, before asking, I want to say, I'm asking you 'in front of Jesus.'" This was not a manipulative ploy, nor words frequently spoken, but Mamma used them as a reminder at those times when she felt we might be tempted to use dishonesty as a defense. Her words, "in front of Jesus," framed a picture accentuating that our Savior was not a distant entity, and our honesty in matters was not an optional issue. I never thought this phrase was used to induce guilt or to breed an atmosphere of condemnation. Rather, it was based on a biblically verifiable truth even redeemed human nature too often forgets to heed: "All things are naked and open to the eyes of Him to whom we must give account" (Heb. 4:13).

The second memory is from the summer I was seventeen years old. Each day at lunch, taking a break from my job to earn money for my college education, I memorized Bible verses from the Navigators card pack I carried. One verse in particular became indelibly etched on my heart as well as my mind:

> The heart is deceitful above all things, and desperately wicked; who can know it? (Jer. 17:9).

I remember asking myself the question: If I can trick myself into believing something's right and it's not, how can I keep my heart from being deceived? In response to that query, the following verses became pivotal to my life and began to govern my habits of thought:

> "How can a young man cleanse his way? By taking heed according to Your Word. With my whole heart have I sought You; oh, let me not wander from your commandments!" (Ps. 119:9,10). It is not enough for me to know God's Word, but my WHOLE HEART must be kept consciously available to His Spirit's correction so I will not inadvertently wander in my own way or in the supposed wisdom of my own flesh.

"Search me, O God, and know my heart; try me, and know my [thoughts] anxieties; and see if there is any wicked way in me, and lead me in the way everlasting" (Ps. 139:23,24). Only by daily welcoming the Lord to walk the corridors of my heart can I know the blessing of HIS PROTECTION against the subtlety of my rationalizing of my sin, my toleration of my selfishness or my tendency to defend arguments designed to justify my preferences without being humble or open to correction from the Lord.

In brief, I began to come to terms with the determinants of true character. The shaping power of such character is the truth of God's Word. The forming hand is His Spirit's "dealings" with the leader. The essential terrain on which this work is accomplished is the human heart, which must be kept fully open to instruction, correction and refinement. I began to learn that God is not so much interested in what I am now as He is in what I am becoming. Thus, I launched upon a journey of opening my heart to Him for scrutiny every day, not as an exercise in self-flagellation or berating introspection, but as an intentional means of maintaining sensitivity to His Spirit's "voice," keeping integrity with His dealings in my heart.

The Bible candidly states, "As he thinks in his heart, so is he" (Prov. 23:7). Jesus pressed this same issue with His disciples, calling them to move beyond the superficial to the essential. He wanted to teach them that what makes a man is not the appearances of his words or deeds, but the content of his heart (see Matt. 15:10-20). This is the reason the writer of Proverbs says:

> Keep your heart with all diligence, for out of it spring the issues of life (4:23).

A leader's character will never rise beyond the flow level of his obedience to the Holy Spirit's dealings with the heart. Although our standard of character is outlined in God's Word and expressed through the person of Christ, the substance of character is fashioned by the accumulated responses of the heart to the Spirit's refining work.

BECOMING "HONEST TO GOD"

At the core of everything a person does lies an inner value system—a commitment to the objectives dictated by a grid of convictions and personal priorities. These values that guide decisions and motivate action are life's "heart" issues. They are rightly referred to as being "of the heart," for they are not only central to our life and thought, but they also transcend our intellect. They point to a fountain from which the outflow of every person's life issues its stream of true "becoming."

For the Christian leader, this fountain must be fed by more than a self-developed set of philosophical principles. Although this grid of our convictions is rooted in biblical principles and in the absolute authority of the Word of God, my applications of that word may too easily be administered in my own best interests or flavored by my opinions. Thus, joined to God's objective Word must be a more subjec tive integrity. It will determine how I "live out" the objective statements of His Word. This brings about the intersection of promise and problem. The "promise" is in God's divinely trustworthy, objective revelation in His Word, given once-for-all by His Holy Spirit. The "problem" is my fallible, subjective perception of God's will, and my need for daily correction by His Holy Spirit.

Without my acknowledgment of the "problem"—and thereby, my constant availability to the Holy Spirit's corrections to my attitude, understanding or perspective—I will inevitably have occasions when I "fool myself," no matter how much objective truth I may know.

That, for example, is the reason "good Christians" show bitterness and unforgiveness toward others, and justify their attitudes on the basis of being the "violated party." It is why "committed Christians" speak critically or condescendingly about believers who hold different doctrinal emphases than they do and justify their judgmentalism with the false supposition that God sees them as "more right" than others. It is why "sincere Christians" become deluded about the nature of an inappropriate relationship, then marry an unbeliever or fall into an evil infatuation or an adulterous relationship.

Honesty requires that I see that my character be determined both by a growing knowledge of God's Word and a willingness to permit His Spirit to continually refine my responsiveness to His will in all the details of my life. My character is not shaped by the sum of my information, but by the process of a transformation that is as unceasingly needed in me.

There is more to my character formation than having learned a set of ideas—even if they are God's. I not only need to *turn to the Bible*, but

I must also keep *tuned to the Holy Spirit*, for with the "grid" of values His Word gives me, He provides His Spirit as the ultimate umpire who comes to apply that Word to my life. His presence is given to every reborn son or daughter of the Most High, to teach us how the Father's will is to flow into the details of our lives.

The purpose of this monitoring is not to produce a mysticized brand of "holiness," but to generate a dynamic, wholehearted, clear-eyed people—people who possess the character of Christ! My character as a leader seeking to reflect the highest of values will distill truth from God's Word to be woven into the fabric of my life. My ultimate objective is to grow, slowly but surely, into the image of Christ—*only as I "walk in the Spirit."* That element—walking in the Spirit—becomes pivotal in determining my character. It is the secret to achieving a heart of integrity. It means I need to learn to recognize when I "grieve" the Spirit (Eph. 4:30), and to readily repent and confess in each situation in which He corrects me.

BEGINNING THIS WALK

A leader's commitment to walk with integrity of heart calls for a refusal to allow even minor deviations from honesty of any kind. Regardless of the disdain demonstrated by those who choose a less demanding standard for their lives, making such a commitment to integrity is not to become the victim of a wearying legalism or the exploited subject of a dignified guilt complex. No, this is commitment to a healthy mind-set, a dedication to an "inner-heart lifestyle" lived in the joy of God's grace and in the fullness of peace we are given in Christ. It does call for a willingness, though, to constantly invite and allow the Spirit of God to make one sensitive to matters that make a difference to God—*no matter how small or insignificant they may seem.*

Having decades now behind me of seeking to keep this openness to the Spirit's correction, I can only rejoice about both His patience and His ways. I have found that the pleasing fruit of a diligent effort at steadfast obedience is at least threefold:

A holy intimacy of fellowship with the Father continually increases because the leader has sought the heart of God and made purity of character a priority. "The secret of the Lord is with them who fear [reverence] Him, and He will show them His covenant" (Ps. 25:14).

We are freed from our human preoccupation with self-defense because of our practice of interpersonal confession and our continual confession and repentance before God (see Jas. 5:16; 1 John 1:6-10).

Our submission to the Holy Spirit's prompting and correction enables us to recognize the voice of God, respond more determinedly to the exposed will of God and more readily discern and reject the works of darkness (see Eph. 5:17,18).

The Scriptures clearly instruct and warn regarding this importance of integrity of heart. In the fifth booklet in my "Real Man's Six Pack," I elaborate on "A Man's Integrity." A developing leader will appreciate the lessons revealed through a study of the lives of men who learned God's ways through a commitment to—or the rejection of—personal "integrity of heart." These insights are revealed in the stories of:

- Abimelech (see Gen. 20:1-6): As we witness his confusion as the result of a lie being told him, we also see the PRESERVING POWER of *integrity of heart* as God shows that if we have integrity He will keep us in spite of our honest mistakes.
- David (see Ps. 25:19-21): As we discover his integrity in depending on God's sustaining grace as His defense, we then observe God's PROTECTING POWER, rather than political diplomacy. (See also David's *first* source of leadership ability and resource—*"integrity of heart"*; Ps. 78:70-72.)
- Solomon (1 Kings 9:1-5): As we hear the Lord's covenant relayed to this new king, we are exposed to the revelation that *"integrity of heart"* has a PERPETUATING POWER that will sustain us unto the realization of God's promises—if His ways are faithfully maintained, from the heart.

ARENAS OF VULNERABILITY

Considering both the manifest rewards and the biblical blessings

attending a heart of integrity, let me point to several arenas of vulnerability I have found we leaders need to guard against if we truly seek
a correctable, teachable heart toward maintaining the utmost integrity.

Matters of Accuracy

Few things are more important to the character of a leader than
exhibiting absolute honesty in all communication with those whom he
leads. Often we face the temptation to exaggerate numbers, such as
church attendance figures. (This is sometimes done in the guise that
"our people need the encouragement," when in fact inflated figures
are nothing more than an ego boost for the leader himself.) "Blurring"
information, so as to make something sound better than it is, is another common ruse of the flesh. To surrender to these or similar habits
dulls the ear of the soul to its call to maximum integrity.

Honest mistakes in conveying information are sometimes made, of
course, and such *faux pas* ought not be deemed "lies" or violations of
integrity. A mistake is not a lie; it is an accident in understanding.
Passing on mistaken facts does not compromise the heart; although
corrections are necessary, embarrassment is not. On the other hand, a
deliberate violation of integrity is something else, and the honest heart
will acknowledge that inner "twinge" to the soul and stand corrected
(and also acknowledge the failing to anyone who has been the recipi-
ent of such a willful misrepresentation of the truth).

Matters of Privilege

Along with the responsibilities of leadership, occasional privileges
may also be enjoyed. The reception of these privileges should be made
known to those to whom the leader is accountable and no attempt
should be made to hide such privileges from those the leader leads.
Those who have hearts of integrity never seek these privileges, and
when they receive them, they never endeavor to unfairly exploit them.
What is given without coercion or prompting may certainly be
received and seen as a grace or gift, but like the privilege of God's
grace, a leader should not impose upon the goodness of others to
manipulate such gain.

One of my earliest lessons regarding the matter of inner accountability took place when I was in my first pastorate. I placed an order for
church supplies from one vendor and was pleasantly surprised to receive
a small, complimentary transistor radio along with the products ordered.

"Ah-hah!" I exclaimed with glee, deeming this small "gold mine" a treasure deserved by virtue of having submitted the order on the church's behalf. My initial justification was that some benefits are a natural right to those who engage in such tasks. The argument—I'm paid so little I ought to be able to enjoy some privilege of office—has captured a million minds, dulled as many souls and stumbled thousands of leaders. After briefly flirting with the radio, I realized it was not mine for the keeping. Privileges *are* to be enjoyed—but not secret ones. If there is a privilege to my office, it ought to be sanctioned by those under whom I serve and understood in that way by those I lead.

Matters of Power

By definition, a leader's position incorporates some arena of delegated authority, or "power" in the personal sense (as opposed to spiritual sense). The meaning of "authority" (i.e., the right to a realm of dominion for the service of a task) is biblically intended to focus on "power for the purpose of serving people." This is Jesus' insistent emphasis (see Luke 22:24-27), and its violation will inevitably destroy the very realm of rule intended to the one assigned the authority. (Study Rehoboam's "show of power" and the folly it worked, resulting in splitting the kingdom in 1 Kings 12.)

The late Dr. David Hubbard, who was the president of Fuller Theological Seminary, made one of the wisest observations I have ever noted about the exercise of power. David and I were members of a panel interacting with a group of pastors on the subject of "the submission of a leader." In that context, this dear brother spoke words that welded a concept into my own soul: *"I never exercise the full extent of the power inherent in my position."*

I registered that wisdom, understanding very well that to ever feel the *need* to exercise the full range of my powers makes it likely I am in a situation best handled by a team rather than by myself. It is also far less likely that power *shared* will ever crush a person being chastised. At the same time, sharing my power provides even greater protection against becoming enamored with the power I may have.

Matters of Perceived Prestige

Fame and recognition, at whatever level, render a leader vulnerable to inappropriate vanity, especially when comparisons are made. I dare not let my heart be stolen by sincere praise or approval. It *is* right to accept kindnesses and affirmation, and it *is* inconsiderate to fend off such remarks with false piety. At the same time, though, it is wise to recognize that there is nothing I may have that I have not received (see 1 Cor. 4:7).

This principle works both ways, too. It is far too common for a leader to pander to the pride of those he leads by playing to an individual's or corporate body's sense of, or quest for, superiority. ("You're the greatest choir this town has ever seen!...The greatest congregation in our denomination!") What may innocently be intended as encouragement often gradually develops a spirit of smugness within the encouraged group. It is not necessary to compare to commend. (Note Jesus' words, "Well done good [not better or best] and faithful servant" [Matt. 25:21].)

Early in my present pastoral tenure, I wrestled with the fear of losing "prestige" when responding to a request to write a magazine article. As I came to a point in writing where I wanted to use an illustration I had received from a friend and fellow pastor, I did not want to credit him as the source for fear that mentioning another leader would distract from my own prominence in the mind of the reader.

It is too long a story to tell, but I confronted the fear of lost prestige and as a result of mentioning the other pastor, a woman who read the article visited his church and received Christ! One wonders how many self-protectionist ruses I may have used through the years of my leadership might have been at the expense of similar results. (It is safe to presume that, in the case of the magazine article, the likelihood of *any* reader having any sense of my "prominence" was slim anyway!) I love to quote my dear friend, the author, Ethel Barrett, who said, *"We would worry a lot less about what people thought of us if we realized how seldom they do."*

Matters of Moral Purity

Aside from the obvious mandate the Bible gives to moral purity in sexual, financial and relational matters, a leader who wants to cultivate a heart of integrity must come to terms with his mind as well as his body. Especially today, considering the proliferation of pornographic resources and the capacity for absolute secrecy while deeply involved in illegitimate moral pursuits, maintaining integrity of heart is all the more challenging.

Some years ago, I was speaking at a retreat where the joyousness of the collegians found warm expression in everyone's hugging one another at the conclusion of each service. Nothing was inappropriate: the Bible fully endorses the practice, and the expressions were void of either giddiness or mushiness. It is an embarrassing memory to relate, though, not because I continued in a violation of my integrity, but because I am ashamed to remember that my mind, even for one moment, was compromised by incipient carnality.

I had "holy-hugged" a half-dozen youth—both male and female— when a rather short girl reached out in simple purity to embrace me, the respected Bible teacher. Without intent, as I reached to hug her, by reason of her small size my arms circled her to the point that my reach extended slightly under her upreaching arms, lightly touching the fullness of the side of one breast. Because the contact not only was innocent and brief, and without any intent of a potential impropriety, it went entirely unnoticed. Except to my mind.

As I already said, it is embarrassing to confess (which I did, to my male associate and roommate, who was traveling with me on the trip). At the moment, though, I was suddenly faced with a horrible realization of my mind's conniving potential. For a few shameful seconds I thought to myself of how such an apparently innocent action could become a means for periodic self-gratification. At the same moment, however, the inner pinching of the heart, prompted by the immediate grief of the Holy Spirit about my mind's indulgence, called me to take a stance of integrity: Never again!

Our congregation is a loving one and has a constant habit of embracing one another, and to this day I participate as freely as anyone. That one day, however, the discovery of a fleshly ruse was encountered and refused. I, of course, have stood firm in that grace, vowing within my own soul to never violate integrity with either my own heart before God or my sisters in Christ.

By relaying the story I know I risk the possibility of being judged unkindly by some critic. Because I have had to counsel too many leaders who have violated points of integrity, only to fall deeper into failure and loss for having taken the first step, I have decided to confess that moment's test while testifying to the victories heart integrity can win. May God's tender Spirit cause my sharing to possibly warn some dear but weakened leader away from any compromise of His call to integrity of heart.

INTEGRITY'S HIGHEST CALL

Every Christian leader is constantly confronted with pressures to take sides against other believers, to criticize styles and doctrines that are different, to pass judgment on leaders or ministries that do not suit their tastes. "Spiritual suspicion" has almost become an article of faith in North America, a deceptive notion fostered by "experts" who pursue their critiques of other Christians in the spirit of the jaundiced investigative reporting of secular news writers. One thing is certain: Far more mud-slinging and attack verbiage are employed than ever could be justified. We would all do well to take note that the biblical warning against *last days error* provides no warrant for *end times judgmentalism* or snobbish posturings against one another in Christ's Body.

It just might be possible that the highest call to integrity we as leaders need to hear today is the call to love one another as we have been loved, forgiving of one another as we have been forgiven. It is often hard to hear the Holy Spirit whispering this call to our hearts when we have been schooled in systems that argue for their own righteousness over others without even suspecting the righteousness of such an attitude.

I have neither preachment nor illustration to make at this point, but my appeal is that we learn to defend rather than attack one another. Differences of viewpoint, practice and preference will exist among the members of Jesus' Body—His Church—until He comes again. Yet, knowing this, our Savior Himself prayed:

> "That they may be one just as We are one: I in them, and You in Me; that they may be made perfect in one, and that the world may know that You have sent Me" (John 17:22,23).

Because that prayer was offered in the power of the Holy Spirit, I can be certain that if I will "tune in," the same Holy Spirit will help me avoid doing or saying anything that contradicts the heart cry of my Lord and Savior.

Nothing is more demanding of my character as a leader than to stand in humility before the corrective promptings of the Holy Spirit. He is the One who has drawn me to the Savior! He is the One whose power has brought regeneration—new birth to my spirit! He is the One who has come to develop in me the traits of Jesus' character as surely as He wants to fill me with the words and works of Jesus' power!

As men and women of His—called to lead in some quarter of God's great Kingdom enterprises—let us refuse any path or pursuit offering a *perception* of achievement without the *penetration* of true holiness. It is too short changed an offer for sons and daughters called to long-range vision, called to see the eternal to maintain a heart that values its rewards above all.

THE JOURNEY CONTINUES

So let me summarize the wisdom I have gleaned from these varied influences that have gradually formed my perspective about shaping a leader's character.

The development of leadership character takes more than the practice of external disciplines, for it involves the heart, not just habits.

Character relates to more than just devotion, for it involves transformation, not simply inspiration.

Character transcends obedience to rules, for it involves the Holy Spirit's speaking to the inner man, offering more than commandments understood by the mind.

Such character involves transparency before, and accountability to, other people. It is not merely a private quest for purity; it is not solely a man-to-his-God humility.

All these phrases that address what character does involve as well as that which is not involved in character development are essential to the heart of integrity.

FIVE

BECOMING A
SPIRITUALLY
MATURE LEADER

GENE GETZ

Several years ago, I was conducting a men's conference in Chicago. I had been asked to speak about "spiritual maturity," using the apostle Paul's profiles in his pastoral letters to Timothy and Titus. I had developed Paul's outline at length in my book entitled *The Measure of a Man*, which formed the basis of that seminar.[1]

As I discussed each quality outlined by Paul in these two powerful and dynamic biblical paragraphs, two distinguished-looking gentlemen who were sitting near the front kept giving me positive feedback, not only with their body language, but also verbally. "That's good, Gene!" one said. "Right on!" responded the other. "That is a great insight!" This was a new experience for me, and frankly, it felt good—particularly because I had never met these men before.

During the coffee break, I made my way to the table where they were sitting and introduced myself. I soon discovered that each held top-level management positions in one of the steel mills in a neighboring city. I also discovered they were new Christians, "neophytes" as Paul would call them—which explains why they felt free to interact with me publicly. They had not yet learned the "Christian rules" that undergird "theological conferences." Frankly, I hoped they never would. They had a refreshing naiveté. It was encouraging to relate to men who had not yet imbibed some of our restrictive cultural traditions.

What affected and intrigued me the most, however, were their comments about Paul's maturity profiles. They readily admitted they had never heard much about Timothy and Titus. One man said, "Gene, I seem to remember hearing about Timothy, but this Titus guy—well, I've never heard of him."

ALL TRUTH IS GOD'S TRUTH!

At this point these businessmen really grabbed my attention! Though they had never read or heard these passages in the New Testament before attending that conference, they were experientially familiar with the characteristics of maturity outlined by Paul and why they were so important. That is why they were responsive to what I was sharing. They were affirming the importance and significance of each quality. Probably without knowing it, they were demonstrating that "all truth is God's truth"!

During that coffee break, they expanded on their public responses. "Gene," one said, "it's amazing how Paul's maturity profiles for leaders aligns with what we've learned by experience in our positions as upper-level managers." Even as new Christians they had learned that they only wanted to hire leaders for middle-management positions who had "good reputations"—the first quality outlined by Paul in both letters (see 1 Tim. 3:1; Titus 1:5).

Furthermore, they said they did not want men in leadership positions who were unfaithful to their wives—the second requirement listed by Paul in both profiles. "If they cheat on their marital partners, they'll also cheat the company," one said. They readily affirmed that leaders who can not give good direction to their own families will never give proper direction to the people they are responsible for in their business positions. For Paul this was also a foundational qualification!

In essence, they told me during that fifteen-minute "break in the action" that Paul's requirements for spiritual leaders in the church were the same requirements they had discovered pragmatically to be what they need to look for in a competent leader in their own corporate arenas.

A LEADERSHIP CHALLENGE

Paul had left Timothy in Ephesus to help establish the church. Though the Christian community was well on its way as a growing and influential church in the broader Asian area, "certain men" had emerged and secured for themselves prominent leadership positions. Unfortunately, these men were anything but qualified to lead, both in terms of what they believed and taught and in the way they lived their lives. Not only were they teaching false doctrine, but they also demonstrated arrogant attitudes and actions (see 1 Tim. 1:3-7).

Some of these men went so far as to be guilty of blasphemy. Paul warned Timothy to avoid being influenced by these false teachers—to "fight the good fight" by "keeping faith and a good conscience" (vv. 18,19). To do otherwise could lead to spiritual disaster, as it did in the lives of Hymenaeus and Alexander and others who had "suffered shipwreck in regard to their faith" (v. 19).

Imagine the challenge Timothy faced! Here was a relatively young man, probably about thirty years of age, facing some men who were no doubt much older than himself, men who were already in influential positions and in the process of leading believers astray.

Problems such as these are not solved easily nor quickly, which helps explain Paul's challenge to Timothy in his second letter. In that Epistle, Paul charged his younger colleague to "fan into flame" the gift God had given him and to never become intimidated by these powerful and influential leaders. He was to face the problem head on with a "spirit...of power and love and discipline" (2 Tim. 1:7).

Titus had a similar challenge on the island of Crete. Also a young man, Paul had left him in this pagan but fruitful mission field to establish the new believers that had come to Christ as a result of their church-planting efforts and to appoint godly leaders who could lead these new congregations (see Titus 1:5).

In some respects, Titus faced an even greater task than Timothy did in Ephesus. Many "rebellious" leaders—"empty talkers and deceivers," to quote Paul—had already emerged and were "upsetting whole families, teaching things they should not to teach" (v. 11b). They "must be silenced," wrote Paul (v. 11a).

Prior to this exhortation, Paul had outlined a list of qualifications to guide Titus in appointing leaders in the churches in Crete that is in essence very similar to the list in Paul's first letter to Timothy (compare

1 Tim. 3:1-7 with Titus 1:5-9). Because of space limitations in this chapter, let's concentrate on the characteristics outlined in 1 Timothy, and include supplementary references to those listed in Titus.

BECOMING A *CHRISTIAN* LEADER

Paul wanted both Timothy and Titus to know in no uncertain terms what to look for in a potential leader. As we outline and elaborate on these requirements, note that Paul said very little about skills or abilities or even gifts. All these characteristics relate to qualities of life: high morals, ethical behavior, right attitudes, pure motives, proper goals, positive habits, quality relationships and a good reputation. Even knowledge is not high on Paul's list of priorities, though it is certainly assumed, particularly in his letter to Titus when he said these leaders were to "exhort in sound doctrine and to refute those who contradict" (Titus 1:9).

There is a reason for this emphasis. Those who have knowledge, skills and abilities without the qualities outlined by Paul can lead people in the wrong direction efficiently and quickly. This was happening in both Ephesus and Crete.

Do not misunderstand! This does not mean that knowledge, skills and abilities are not important, even when looking for qualified spiritual leaders. The Scriptures warn against "zeal without knowledge" (Prov. 19:2, *NIV*). A person devoid of knowledge, skills and abilities will flounder as a leader. Giftedness without character, though, is lethal. When appointing leaders, if we get the "cart before the horse"—abilities before character—we can literally destroy a church or any other Christian organization. All it takes is one strong ego-driven person to disrupt unity and create almost intolerable divisiveness.

Leadership Principle 1:
A leader should be living an exemplary life that is obvious to both Christians and non-Christians.

Related Spiritual Principle:
A leader must be above reproach.[2]
When looking for a potential leader, Paul listed this character quality first. Significantly, it is at the top of the list in both his first letter to

Timothy and in his letter to Titus. Paul was not talking about perfection, because Jesus Christ was the only perfect leader who walked on planet Earth. Rather, Paul was referring to a person's reputation—how others view this person.

Timothy's character was perhaps his greatest strength as a leader. This was a key reason Paul asked him to serve as his assistant in ministry. When he and Silas arrived in Lystra on their second missionary journey, Luke records that Timothy "was well spoken of" in his home town (Acts 16:2). People were talking about this young man and his commitment to Jesus Christ, not only where he lived, but also in Iconium, a neighboring city. His reputation had spread beyond his local community. Paul was impressed because he knew the leadership challenge that lay ahead. If new congregations were to survive and grow, they would need godly leaders.

Paul also knew that he needed a fellow missionary on the second journey who could discover and approve these leaders. More importantly, he needed an associate who was "practicing what he preached." In short, it takes a leader who has a "good reputation" to direct, train and appoint others with "a good reputation."

Imagine what would have happened if Timothy had preached a message in Ephesus regarding the need for leaders who have a "good reputation" without demonstrating this quality in his own life. He faced a task that was tough enough without giving people the opportunity to question his own character.

Notice that Paul wanted Timothy to appoint leaders who not only had a good reputation in the "believing community," but also in the "pagan community." Consequently, he culminated his character profile for elders and pastors by stating that every spiritual leader "must have a **good reputation with those outside the church**" (1 Tim. 3:7, author's emphasis). Paul did not mean that these potential leaders would not be criticized or ridiculed because of their faith. Rather, he wanted leaders in the church who demonstrated honesty and integrity in their relationships with nonbelievers. In essence, Paul was saying the same thing Peter said to all Christians when he wrote:

> And keep a good conscience so that in the thing in which you are slandered, those who revile your good behavior in Christ may be put to shame (1 Pet. 3:16).

Leadership Principle 2:
A leader should be morally pure, maintaining God's standard of righteousness.

Related Spiritual Principle: A leader should be the husband of one wife.[3] When Paul exhorted Timothy to seek individuals who had been "the husband of one wife," in essence, he was referring to moral purity. We could fairly translate Paul's phrase as a "man of one woman." In other words, any man who served the church as an elder or pastor was to have only one woman in his life sexually—namely, his wife.[4]

One reason this was such an important spiritual requirement in the New Testament world for leaders is that many men—particularly those who were well-to-do—had more than one woman he related to at a sexual level. Besides his wife, he had a slave girl who was available to him, and he often acquired the services of a temple prostitute. This was common within the Roman Empire. When any man became a Christian, however, he came face-to-face with a new standard of morality: God's standard. He was to have only one woman in his life in terms of sexual intimacy: his legal wife. The same standard applied to any Christian woman. In terms of sexual relationships, she, too, was to have only one man in her life: her husband.

In both letters, being the "husband of one wife" is listed second after being "above reproach." This is by divine design. Moral purity is the most important quality for building a good reputation. Any Christian leader who violates this principle becomes suspect in terms of being trustworthy. As my new friends stated during the conference coffee break referred to earlier, if you cannot trust a man to be loyal to his wife, you cannot trust him to be loyal to his organization, be it Christian or non-Christian. The same applies to any woman in a leadership role. A woman who cheats on her husband will more often than not cheat the company—or the church.

This biblical requirement for Christian leaders raises an important question. Should a person who has committed adultery and truly repented of that sin ever be allowed to occupy a top leadership position in the church (pastor, elder, deacon, deaconess)? This question is not easily answered. One thing is clear, though. If this kind of behavior hurts our reputations, making it difficult for us to minister to others, we are violating the first requirement—being "above reproach." For some it *is* possible to start over, especially in another community. For others, however, their reputations are so tainted because of their high profiles in the Christian community that it is virtually impossible to start over.

I remember talking to a well-known pastor who was guilty of adultery with many women. Relieved of his duties where he pastored, he wanted to immediately start a new church in the same geographical area. I reminded him one day that the "whole city" knew about his affairs because his moral crisis had been reported in the major newspaper. Furthermore, he was an author whose books were read widely and he was featured on a national and international television ministry. He could go very few places in the world without being known as the pastor of a large and growing church who had committed adultery, many times with many women. Unfortunately, he did not listen to me (or several other concerned people). It was just a matter of time before he repeated his sinful behavior, devastating more people and bringing further reproach on the cause of Christ.

Having a "good reputation" is a fundamental criteria for answering the earlier question. More important, sufficient evidence must be made available to know whether or not the person has truly repented of the sin. Sadly, in the case just illustrated, it was revealed that this man was not telling the whole truth. After our conversation, it soon became evident that he had been involved with more women than any of us knew about. His so-called "repentance" was not real. Sadly, this, too, was reported in a well-known and sophisticated secular periodical. Unfortunately, many leaders who are trapped in this kind of sin and are found out are more "sorry" they were caught than that they hurt the Savior and deeply offended the Holy Spirit.

Leadership Principle 3:
A leader should walk by faith, demonstrate hope and manifest true biblical love in all relationships.

Related Spiritual Principle:
A leader should be a temperate Christian.[5]
When Paul used the term "temperate," he was describing a Christian who had a clear focus on life. More broadly, this kind of Christian has a philosophy of life that is built foursquare on the Scriptures.

Leaders who are temperate have a biblical view of history. They understand God's sovereign control of the universe, but at the same time they carry out their human responsibilities diligently. They are balanced as they approach problems and they avoid extremes that sidetrack them from the purposes God left us in the world to fulfill.

In his letter to the Thessalonians, Paul described a "temperate" Christian as one who has "put on the breastplate of **faith** and **love**, and as a helmet, the **hope** of salvation" (1 Thess. 5:8, author's emphasis). Interestingly, Paul used these three words frequently to describe maturity among Christians generally (see Eph. 1:15,18; Col. 1:3-8; 1 Thess. 1:2,3; 2 Thess. 1:3; 1 Cor. 13:13). If all Christians together are to reflect these qualities, how much more must Christian leaders possess them?

More specifically, how do we recognize a Christian who is "temperate"?

Faith is reflected in Christians who are willing to step out and believe God's promises. They do not fear the unknown, because they know that God is in control. At the same time, people of faith do not take foolish risks, ignoring the human factors in decision making. In essence, they practice the following proverb:

> Trust in the Lord with all your heart, and do not lean on your own understanding. In all your ways acknowledge Him, and He will make your paths straight (Prov. 3:5,6).

Hope is reflected in Christians who are secure in what they believe. They are stable and steadfast, particularly in the face of adversity. They know where history is going and ultimately, no matter how much their society deteriorates, they know they have "an inheritance which is imperishable and undefiled and will not fade away, reserved in heaven" for them (1 Pet. 1:4). Furthermore, they are not "carried about by every wind of doctrine" (Eph. 4:14).

Love is reflected in several characteristics that are beautifully illustrated in Paul's first letter to the Corinthians, in which he describes love as being patient, kind, not jealous, not arrogant, not acting unbecomingly, not seeking its own, not provoked, not taking into account a wrong suffered and not rejoicing in unrighteousness. Love is also described as rejoicing with the truth, bearing all things, believing all things, hoping all things and enduring all things (1 Cor. 13:4-7).

Leadership Principle 4:
A leader should be wise, discerning and experienced; the kind of

Christian who reflects true humility and is disciplined by God's grace to live a godly life and to be a person of prayer.

Related Spiritual Principle:
A Christian leader is a prudent person.[6]

The Greek word translated "prudent" is *sophron*, which literally means "sound in mind." This word can also be translated "discreet," "sober" or "sensible," depending upon the context. Frankly, I like the word "prudent" because Webster reminds us that a prudent leader is "shrewd in the management of practical affairs." Consequently, we can conclude that a prudent person is a "person of wisdom."

When Moses faced the awesome responsibility of leading two million plus people through the wilderness, he was directed by the Lord to "Choose **wise** and **discerning** and **experienced** men" from each tribe and to appoint them as leaders to help in his own management role (Deut. 1:13,14, author's emphasis). In short, "wise," "discerning" and "experienced" people become prudent leaders.

More specifically, how do we recognize a "prudent" Christian?

First of all, such a person is a humble leader. Paul underscored this reality when he wrote to the Romans that no person should "think more highly of himself than he ought to think; but to think so as to have **sound judgment** [that is, to think soberly, sensibly or prudently], as God has allotted to each a measure of faith" (Rom. 12:3, author's emphasis). Put another way, prudent leaders will "do nothing from selfishness or empty conceit"; rather they function "with humility of mind." They regard others "as more important" than themselves; they will "not merely look out for" their "own personal interests, but also for the interests of others" (Phil. 2:3,4).

Second, a prudent Christian is one who possesses a proper view of God's grace. Paul underscored this point when he wrote to Titus:

> For the grace of God has appeared, bringing salvation to all men, instructing us to deny ungodliness and worldly desires and to live sensibly [or prudently], righteously and godly in the present age (Titus 2:11,12).

Finally, a prudent person is a person of prayer. Peter acknowledged this when he admonished his followers: "Be of **sound judgment** [be **prudent**] and sober of spirit for the purpose of prayer"

(1 Pet. 4:7, author's emphasis). A "prudent" leader will go to his knees in humble and prayerful adoration, and then rise to a new level of righteous and holy living.

Leadership Principle 5:
A leader should live a well-ordered life that makes the gospel attractive to unbelievers.

Related Spiritual Principle:
A leader must be a respectable Christian.[7]
If a **temperate** Christian reflects "a well-ordered *philosophy of life*," a respectable Christian lives "*a well-ordered life*." The former involves a person's ability to think clearly; the latter reflects the ability to translate "good thinking" into "proper actions."

The Greek word translated "respectable" is *kosmios*. Our English word "cosmetics" comes from the same basic word. We see this connection when the verb *kosmeo* is translated "to adorn." For example, slaves were to be "well-pleasing, not argumentative" and they were not to steal from their masters. Rather, they were to "adorn [*kosmeo*] the doctrine of God our Savior in every respect" (Titus 2:10). In essence, Paul is teaching that a mature leader's life will be like "cosmetics to the gospel." When non-Christians observe their attitudes and actions, they should be attracted to the gospel message and to the One who incarnates that message.

When I speak about the subject of leadership qualities, I like to share the following modern parable:

> A certain man and his wife in a certain city bought a home and moved in. This man was a Christian and the man from whom he purchased the house was also a Christian. Both were Christian ministers.
>
> After a few days it became apparent that certain neighbors were disturbed that another minister had moved next door. For behold, the former minister had paid little attention to the outward appearance of his property. He allowed the grass to grow long and unattended, and when he did mow the lawn, certain sections were left uncut, and where he mowed, mounds of dry grass accumulated, creating a shabby appearance. Dandelions grew rampant, and other assorted weeds

became a permanent part of the landscape. This man had planted no trees or shrubs, but allowed his large and spacious lawn to become a hay field.

It just so happened that certain neighbors in this particular community paid special attention to the outward appearances of their homes. True, many were not Christians and they were materialistic. Their houses and lawns appeared to be their "gods."

But the neighbors were totally turned off by this minister's irresponsibility and lack of orderliness and unwillingness to do his part to add to the natural beauty of the neighborhood. Consequently, the minister moving in after the former one moved away found great communication barriers with his non-Christian neighbors. They were utterly convinced that ministers are a bad lot, that they are disorderly, unconcerned and irresponsible about keeping up their property.

This is a true parable. It happened to my wife and me. Because of this man's actions, it took us months to build bridges to the people next door. Eventually, we won respect by working hard to do what this Christian leader had not done. After days of mowing, planting trees and shrubs and eliminating the weeds, we overcame this communication barrier. We became "respectable" in that neighborhood and once again we were able to "adorn" the gospel of Christ by living a lifestyle that was commensurate with the character of God.

Leadership Principle 6:
A leader should be unselfish and generous, willing to open his home for ministry and to share his earthly blessings with both Christians and non-Christians.

Related Spiritual Principle:
A Christian leader should be hospitable.[8]
Generally speaking, "being hospitable" refers to the way we use our material possessions—particularly the homes we live in and the food we eat. Interestingly, showing hospitality is not distinctive to Christianity. For example, consider the following description of the Muslim culture: "A traveler may sit at the door of a perfect stranger and smoke a pipe until the master welcomes him with an evening meal and then tarry a

limited number of days without inquiry as to his purposes, and depart with a simple 'God be with you' as his only compensation."[9]

It is clear from the New Testament that Christians, of all people, should be hospitable. Listen to the following exhortations:

- Be devoted to one another in brotherly love; give preference to one another in honor...contributing to the needs of the saints, practicing hospitality (Rom. 12:10,13).
- Let love of the brethren continue. Do not neglect to show hospitality to strangers, for by this some have entertained angels without knowing it (Heb. 13:1,2).
- Above all, keep fervent in your love for one another, because love covers a multitude of sins. Be hospitable to one another without complaint (1 Pet. 4:8,9).

"Showing love" and "demonstrating hospitality" are inseparable concepts. **Love** is the foundational quality that reflects the unselfish way Jesus Christ gave His life to save us. **Hospitality** is a specific way we can imitate Jesus Christ and demonstrate His love to others. To fail to show hospitality is to fail to love as Jesus commanded.

If all Christians are to show hospitality—and they are—they need to see it in their leaders. This was imperative in the early days of Christianity because the church could not own property. Consequently, they had to meet in homes—especially in the homes of church leaders. Though cultural situations have changed, it is still important that a Christian leader be hospitable.

Leadership Principle 7:
A leader should be able to communicate in a nonargumentative, nondefensive and nonthreatening way—demonstrating gentleness, patience and teachability without compromising the message of the Word of God.

Related Spiritual Principle: A leader must be able to teach.[10]
On the surface, it may appear that Paul was talking about the "**gift of teaching**," or an **ability** or **skill** in communication. Not so—at least not in the way we describe teaching methods today. Rather, to be "able to teach" is a quality of life, an aspect of a person's character.

Let's allow Scripture to interpret Scripture. The Greek word translated "able to teach" is *didaktikos*. This word is used only twice in the New Testament—here in 1 Timothy and in 2 Timothy 2:23-25. In this latter passage, the main idea is "communication," which is described as *didaktikos*. Note the words Paul used that cluster around the quality of being "able to teach." Paul exhorted Timothy to "not be quarrelsome" or argumentative. He was to be "kind to all," referring specifically to everyone he was teaching. While teaching, he was to be "patient when wronged." When anyone opposed the message of the Word of God, he was to "correct with gentleness."

Needless to say, these are qualities of maturity that are reflected in a nondefensive approach to communication and an openness to learn. In classical Greek, the word *didaktikos* meant "teachable." In essence, a person who is "able to teach" demonstrates a sense of security, teachability and a nonthreatening response to those who may disagree.

I love to illustrate this quality of life by telling a true story of a man and his wife who have served with me as lay leaders for several years at Fellowship Bible Church North where I am senior pastor. Mike and his wife, Sharon, are wonderful dedicated Christians and have always challenged me with their own walk with God.

Mike is a banker. One Saturday morning, he and Sharon were eating breakfast. As they looked out their kitchen window, a bus pulled up in front of their home. A number of people got off the bus, picked up placards and began to picket in front of their house.

In a few minutes, a man knocked at the door with a document in his hands. He wanted Mike to sign a statement that his bank—a large Savings & Loan conglomerate throughout Texas—demonstrated prejudicial decisions against minorities in making loans. Standing beside this man was another individual with a camera, ready to take a picture of Mike's reactions—assuming they would be negative, which would probably be displayed the next day in *The Dallas Morning News*.

In reality, what had happened was that the United States government had passed legislation that had been interpreted by minorities as prejudicial treatment. Since Mike was the CEO of this large Savings & Loan association, those minorities targeted him as a means to make their point. In short, Mike was set up.

As a Christian, what would you have done in this situation?

Frankly, my own reactions might have been less than mature. Mike's response illustrates in an incredible way what Paul meant by being "able to teach." Rather than defending himself or reacting negatively, Mike invited all of the picketers into his home. Naturally, the man at the door with the document in his hands was totally nonplused—as was the entire group. However, recognizing Mike's offer was sincere, they laid down their placards in a pile on the front lawn and all marched into his family room. Sharon served them coffee while Mike explained his personal concerns for minorities, as well as the history of his own involvement with minority groups in the city of Dallas.

When the natural opportunity came, Mike shifted his focus from his involvement in social activities to an experience that he had several years before. Mike had come to know Jesus Christ as his personal Lord and Savior which, he told the group, even intensified his concern for helping others.

At that point, there was a decided change in the reactions of the group. Mike even began to get some affirmations from some of these strangers. Mike had won their hearts. They began to see more clearly his own perspective on what was happening in our society.

After a period of time together, the people stood up, thanked Mike and Sharon for their hospitality, and one by one walked out the door and got on the bus and left. They were never heard from again.[11]

When I heard Mike share this experience, I thought immediately of what Paul wrote to Timothy about being "able to teach." Mike and Sharon both demonstrated unusual maturity in that situation. Very quickly, a negative response on Mike's part could have led to an argument. If he had "slammed the door"—which I would have been tempted to do—he would have played into their hands. More importantly, he would have missed the golden opportunity to share both the message of Christ and Christlikeness.

By "keeping the door open" and being "patient when wronged" and "with gentleness correcting those who were in opposition" to him, Mike was also given an "open door" to correct the thinking of the people in this group. Right there before his very eyes he began to see attitude changes, which happens when people begin to listen and to come "to the knowledge of the truth."

What Mike did in no way justifies anything that may have been inappropriately done by the United States government or any other organization. Mike, however, took this opportunity to share his desire to be fair, honest and nonprejudiced in his dealings with people, both in his personal life and in his business. By practicing this quality of life in a nondefensive and open way, he was "able to teach."

Leadership Principle 8:
A leader should not be in bondage to any sinful cravings of the flesh; furthermore, that person should carefully consider the way his or her freedoms in Christ might lead others to sin.

Related Spiritual Principle:
A Christian leader must not be addicted to wine.[12]
This particular requirement for leadership has often confused people. The fact is the Bible does not teach total abstinence. Most scholars agree that references to wine in both the Old and New Testaments refer to fermented grape juice. This is why Paul wrote that a spiritual leader should not be "addicted to wine." Obviously, we cannot be "addicted" to nonalcoholic grape juice. If Paul were teaching total abstinence, he would have stated that a spiritual leader should never partake of wine. What does the Bible actually teach about drinking wine?

The following guidelines are provided in the Bible.

1.   It is always outside God's will to overindulge and over-drink. Listen carefully to the following warnings in the book of Proverbs:

      Who has woe? Who has sorrow?
      Who has contentions? Who has complaining?
      Who has wounds without cause?
      Who has redness of eyes?
      Those who linger long over wine (Prov. 23:29,30).

2.   It is always outside God's will to become **addicted** to wine. Listen to the words of Paul in his letter to the

Corinthians: In 1 Corinthians 6:12 Paul wrote, "All things are lawful for me, but not all things are profitable. All things are lawful for me, but I will not be **mastered** by anything." In essence, this is what Paul had in mind when he established this requirement for spiritual leaders. Today we classify this kind of person as an alcoholic.

3.   It is always outside God's will when we cause others to sin. Paul spoke to this particular issue when he said, "It is good not to eat meat or to drink wine or to do anything by which your brother stumbles" (Rom. 14:21). This principle is applicable to all relationships. However, it is particularly applicable to parents. The National Council on Alcoholism states that children of alcoholics run a risk of becoming alcoholics themselves that is four times greater than that of children of nonalcoholics. This demonstrates the power of modeling and example. Furthermore, we must remember that some children (some say one in five) are born with a propensity toward alcoholism. When children have this natural tendency to become addicted, modeling by parents simply moves them in that direction more quickly.

4.   It is always outside God's will to become addicted to anything. Paul's exhortation to not be addicted to wine has a broader application. A Christian should not be addicted to anything: drugs of any kind, sex, material things or food. For example, some Christians regularly overeat, but they never drink wine or any kind of alcoholic beverage. Yet the Bible condemns both addictions (see Prov. 23:20,21).

Within a period of two weeks, two men in the church I pastor separately approached me regarding drinking alcoholic beverages. Both men were growing Christians who desired to do the will of God. The factor that triggered their concerns about their actions, however, was their young children. Both these men were well aware of the problems in our society. They knew the dangers of alcoholism, and they were concerned about the example they might set for their children. Was it worth the risk to drink, although drinking might not be sin for them? Would their freedom in Christ eventually cause one of their children to fall?

As we discussed the matter, they both came to the conclusion that drinking alcoholic beverages in front of their children was not worth the risk. One decided on total abstinence. The other decided on abstinence in front of the children. Both made decisions based on principles of Scripture (see Rom. 14:1-23).

Leadership Principle 9:
A leader should be able to control angry feelings, never expressing these feelings in hurtful ways nor allowing them to linger indefinitely.

Related Spiritual Principle: A leader is not pugnacious.[13]
The Greek word translated "pugnacious" is *pleektees*. Thayer defines this kind of person as a "bruiser," one who is "ready with a blow"; a "pugnacious, contentious, quarrelsome person."[14] Pugnaciousness is really anger out of our control. It is not surprising that Paul stated this requirement for spiritual leaders following his warning against being "addicted to wine." Drinking and particularly drunkenness often lead to arguments, brawls and fights.

Even more fundamental to not being pugnacious is to avoid being "quick tempered." Paul referred to this characteristic in his letter to Titus (1:7). "Quick temperedness" is also a form of anger.

At this point, we must understand that not all anger is sinful. It is a normal emotion. Paul acknowledged this when he admonished the Ephesians: "Be angry, and yet do not sin" (Eph. 4:26). Jesus Christ, the perfect Son of God, demonstrated that it is possible to express anger without sinning when He drove the money changers from the Temple (see John 2:13-17).

When does anger become sinful?

1. When it results in "quick tempered" behavior. The Greek word *orgilos*, which Paul used in Titus 1:7, literally means "prone to anger." The English word that probably comes closest to describing this kind of quick-tempered person is "irascible," meaning "hot tempered" or "easily provoked" to anger. A quick-tempered person "flies off the handle," "loses control" and usually says and does things that hurt and offend others.
2. When it hurts people physically. This is what Paul had in mind when he used the Greek word *pleektees*—which

is translated "pugnacious." This can also happen when anger gets out of control.

3.   When it persists and results in bitterness. After Paul exhorted the Ephesians to "be angry and yet do not sin," he elaborated by warning them that all of us need a cooling off period when we get angry. It is virtually impossible to suddenly flip the switch and dissipate angry feelings. Time, however, becomes our friend. It gives us an opportunity to understand what is causing our anger and to become more objective. If this does not happen, angry feelings can turn to bitterness, which is sinful.

4.   When we hurt people emotionally and spiritually. Anger that leads to verbal abuse can be even more devastating than physical abuse. Some Christians would never strike out at others physically, but they use their tongues to put others down, to control people, to embarrass them and to misplace their own hostility. Unfortunately, children are more vulnerable to this kind of abuse than adults simply because they have no way of protecting themselves.

5.   When we become vengeful. It is natural to want to hurt those who have hurt us—to get even. That, however, God says, is not our right nor our responsibility. Paul wrote: "Never pay back evil for evil to anyone....Never take your own revenge, beloved, but leave room for the wrath of God, for it is written, 'vengeance is mine, I will repay,' says the Lord" (Rom. 12:17,19).

Leadership Principle 10:
A leader should be able to demonstrate strong convictions and directness in taking a stand for righteousness, but to also balance these attitudes and actions with a loving spirit.

Related Spiritual Principle: Be gentle.[15]
Paul contrasts "pugnaciousness" with "gentleness." Interestingly, several Greek words are translated "gentle." Paul, however, chose this particular word (*epiikees*) to describe a particular kind of gentleness: "a spirit of forbearance." Thayer defines the word as being "equitable" and "fair," and we might add "reasonable."[16]

I like to use Tom Landry, former coach of the Dallas Cowboys, to illustrate this particular quality. Coach Landry was a fair-minded man. Tony Dorsett, a premier running back who at times frustrated Landry, made the following comment as he reflected back on his years with the Cowboys: "Maybe you didn't always like his decisions, but he was fair. He would listen to all sides of an issue and then decide what was best for the team."[17]

Dorsett was not the only Cowboy who at times caused a lot of difficulties for Landry. Dwayne Thomas, another powerful running back, helped lead the Cowboys to a Super Bowl victory. Thomas later got hooked on drugs, however, and his behavior became so bizarre that it became ridiculous.

Then Thomas (Hollywood) Henderson blew a potentially brilliant career for the same reason and later became a public embarrassment to the entire Cowboy organization.

As tough-minded as Landry could be, he demonstrated incredible patience and forbearance (gentleness) with these men on his team. In his book *The Landry Legend*, Bob St. John summarized Tom's approach: "Faith was certainly a factor in helping him to try to understand and cope with a much troubled Dwayne Thomas and to be more fair and understanding of a person such as Thomas (Hollywood) Henderson and the somewhat different behavior patterns of Tony Dorsett."[18]

Randy White, an All-Pro Defensive lineman put it this way, "Hey, I was there when he had a lot of those misfits, and Coach Landry would bend over backwards in giving them a second and even a third chance. That's two or three more than they'd have gotten from anybody else— or from anybody in any other kind of business. He did it because he has faith in people."[19]

Mike Ditka, who both played for the Cowboys and later coached the Chicago Bears added, "Tom Landry is probably the fairest guy I've ever been around. He let a lot of players push him to the limit. But when they did, that was it!"[20]

I use this Tom Landry illustration because it is not often we find a Christian man who is so well-known as a leader and who has demonstrated so dramatically what Paul had in mind with the word *epiikees*. Strange as it seems, this form of "gentleness" and "patience" is unique. The translators of the *Amplified New Testament* captured this meaning with these words, "not combative but gentle and considerate" (1 Tim. 3:3).

Leadership Principle 11:
A leader should relate to others by using a style of communication
that does not make them feel controlled, manipulated and defensive.

Related Spiritual Principle: Do not be contentious.[21]
I have a close friend who now serves with me as a lay elder at
Fellowship Bible Church North. Those who knew him best called him
"Mr. Charge Ahead." In his young days, he was known as "Fast Eddie."
He loved to debate—which at times was interpreted as being argumentative, insensitive and even contentious. Before this man was
selected to be an elder, we followed a standard procedure we regularly
use in evaluating whether a man and his wife are qualified for this level
of leadership. We asked all our other elders (and their wives) and our
staff pastors (and their wives) to fill out an evaluation form on each
prospective candidate and his wife (if married). This form is based on
the characteristics we are looking at in this chapter. We ask each person
to use a seven-point scale to express his or her degree of satisfaction or
dissatisfaction with this person's behavior on each characteristic. (The
questions are contained at the conclusion of this chapter.)

When Eddie was being considered for eldership, we followed this
procedure. When the forms were returned, he was consistently
marked down in several related areas, one being "contentious." As
senior pastor, I and one other lay elder sat down with this man and his
wife to report these responses. Frankly, I was nervous about it, as I
always am in these circumstances. This kind of communication is
always difficult for me, especially when it involves a close friend.

A wonderful thing happened. Eddie sat and listened, obviously
surprised. He was totally open and nondefensive and thanked us for
our time and openness with him and assured us he would think and
pray about what we had shared.

Later, he asked his wife—who had received perfect scores—for her
opinion. Did she agree with our evaluation? She did. What she said
surprised him. In retrospect, the following is Eddie's own personal
account of what happened!

> When Maureen said that she agreed with the evaluation that I
> could be contentious, argumentative and too bold in defend-
> ing the views I held strongly, I knew that God wanted to get
> my attention—big time. I also knew down deep that the eval-

uation was correct. As I asked God for help, He made it clear to me that I needed to develop the fruit of the Spirit known as gentleness. He also gave me a plan. I was to get my family to hold me accountable. One evening I called my family together and asked each one to forgive me for not being gentle and to ask for their help. I explained to them that every time they saw me using my verbal skills to steamroll over them, raise my voice, show anger or be contentious in any way, they were to put an X on the family calendar in the kitchen.

To my dismay, the next day I got five Xs. I considered changing the rules! But I was committed and my family helped me learn to be gentle. What started out as a crushing blow to my "Mr. Charge Ahead" ego had turned into a wonderful blessing in my life. I now know a viewpoint spoken in gentleness with energy is much more acceptable and effective with the listener. I certainly have not arrived at my goal, but I'm on my way.

Eddie's response to this process in itself demonstrates his growing maturity. The changes he made were immediately obvious to all who knew him well. He eventually became an elder and today I consider him one of our most faithful board members. He has a heart for God, a heart for the ministry and a heart for people. The facts are, he really always did. He simply needed to change his style of communication. He did not mean to appear contentious, authoritarian, argumentative and controlling. When he learned that other mature leaders—including one within his own family—thought he was, however, he made some permanent and lasting changes.

Leadership Principle 12:
A leader should be a generous Christian, giving regularly, systematically, proportionally and joyfully to the Lord's work.

Related Spiritual Principle:
A leader must be free from the love of money.[22]

A mature Christian leader does not love money. This is true of all mature believers. Do not misunderstand. The Scriptures do not teach that "money," per se, is evil. Nor do they teach that it is wrong to have lots of money. What they do teach is that it is a serious violation of God's will when we love it. That is why Paul said that when a

Christian is selected for a leadership position, that person should be "free"—not from money, but "from the love of money."

I had the unique experience of joining a group of men who studied everything the Bible says about material possessions. Later I wrote a book entitled *A Biblical Theology of Material Possessions*, in which I compiled the findings. To our amazement, we discovered that God says more about the way Christians should use their material possessions than about any other subject other than God Himself. Unquestionably, the greatest hallmark of Christian maturity is generosity.

Some researchers tell us that the average Christian gives only about 2 percent of his or her income to the Lord. Because approximately 15 percent of the Christian population tithe (i.e., give 10 percent of their income), this means that the majority of Christians give next to nothing. This simply indicates that most of us are "lovers of money." Christians as a whole have become materialists, which is a direct violation of the will of God.

In our culture, I personally believe this admonition should mean that we give a *minimum* of 10 percent of our gross income. If at all possible, this should be a starting point. If it is not possible, it should be our goal—one that we should ask God to help us reach as soon as possible.

Leadership Principle 13:
A leader who is also a parent should have a good relationship with his or her children, giving proper direction to the family unit.

Related Spiritual Principle:
A leader manages his own household well.[23]
Because Paul was addressing men with this maturity profile, he compared the father role to both the pastoral and deacon role (see 1 Tim. 3:12). The basic criteria for determining whether or not a man is ready for a key leadership role in the church is how well he is functioning as a spiritual leader in his home. His children particularly will reflect how well he has fulfilled this God-ordained function. If he is mature, a man will be able to keep "his children under control with all dignity" (1 Tim. 3:4). Paul told Titus that this kind of father will have "children who believe" and who are "not accused of dissipation or rebellion" (Titus 1:6).

Paul viewed a well-ordered family as the true test of a man's maturity and ability to lead other Christians. When the whole household is committed to Christ, you can be sure the father is spiritually and psychologically mature. When this is not true, however, if that man is appointed as a spiritual leader, the church will experience the same problems his family did. The very weaknesses that made this man a poor husband and dad will cause him to be a poor leader in the church. Furthermore, if a man who is not a good leader at home accepts this kind of leadership role, his family members will have less respect for him, which in turn will cause greater problems.

Do not misunderstand! Paul was not saying a person had to have children to be a good leader. He was simply saying **if** a man **is married**, and **if** he **has children**, then he should have a well-ordered household.

Neither was Paul referring to young children and the natural phases they go through as they are growing up. Rather, he was talking about older children who still lived in the family complex and who were guilty of "dissipation" and "rebellion" (see Titus 1:6)—or more specifically, a riotous and immoral lifestyle. The rebellious sons of Eli, who served as priests in the Tabernacle, illustrate what Paul had in mind (see 1 Sam. 2:12ff.).

Women who serve in leadership positions should also be tested in the same way. For example, Paul commended Timothy's mother, Eunice, for her diligence in nurturing this young man in biblical truth. She had taught him the Scriptures from the time he was a child (see 2 Tim. 1:5; 3:14,15). Because Timothy's father was not a Christian, Eunice served as both the mother and father in terms of spiritual nurture.

Note also that when Paul outlined qualifications for women who would serve in deacon roles, he stated they must "be dignified, not malicious gossips, but temperate, faithful in all things" (1 Tim. 3:11)—which certainly implies being good "managers of their own household."[24]

Paul also addressed this issue when writing to both older and younger women. Older women were to serve as leaders to younger women. To be qualified to do so, Paul outlined very specific leadership qualifications in Titus 2.3-5.

BECOMING A CHRISTIAN LEADER

It is important to understand that the criteria for selecting leaders in the church is not just a profile for pastors, elders or deacons. Rather, what Paul outlined in his letters to Timothy and Titus are the marks of a mature Christian. In essence, Paul was stating, "If you want to be a spiritual leader in the church, that's great! But just make sure you are mature!" He then outlined what a mature Christian looks like, whether male or female. The specific characteristics Paul pulled together in these succinct and power-packed paragraphs are listed elsewhere in the New Testament as marks of maturity and goals for all Christians.

Note again that Paul was not saying a Christian must be perfect to be a leader. That would disqualify all of us, including the apostle Paul (see Phil. 3:12-14). Along the way each of us fails in certain areas of our lives. The mark of true maturity, as illustrated by my friend Eddie, is what we do about our weaknesses. A mature Christian is open to correction and takes steps to make changes!

Should the qualifications Paul listed for elders or pastors be used to select **all** leaders in the church? This would be ideal because these profiles present the marks of a mature Christian. Realistically, however, new Christians can serve in many positions that do not require the same standards. It takes time to grow in Christ and reflect His character, and often the most conducive place to mature is in a leadership position. We must remember that the apostles became leaders before they became mature. They often demonstrated incredible egocentric and childish behavior. Jesus gave them selective responsibilities under His supervision and guidance, however, to prepare them for the Day of Pentecost when they became responsible to launch and lead the Church under the direction of the Holy Spirit.

When all is said and done, however, those who serve as pastors and other top leaders of the church should, of all people, be mature in Christ. If they are not, the whole Body of Christ will suffer, including the person who is assigned to a leadership position, but is not truly ready to provide such leadership.

ADDENDUM: PRINCIPLES TO LIVE BY

The following are the thirteen leadership principles we have looked at in this chapter. Fifteen qualifications for "eldership" are actually listed in 1 Timothy 3:1-7. The last two are not being a "new convert" (3:6) and having "a good reputation outside the church" (3:7). In this chapter, the last quality has been combined with the first requirement—being "above reproach." Not being a new believer is vital and important for those in key leadership roles, not only in the church, but also in other Christian ministries. Many new believers have been defeated by Satan when they are given a prominent position too quickly, including speaking and singing. As Paul states, they can quickly "become conceited and fall into the condemnation incurred by the devil" (3:6). Personalize these principles by answering the following questions and circling the appropriate number on the seven-point scale:[25]

1. To what extent am I living an exemplary life that is obvious to both Christians and non-Christians?

1	2	3	4	5	6	7
Never						Always

2. To what extent am I morally pure, maintaining God's standard of righteousness

1	2	3	4	5	6	7
Never						Always

3. To what extent am I a temperate Christian, one who walks by faith, demonstrates hope and manifests true biblical love in all relationships?

1	2	3	4	5	6	7
Never						Always

4. To what extent am I a prudent Christian, a person who is wise, discerning and experienced; furthermore, to what extent do I reflect true humility and a godly and prayerful life that is motivated by God's grace?

1	2	3	4	5	6	7
Never						Always

5. To what extent am I a respectable Christian, a person who lives a well-ordered life and makes the gospel attractive to unbelievers?

1	2	3	4	5	6	7
Never						Always

6. To what extent am I a hospitable Christian, one who is unselfish and generous and willing to open my home for ministry to share my earthly blessings with both Christians and non-Christians?

1	2	3	4	5	6	7
Never						Always

7. To what extent am I able to communicate in a nonargumentative, nondefensive and nonthreatening way—demonstrating gentleness, patience and teachability without compromising the message of the Word of God?

1	2	3	4	5	6	7
Never						Always

8. To what extent am I free from the sinful cravings of the flesh; furthermore, to what extent do I use my freedom in Christ in a way that does not cause others to sin?

1	2	3	4	5	6	7
Never						Always

9. To what extent am I able to control angry feelings, never expressing these feelings in hurtful and sinful ways?

1	2	3	4	5	6	7
Never						Always

10. To what extent am I able to demonstrate strong convictions and directness, not only taking a stand for righteousness, but to also balance these attitudes and actions with a spirit of gentleness that is fair, equitable, reasonable and sensitive?

1	2	3	4	5	6	7
Never						Always

11. To what extent am I able to relate to others with a style of communication that does not make them feel controlled, manipulated and defensive?

1	2	3	4	5	6	7
Never						Always

12. To what extent am I a generous Christian, giving regularly, systematically, proportionally and joyfully to the Lord's work?

1	2	3	4	5	6	7
Never						Always

13. To what extent am I a parent who has a good relationship with my children, giving proper direction to the family unit?

1	2	3	4	5	6	7
Never						Always

Notes

1. Gene A. Getz, *Measure of a Man* (Ventura, Calif.: Regal Books). This book was first published in 1974, then was extensively rewritten and republished in 1995. It continues to be the basis for men's Bible study groups and is also used extensively as a discipling tool to prepare men for leadership roles in the church. The book is based on a timeless outline and Scripture taken from 1 Timothy 3 and Titus 1.
2. See 1 Timothy 3:2a and Titus 1:6a.
3. See 1 Timothy 3:2b and Titus 1:6b.
4. Before we look carefully at this characteristic of maturity and what Paul had in mind, note that the profiles outlined by Paul in his letters to Timothy and Titus are applicable to both men and women in leadership roles. It is true that Paul was referring primarily to men when he listed this quality, but other references to a woman's leadership position emphasize the same quality of life. For example, a widow who served the church on a remunerative basis was to be "the wife of one man" (1 Tim. 5:9).
5. See 1 Timothy 3:2c.
6. See 1 Timothy 3:2d.
7. See 1 Timothy 3:2e.
8. See 1 Timothy 3:2f.
9. Merrill F. Unger, *Unger's Bible Dictionary* (Chicago: Moody Press, 1967), p. 502.
10. See 1 Timothy 3:2g.
11. This story has been previously published in *The Walk* by Gene A. Getz (Nashville: Broadman & Holman Publishers, 1994), pp. 201, 202, 218.
12. See 1 Timothy 3:3a and Titus 1:7d.
13. See 1 Timothy 3:3b.
14. Joseph H. Thayer, *Greek-English Lexicon of the New Testament* (Grand Rapids: Zondervan Publishing House, 1962), p. 516.
15. See 1 Timothy 3:3c.
16. Thayer, *Greek-English Lexicon of the New Testament*, p. 238.

17. Bob St. John, *The Landry Legend* (Dallas: Word Inc., 1989), p. 283.
18. Ibid., p. 156.
19. Ibid., p. 291.
20. Ibid., p. 157.
21. See 1 Timothy 3:3d.
22. See 1 Timothy 3:3e.
23. See 1 Timothy 3:4.
24. When Paul referred to "women" in 1 Timothy 3:12, it is my personal opinion he was referring to women in "serving roles." Consequently, this concept could be translated "deaconess."
25. This evaluation is based on *The Measure of a Man*, which is based on the twenty qualities outlined in both 1 Timothy 3 and Titus. The book is highly recommended as a resource to use to disciple and develop Christians who have leadership responsibilities.

SIX

BEING A TOUGH
BUT TENDER
LEADER

H. B. LONDON JR.

Following thirty-two years pastoring churches of all sizes—the last twenty years or so leading a "megachurch"—I now devote my energy to working with pastors and churches around the world. What I observe is an increase of contentiousness within congregations. I have further observed an increase in forced pastoral terminations and failed assignments. I have seen an upswing in the number of Christian leaders who, because of burnout and frustration, have opted out of their calling. In many cases, this choice has not necessarily been because they wanted to make such a transition, but because they could no longer stand the pressure of a contentious laity. Too much was at stake. The leaders valued their families and their own sanity far too much to stay and jeopardize their own future. I have talked to many of these people and have felt their total frustration at the inability to work out the "mess" that threatened their leadership.

In truth, some situations are just too tangled to correct, but from my experience and from the situations I have observed in which leaders successfully worked their way through the mine fields, I would argue that most conflicts between leaders and followers can be resolved. It is simply a matter of knowing when to be tough and when to be tender.

I would like to take you through some of the challenges I faced in my more than three decades of pastoral ministry. It might just be that you will see yourself in some of these snapshots of my past. How I handled these situations is where we might differ. First, however, let me share a bit of who I am and how I came to develop my style of balancing toughness and tenderness.

PREPARATION FOR LEADERSHIP

I am an only child born into the home of a minister. My dad was driven by his calling and did whatever he could to avoid conflict. My mother was also a people pleaser, but very much in control of every situation. Until my mid-teens, I was sheltered from conflict and dissension in the church world. We lived in a home where our love for each other was verbalized infrequently. We were not a demonstrative family and handled most of our problems either through avoidance or compromise. I do not remember any knock-down, drag-out battles between us. When a problem arose, we just worked it out.

I was generally sheltered from trouble until age sixteen, when my father was accused of an indiscretion by some members of the church he pastored in a midwest city. It was devastating for me. The accusation eventually cost our family more than I would realize. I think if I had known more about conflict management it might have played out differently, but it took me by surprise. The entire episode dulled my senses and created a huge distrust within me toward those who represented themselves as authority figures. To this day, I harbor a degree of distrust for folks who want to get too close, too quickly. I remember as a young man headed for college vowing in my heart never to be hurt that badly by anyone again.

You see, I wanted my dad to fight back, but he refused. Oh, I think a token defense was laid out for him by a half-hearted team of pastors, but in the end we packed up our "stuff" and headed into limbo. It would be seven years before our family would be together again in our own home.

As I look back at the forty years that have gone by, I realize our lives were never the same again. When you misspend seven years of your life, no amount of "good years" can recoup the loss. My dad was restored and was allowed a profitable and extensive ministry. My dad passed away in February 1996. For four months prior to his death, I watched the 87-year-old man sitting in a care home suffering the ravages of stroke dementia, and I can't help but wonder what our lives would have been like if he had taken the "bull by the horns" and faced his accusers. Of course, nothing can be gained by dwelling on the "what ifs" or the "how comes." Life just goes on. You can't hold back the dawn, as they say, and so much of what plagues each of us in life depends on how we handle the immediate. Your life is shaped by how you deal with the hand that has been dealt to you, just or not.

I am not writing these words so you will draw any conclusions about me or my leadership style. My purpose is to acknowledge that when each of us faces conflict, our decisions are influenced by the way our parents handled their challenges and, in some cases, the ways in which we have addressed our own past disappointments.

THE CATEGORY OF CHALLENGES

Of course, there is no way to list every challenge you might face as a leader. I am amazed at how many new dilemmas can surface in the course of an assignment. To frame the remainder of this discussion, let me address six common challenges to consider.

Self. My wife, Beverley, has often said I am my own worst enemy. She speaks with some authority about this matter: We have been married for more than thirty-nine years. She has seen me through my good times and bad. She has spoken her piece and held her tongue, but always she has spoken the truth in love.

The bottom line is that most of us know ourselves better than anyone else does. We are aware of our faults and shortcomings. We know when we are being stubborn, difficult to talk to, selfish, unbending, jealous and often unreachable, and we have many ways of hiding our faults even to the point of blaming someone else.

In the midst of conflict, every pastor-leader must first ask himself: Am I being fair? Have I looked deeply inside my own soul? Have I been willing to pray the psalmist's prayer, "Search me, oh God, and know my heart;...see if there be any offensive way in me" (Ps. 139:23,24, *NIV*). You have to be honest with yourself. Is there pride that must be confessed, sin that needs to be forgiven, an attitude that must be changed, arrogance that must be humbled? Remember the little song: "Let there be peace...and let it begin with me."

When conflict arises, the first place to look is in one's own life.

Criticism. Arlo Walker once wrote, "Coping with critics, complainers, and even the not-so-occasional loud mouth is routine ministry. But not all flack is routine criticism."[1]

There is a fine line between being thin-skinned and hardnosed. I remember hearing Stuart Briscoe say, "To be a successful pastor one must have the mind of a scholar, the heart of a child, and the hide of a rhinoceros." What if we do not have that hide? What if we are vulnerable or hypersensitive?

The answer: We must either get tough or we will be destroyed. We must develop a mind-set, a self-image and a skin that is not easily torn. To be honest, I have never managed to succeed in taking my own advice.

In Proverbs 17:10 *(NIV)* we read, "A rebuke impresses a man of discernment more than a hundred lashes a fool." The question is: When do we take criticism seriously? For starters, ask yourself this question: Is there a thread of truth in the criticism? Such a question raises many others: Are my motives appropriate? When I share my criticism with another, can the person help me honestly separate the truth from the fiction?

Thomas à Kempis, the fifteenth-century church leader, talked about the "medicinal use of criticism." He said, "It's good that we at times endure opposition and that we're evilly and untruly judged when our actions and intentions are good, because often these experiences promote humility and protect us from vain glory. For then we seek God's witness in our heart."[2]

Kempis is referring to the all-too-common humblers in life. Frankly, in my own ministry I have usually attempted to confront my critics. I do not think I do it to win them over as much as I do it to make sure that all the facts of the issue are correct. In more than one case I have found the "instant relief" of a solved conflict when during lunch or iced tea I asked with sincere wonder, "What do you think we can do to resolve our problem?" Call it the Matthew 18 strategy, if you wish; I call it common sense. Do what you need to do. If you can do something to make things better, do so. If you can't, knock the dirt off your shoes and go on.

Communication. Most leaders have little problem speaking, but severe limitations when it comes to listening. A majority of the problems we face in the church occur because we usually communicate on a "me" level. Sometimes we fall victim to conflict because we do not have a common vocabulary: We do not know how to describe what we are seeing and feeling without initiating an argument.

Take preaching, for instance. Preaching usually represents one-way communication. When pastors are taught how to preach but do not learn other forms of communication, they are severely handicapped. When they experience stress and tension in the congregation, they revert to the form of communication they know best, and that is preaching. Not listening, mind you, but preaching. We have learned well how to speak our opinions, but we have not learned how to hear or respond equally well to the opinions and positions of others. Often, once we stake out a position within a conflict scenario, we are immovable.

One of my most powerful experiences as a pastor was a situation of miscommunication that was never resolved. We tried, but we just could not make it work. We parted friendly, but not friends. To bring closure to the relationship I had an early-morning meeting with the couple in question and a staff member they admired. I allowed them to express their opinion of me and my ministry. The pain was excruciating, but like a dental appointment, it ended quickly. During the interchange, the couple made their point well. I listened. We shook hands, and they walked out of my life. Had we been unable to communicate, we would never have had closure. I only wish it could have ended differently. I have agonized about the failure of that relationship for years.

At times we must just cut our losses, but never, if possible, without a controlled confrontation that brings closure.

Staff. By definition, leaders have the responsibility to lead people. In many churches, that includes leading staff, whether laypeople or clergy. Often the greatest conflicts in an organization result from the inability of senior leadership to coexist effectively and cordially with their colleagues. To make matters worse, often a third party's apparent job is to ensure that calm is impossible.

I think it was Bill Hybels who said that three things are required from every staff member at a church: godliness, competency in the person's area and loyalty to the senior leader. Godliness takes time and devotion; competence you can help a person achieve; but if a colleague is not loyal, you can't help the person. The moment a staff member can no longer be supportive of his leader, he should leave. This is true regardless of that person's value to the Body or how deeply entrenched he is within the congregation. To prevent deeper divisions, festering animosities and other unnecessary conflict, the person should leave immediately.

I have had good success with staff relationships, but there have been exceptions. Like many leaders, I was once asked to inherit another man's group. They were loyal to the former leader—as they should have been—but they found it difficult to adjust to my way of doing things. The transition was tough on them and tough on me. My biggest mistake—and, I might add, injustice to them—was to temper my leadership by allowing my emotions to get the best of me. After all, I reasoned, these good people had homes, friends and a network of support, and I did not want to jeopardize any of that. My solution, instead, was to jeopardize my own effectiveness.

I recall with admiration one pastor's approach to his newly inherited staff: "These are my requirements. I am going to allow a few months for us to consider my expectations. In time, if I feel that you will be happier and more effective somewhere else, I will tell you that."

Indeed, staff difficulties should be resolved swiftly. They are like a cancer in that these crises rapidly infest the total Body. My experience has shown me that no matter what else, trust and loyalty are the two common threads that must exist if the leader-colleague relationship is going to work.

A few years ago I needed to ask a well-known, talented staff member to work somewhere else. Because of his national reputation and his connections with an important segment of our community, I was reluctant to do so. My reticence caused matters to deteriorate to a point where it was becoming obvious to our people. I was sitting at home late one evening when the telephone rang. It was a member of my church board. "We have just done what you should have done—we have terminated the employment of a staff member that should have been terminated weeks ago." I can't tell you how relieved I was. The fallout was painful, but the peace that permeated our staff from that day forward was worth the pain. For me, it was a harsh but important lesson.

Thus, my advice: Face staff issues quickly and honestly. Ask the three questions previously explained. If you cannot get a positive and affirmative response to all three items, a change must be made swiftly. Does that sound overly tough? It is not, really. In the long run, it is a more tender reaction. I beg you to be decisive.

Change. Change always costs something. We are presently in a period—both in and outside the church world—that is pulsating with rapid transformations. From the way we minister to the way we worship to the way we respond to the leaders who instigate change, people are being bombarded with new and different ways of doing things.

We minister in the age of the baby boomer whose credo is: If it's broken, don't fix it—get a new one. Boomers insist upon quality. Their generation does not say, "Oh well, if you want it done that way, even though we don't understand it, we'll go along with it." Rather, they say, "We don't understand that and we're not going to budge until we get some answers." If the right answers are not forthcoming, they persevere until they receive the one they want.

On the other hand, we also work with people who resist even an overture to create anything different. The conflict comes when the leader has to make a choice. Should we resist change and thus stay where we are? Should we make wholesale changes? Or should we attempt to pacify both sides? Trying to keep both groups happy is like the story of the Civil War soldier who one day mistakenly put on a blue shirt and gray pants and was shot at by both sides, the North and the South. To avoid such decision-making paralysis, here are my thoughts concerning ways to facilitate change.

√ **Build on your gifts and your personality.**

Because many leaders never learn to be themselves, they chase the elusive dream that God gave another. Be the best you can be. Hear God speaking to you. Never try to be a clone of anyone; be an original.

√ **Sell your vision to spiritual people.**

Conflict often begins when we "cast our dreams" to those who are not prepared to receive them. In every ministry, certain people have wealth, are very vocal or are the power brokers in the group. When you project the possibility of change, they can stifle your dreams quickly. Take time to get together with truly spiritual people in whom you have trust and confidence. Ask them to be honest with you after they have prayed about the vision and direction you have described to them. After this time of protected refinement, sell your dreams to your leadership team—one or two people at a time. You can't blame others for not accepting what they do not understand.

√ **Count the cost of change.**

I guarantee you it will cost you a great deal to make major changes in your organization. The price will be paid in people, finances and unity. I have seen churches, for instance, that were moving along smoothly. Everyone was satisfied just to be a part of the group, when all of a sudden a simple thing such as a change in worship style was just dropped on the people one Sunday. The days that followed were filled with phone calls, letters to the pastor, closed-door meetings and damaged emotions. Why? Because the leader did not count the cost of change. In the end it cost him his permission to lead his congregation any further.

I read that in a major denomination (to remain nameless) last year, twenty-five hundred pastors were forced to resign. This represented nearly 7 percent of their churches. I would almost guarantee that a major portion of those resignations came because of change, and the cost was never really determined until the pastor became the sacrificial lamb. Please never underestimate the ability of those you lead to resist with almost supernatural power the very notion of changing the way things used to be.

Expectations. In *Pastors at Risk*, Neil Wiseman and I wrote:

> Actual or assumed expectations smother vitality out of a leader's spirit. Then what "they" think or what "they" want tortures him with bad scenarios of what might happen. As a result, disquieting fears nag every expression of ministry, and leaders become so spoofed they cannot see the difference between a pesky mosquito and a ferocious lion. Without extreme care, these debilitating feelings shut a leader off from two energizing forces for ministry: intimacy with Christ and tenderness with family. A mature leader warns: "In the overload frame of mind, a pastor often gives up on a fruitful devotional life and a robust, satisfying family life. As a consequence, many wrestle with empty souls and a loss of family through divorce or rebellious children."[3]

Because of the exigency of expectations, it is easy for a leader to barter the important for the immediate. Describing his frayed emotions, a veteran spiritual leader writes about the complicated demands he is experiencing: "Exhaustion comes to me from just thinking of the many more complex predicaments people bring to their leaders these days, let alone trying to help them with the problem." Like cancerous cells in the human body, these priorities and unrealistic expectations may multiply and feed on themselves. A serious attempt to reconcile grace with expectations and dependence with duty may provide the much-needed answers we seek. Liberating freedom comes to a leader's mind when he realizes his best self and his noblest efforts are good enough for God. It is vital that you not let your assignment determine your lifestyle. If that happens, you will become paranoid, and the very people you have been asked to lead will become the enemy rather than your colaborers.

The secret is to determine the parameters within which your ministry will operate. Help those you lead understand your values and your priorities. Constantly reiterate your understanding of the expectations required to perform your task. If you fail to make this clear, you will constantly be drawn back and forth from one group to another, attempting to make everyone happy. The unhappiest of all will be the leader.

Remember the counsel Jethro gave his son-in-law Moses: "'What you are doing is not good. You and these people who come to you will only wear yourselves out. The work is too heavy for you; you cannot handle it alone'" (Exod. 18:17,18, NIV). Jethro advised Moses to select capable men to assist, and then said, "'That will make your load lighter, because they will share it with you'" (v. 22, NIV).

FIGHTING: THE NATURE OF MAN?

Why is conflict so prevalent these days? It seems that much of the leader's time is devoted to handling conflict situations instead of moving the people forward in a more efficient and productive way. Much of the conflict and division that consumes the energy and attention of church leaders is a result of spiritual immaturity. This immaturity is most often manifested through the wickedness of the human heart (see Jer. 17:9); our self-centeredness (see Isa. 53:6); and individual pride (see Prov. 13:10).

Sometimes the leader himself becomes the target of derision and must show a tough side. Mark Albertson, a counselor, believes that conflicts focused on the leader fall into five general categories: communication problems; the breakdown of systems within the church, creating widespread frustration; unresolved tensions that spawn gossip and other backbiting; personality clashes; and philosophical differences.

Regardless of whether the conflict is focused upon the person of the leader or upon other people or factors, resolving conflict is critical if a leader is going to do what he does best: lead. Lyle Schaller, a church consultant, claims that "three-quarters of all church ministry is significantly reduced because of nonproductive and destructive conflict." He adds that if the conflict is not resolved, the church will be unable to continue any level of effectiveness. The average church leader spends roughly 20 percent of his time handling conflict in his church. That is a high price for any leader to pay.

Dr. Norman Shawchuck's research confirms the devastating effect of intrachurch conflict. He told me the number one reason for conflict is that leaders generally have poor interpersonal skills. A second major reason is that many congregations are determined to resist change even though they must inevitably come to grips with the sweeping changes all around them. When a church resists a leader's efforts to change strategically, it is only a matter of time before the church becomes riddled by conflict.

Shawchuck's view about church conflict: he believes it is inevitable. The important issue relates to how churches handle conflict. In too many churches, the leader allows conflict to become a habit. In these instances, the leader is most likely shirking his responsibility to be tough and lead. There are times to be tender and times to be tough; when seeking to break the back of an unhealthy conflict, the leader must be firm in his stance and committed to resolving the tensions and fissions that are undermining the Body. In many cases, the conflict takes on a life of its own because it is a political struggle: a power play. These circumstances raise the issue that you, as a called leader, must answer: What does it mean to lead God's people? What does pastoral leadership look like when the going gets tough?

THE CHALLENGE OF BEING TOUGH ENOUGH

I think one of the great challenges for many of today's pastors is to exert firm leadership. Most of us come into the pastorate having tender hearts, and desire to demonstrate servantlike love and mercy. The church, however, is a spiritual battlefield and it often requires a strength of leadership that is uncommon in the secular world.

A good friend of mine described his tenure as pastor at a church. When he first arrived, he was repeatedly asked if he thought he was strong enough to lead a church comprised of very strong people. Five years later he discovered the reason for the question. After four positive years of ministry, the founders of the church thought their power was being threatened. One of those people told my friend at a private lunch meeting, "You had five very good years here, and you ought to feel good about it. We do. We change pastors every five years. Do you understand what I'm saying?"

As he told me this story, I could feel his pain as if it were my own. As we reflected on this all-too-common experience, I asked him what lessons he would impart to other pastor-leaders. "I would begin by saying there is a cost to our calling. The Man that we're following has said to us, 'Come after me, take up your cross and follow me.' So what we're doing is going to be marked by suffering, servanthood, pain, sacrifice and submission. As the apostle Peter said, we ought not to be surprised at the fiery trial that is a part of us. There is really no way to avoid all of it. There may be preparations that we can make, but I don't think there is any way to totally avoid it."

Perhaps conflict in ministry is a given, but it does not have to be unmanageable. We read in Scripture that Jesus Christ came to tear down the walls of hostility. He did His very best to bring people together. He realized He could not win them all, and He didn't. In time, His desire to bring peace to all men cost Him His life. Yet it was a worthy goal and remains so today for all of us who lead. In Ephesians 2:14 (NIV) we read, "For he himself is our peace, who has made the two one and has destroyed the barrier, the dividing wall of hostility." Jesus was a reconciler. He attempted to bring men to a place of confrontation where they could in an open, honest manner look at the issue. This will not always mean agreement or understanding on every issue, but it might result in unity, if not uniformity.

In my ministry I have tried to follow His example by doing the following:

1. Identify the point of understanding;
2. Make reconciliation the primary objective;
3. Reestablish oneness of heart;
4. Accept one another for who we are.

In one of the interviews I conducted for my bimonthly audiotape series "Pastor to Pastor," my guest Horace Fenton Jr. was speaking about his life experience with church conflict. This elder statesman had seen it all! His philosophy about leading in the midst of conflict was soaked with wisdom.

> I would say to any leader to take conflict very seriously. Don't ever make light of it. Don't postpone doing whatever you can do about it. Recognize that conflict among Christians—true believers—is not the will of God and therefore you can count on all the resources of heaven to help you in what otherwise is an impossible situation. Get to the people as soon as possible, draw in outside help when it is needed, and let your own life be characterized by love, the love of Christ. It is vital to recognize that the solution to our differences does not lie in our seeing things exactly the same way, but by learning the mind of Christ. His will must rise above the convictions and opinions that we hold onto so tenaciously.

STRIKING THE BALANCE

When a person is "leadership tough," he needs to perform his leadership duties as a winner. When we view our problems in leadership as a win/lose proposition, it creates exactly that—winners and losers. Tender leadership attacks conflict with a win-win attitude. It wants to come out of the fray with as few scars and hurt feelings as possible.

I have learned a lot of lessons in my years as a pastor and now as an executive in a parachurch ministry. I sincerely want to be a "tender leader." In addition to enacting the strategic functions of a leader, success in minimizing or addressing conflict requires that I do three things:

1. Always accept personal responsibility for the situation. It may or may not be my fault, but a true leader must take the initiative for reconciliation.
2. Make any effort necessary to move toward the person or persons involved in the conflict. I can play the "blame game," but it will not do any good. As a leader I must make strategic use of my limited leadership resources. In those calculations must be a determination to use

some of my leadership capital to control conflict-oriented circumstances.

3.   Take the risk of confronting the issue for the sake of the relationship. In the end it will make little difference who wins or who is right, but what really matters is how we walk away from one another.

I am reminded of a quote from *Peacemaking, The Quiet Power.* My prayer is that it will become your leadership style as well.

> The Christian church has been in existence for several thousand years now. In its history there have been innumerable fights and conflicts and battles, and yet, the church has survived. This certainly gives credence and evidence of the Holy Spirit of Christ and His power to mediate when we have differences. But the intensity and frequency of conflict has become more increasingly apparent in the last two decades. The reason? Well, they are many and varied. Furthermore, these reasons certainly mirror the changes in our society as a whole. Mediation can give greater stability and more hope to the church in our complex time. The Holy Spirit of Christ has so many ways of working. We're living in a time when this Holy Spirit is ready to take the means and vehicles of grace that Christ continually offers and show them to us. We are vehicles through which the Holy Spirit can work. Mediation is a vehicle in which the Holy Spirit can create, through us, the process of keeping peace. The goal is peacemaking, and it is Christ our Lord who towers over all of us, the One true mediator, the Prince of Peace.[4]

May God bless you with the patience and the will to become a tender leader—never compromising that for which you stand and Him who called you, but always seeking the best for His kingdom and those for whom He gave His life.

Notes

1. "Are Pastors Abused?" Arlo Walker, *Leadership* XIV, no. 1 (1993): 80-84.

2. Thomas à Kempis, *The Imitation of Christ* (New York: Harper & Row, 1942).

3. H. B. London Jr. and Neil Wiseman, *Pastors at Risk* (Wheaton, Ill.: Victor Books, 1993), pp. 61-62.

4. Terje Hausken, *Peacemaking, The Quiet Power* (West Concord, Minn.: CPI Publishing, 1992), pp. 167-168.

SEVEN

HELPING LEADERS
GROW

LEIGHTON FORD

Not long ago, a father and son took a sentimental trip to the father's boyhood hometown. They saw the houses where he grew up, the store where his parents worked, the schools he attended and the park where he played. They went to the civic auditorium, closed for the summer, and persuaded the janitor to open up the locked and darkened theater.

"Here is where we had our youth rallies," the father said to the son as they stood on the stage. "Hundreds of our friends would come. I loved having the opportunity to emcee the meetings. We saw many kids touched by Christ."

Then he grew reflective. "But I remember the night we had a very famous evangelist come. We were sure that most of our friends would accept Christ. The place was packed that night but I was disappointed. Only one person came forward."

Then the father pointed to the wings at the side of the stage. "I went over and stood there, very discouraged. I remember that the evangelist came over, put his arm around me, gave me a hug, encouraged me. He said he would pray for me and believed God would use me if I stayed humble." The father paused and looked his son in the eyes. "I have never forgotten that arm around my shoulder."

The father in that story is me; the son is my own son, Kevin. The evangelist was Billy Graham, later to be my brother-in-law and Kevin's uncle.

I have often thought back to that arm around the shoulder and the fact that Billy Graham spoke to the crowd, but took time for one young man. I have reflected that the doors to leadership were opened for me by mentors who cared for those who were coming after them. Early in my life, my adopted mother held before me the vision of serving Christ. Later, Evon Hedley, the field director for Youth for Christ in Canada, appointed me as president of our local rally. At the time I was only fourteen, but I was tall and Evon thought I was seventeen. I am sure when he learned my true age he must have nearly had a heart attack! He stayed with me, though, encouraged me, cuffed me a bit when I needed correction and saw the potential in a lanky teenager.

NEW WORLD, NEW LEADERS

Today our rapidly changing world presents a constant universe of challenges to its leaders. In such a time, it is not enough to have managers who know how *to do things right*. It has been said we need leaders who can articulate and envision *the right things to do*.

The need to raise up transforming leaders is matched by the opportunity. As the psalmist said, "For no one on earth—from east or west,...can raise another person up....God alone...decides who will rise and who will fall" (Ps. 75:6,7, *NLT*). God in His sovereignty has always raised up leaders for His people—the Moseses and Joshuas who helped His people move from Egypt into the Promised Land, the Peters and Pauls who helped the Church shift its focus from Jews in Jerusalem to peoples of the entire world.

God is already raising up young women and men of vision throughout the world. These emerging leaders are eager to follow the call of Christ. The big question is whether those of us who are now in senior leadership positions will have the vision to nurture them. Will we be like Paul who urged young Timothy to "stir up the gift of God" that was in him (2 Tim. 1:6)? Or will we be like the banyan tree, whose extensive and dense branches do not permit enough sunlight through to nurture its seedlings, so conscious of our own positions and power that we will stunt the young seedlings who are poised to grow into branches? Will they be forced to move away from our shadow to pursue God's call to them?

THE LEADERSHIP PARADIGM

Jim Crupi, a leadership specialist, once asked me during a conversation to put in one sentence the aim of our work. I was a bit startled. Although we had developed a clear mission statement, I had never tried to focus it into one sentence. These words then came to me: We are seeking to help young leaders worldwide *to lead more like Jesus and to lead more to Jesus.* Leading **like** Jesus is a matter of character and style. Leading **to** Jesus has to do with effectiveness and results.

If we are setting out to help develop young leaders, we need to have the outcome and goal clearly in focus. We need a paradigm and a model.

For us who follow Christ as Lord and leader, He is that paradigm. He embodies, surpasses and critiques all other leadership standards.

Warren Bennis and Burt Nanus, in their best-seller *Leaders*, interviewed ninety leaders known for their transformational influence. He asked these men and women (who led in the arts, education, business and sports) about their strategies for change. He found they were able to bring transforming leadership through four basic strategies:

1. They got **attention** through **vision**—"vision grabs" write Bennis and Nanus.
2. They brought **meaning** to people through communication.
3. They engendered **trust** in those who followed them through positioning—they had a firm direction, but were also flexible.
4. They practiced **self-deployment** through **empowering**—they did not try to do it all themselves. They had sufficient positive regard for what they, personally, could do, but also knew they needed others to share in the vision.

Jesus Christ not only embodies all these traits, but He also transcends them! Unfortunately, too much of what has been promoted as Christian leadership has simply meant taking secular management and leadership concepts and attaching a few Scripture verses to the concept. Our challenge is far more radical: to *start* with Jesus as the leader and to let Him shape us into His model. "Follow Me," he said, "and I will make you" (Matt. 4:19)—not just fishers of men, but also leaders of people.

In my book *Transforming Leadership*,[1] I use the Gospels to provide a credible portrait of Jesus as leader. I also seek to interact at several points with aspects of transformational leadership as presented by today's leadership specialists. In writing that book, I came to understand more profoundly than ever why the early Christians believed Jesus was the fulfillment of Isaiah's prophecy of one greater than David who would be "a leader and commander of the peoples" (Isa. 55:4, *NIV*).

Transforming leaders get attention through vision? Jesus is the **Seer** for whom vision is not an entrepreneurial scheme, but seeing the kingdom in the person at the next corner (see Mark 1:16ff.).

Leaders bring meaning through communication? Jesus is the **Storyteller** who communicated His vision through His "value stories," His parables (see Mark 4:2,34).

Leaders earn trust through their positioning? Jesus is the **Servant Savior** who set His face to the cross (see Mark 10:45).

Leaders deploy themselves through empowering others? Jesus is not only the Shepherd who seeks the sheep, but also the **Shepherd Maker** who turns sheep into shepherds (see Mark 3:13ff.).

Beyond all this, at the core of His being, Jesus is the Son whose leadership grows not out of insecurity, but out of a deep relationship with His Father (see Mark 1:11).

To put this another way, we need to ask ourselves the purpose of our leadership development programs. Is it primarily an organizational purpose: to help emerging leaders fill leadership roles? Or is it far more personal, organic and transformational: to help young leaders lead more like Jesus? At one level, leadership roles and skills can be taught and learned. Leadership can only be experienced and lived on a far deeper level. Both the being and the doing, the character and the skills are important. The *being like Jesus*, however, brings to the doing the eternal kingdom perspective.

A LEADERSHIP CONFESSION
GOD CALLS US AS KINGDOM LEADERS,
TO BE LED MORE BY JESUS,
KNOWING HIM AND UNDERSTANDING HIS WILL,
TO LEAD MORE LIKE JESUS,
ENABLING HIS PEOPLE TO BE A
RECONCILING COMMUNITY,

TO LEAD MORE TO JESUS,
SERVING HIS REDEMPTIVE PURPOSES
IN OUR GENERATION.

THE LEADERSHIP
DEVELOPMENT PROCESS

In the early years of our leadership ministry, I was encouraged and helped a lot by a visit from Larry Donnithorne, who at that time was assistant to the superintendent at the U.S. Military Academy at West Point. Colonel Donnithorne, who is by training a philosopher and educator, was responsible for developing the new leadership program at West Point. He helped us think of leadership development in three ways.

"At first," he said, "leadership training is like making a mosaic. You teach people to learn certain skills and use them to make a pattern. Then you help people to learn that leadership is an art in itself. Beyond growing skills, it is the ability to paint the picture. But then most important is to help people to see that becoming a leader is becoming God's person over a lifetime."

At the elementary level, we may have leadership training that passes along certain skills in organizing and communicating. At a more advanced level, leadership development must help potential leaders develop their own particular God-given vision. At the most mature level, leadership development means walking with a leader as he becomes the complete person God has called him to be, so in turn he can help another become all God wants him to be.

Thus, leadership training is only one part of a much broader and deeper process that must take place in the life of one who is called to leadership.

It has been said the final test of a leader is that he leaves behind others who have the conviction and the will to carry on. In this regard, Jesus the Shepherd Maker is also a model. Mark 3 tells of a key decision that Jesus made at a crisis point in His ministry. The crowds were growing. Many of the religious leaders were becoming hostile. Jesus strategically withdrew into the hills (see Mark 3:7-13) and spent the entire night in prayer (see Luke 6:12). How could He multiply what He was doing? Deepen it? Continue it after He was gone?

The time had come to focus on a few, and that is when He selected Peter, James, John and the others.

THE MAKING OF A LEADER

How do we make leaders? Let's take Peter as a test case. How did Jesus make Peter into a leader?

I described Jesus' process in my book *Transforming Leadership*, using an imaginary interview with Peter. Consider this abbreviated version of how Jesus made leaders.

He called them. Jesus found His future leaders fishing by a lake and in other everyday activities. He picked them just as they were. Leadership development begins with a call. When we call someone in Jesus' name, it is a ministry of powerful affirmation.

He named them. In Peter's case, He looked straight into his eyes and said, "You are Simon, you are going to be Peter." Similarly, when we develop leaders, we need to know what their names stand for—that is, we must get to know them well—understand their strengths and weaknesses and call them by the new vision of what they will become in Christ.

He made them a team. Peter and the other fishermen knew that in a fishing boat without good teamwork they could go broke. Jesus believed in teams. He sent His disciples out by twos. Leadership developers need to know the power of teams. *It is important to work with individuals, but also to bring them into a group, where strengths and weaknesses can be balanced and visions shared.* He did this in every possible way. The disciples were grown men when Jesus called them, not little kids. Adults learn best when they can be a part of what is already taking place. Jesus' leadership program was not like school; it was life. The disciples were apprentices to Jesus. It teaches us the lesson that leaders learn in real life situations.

He trusted them. At the very beginning, He told them to follow Him, then taught them by letting them live with Him and watch Him. He then sent them out to go and to do, entrusting them with a task. Jesus shows us that leaders are made not just by telling them what to do, but also by trusting them to do it.

He tested them. Actually, you might say He terrified them! When a big storm came upon them on the lake while they were sleeping on the boat, He asked them repeatedly, "Where is your faith?" He pushed them beyond their safe depths. Leaders grow when they are in situations beyond their own control and strength, where they learn that they will fail unless they trust in God.

He included them. From the crowds He picked seventy, and from the seventy He selected twelve, and out of the twelve, three. He often took his inner three, Peter, James and John, off by themselves—when He healed the little girl, spoke with Moses and Elijah on the mountain and prayed in the garden. To make leaders, we have to focus on the few who have the potential, as well as some who may not seem to have it. Of course, this involves risks. These are risks we must take, though, if we want to grow leaders in depth.

He made them His friends. Jesus' leadership program was not a formal, hierarchical structure, but a community of friends, and the Friend was at the center. The night He left them, He said to them, "I no longer call you servants,...I have called you friends" (John 15:15, *NIV*). Imagine being one of those disciples and exclaiming, "He called me His friend. I am the Lord's friend!" Leaders-in-the-making need to sense they are persons, not projects—persons who, in the best sense of the word, are friends.

He warned them and restored them. Jesus warned His disciples of dangers ahead. He particularly warned Peter that he would betray Him and let Him down; and Peter did. What changed him back? Jesus did. Although Peter denied Jesus three times, three times he was given a chance to reaffirm his love and his commitment to feed Jesus' sheep. Peter learned something about rebuke from Jesus; it can be the most loving thing in the world. In developing leaders, we need to know they will fail. When that happens, they need correction, encouragement and a chance to start again.

He made them understand. At the end, it all came together. Jesus' disciples realized He had chosen them, prayed for them, died for them and now He was trusting them. He had put Himself in them. Now He was sending them to find His sheep and care for His people.

Jesus' way of making leaders can be put in a simple phrase. He said, *"Follow Me, and I will make you."* Leadership development is not training people for our programs; it is helping others follow Jesus and become the leaders He calls them to be.

Leadership development is sharing—a sharing of life and goals, a sharing of partnership and learning, a sharing of time and risks and power. Jesus' leadership development was not a lock-step program. It was an ongoing process. In that process, Jesus did the following with His trainees:

- He began by identifying, recruiting and assessing leaders who had potential.

- He gave personal attention to their formation by modeling for them, being with them and praying for them, and motivating them through His attention, support, correction and feedback.
- He built them into a community—in today's parlance, a team—where they learned not only from Him, but also from each other.
- He was constantly involved with them in life-related teaching—real life demonstrations, questions and answers, action followed by reflection.
- He gave them responsibility and provided feedback.
- He empowered them, giving them not a plan but His Spirit, and He let them go, to be kingdom-seeking leaders.

LEARNING TO LEAD

Leadership is a hot topic these days. Effective leadership is widely acknowledged to be lacking. The result? Leadership-building programs are exploding. Which ones are effective? If they do produce leaders, why?

It is a complicated topic, one intriguingly addressed in *Learning to Lead* by J. A. Conger. An associate professor of organizational behavior at McGill University, Conger also is a consultant to many corporations and nonprofit organizations. To determine who is doing what in the world of leadership development, and to evaluate what seems to be having a positive influence, one of Conger's associates went "undercover," so to speak, to take part in five of the most popular leadership programs. In *Learning to Lead*, he offers personal insights and assessments of these programs, organizing them into a typology of four approaches:

- **Personal growth** is the approach taken by the Pecos River Learning Center and Vision Quest. By means of outdoor adventures and psychological exercises, these programs seek to help participants be in touch with their deeper, truer selves.
- **Conceptual understanding** is emphasized in the Leadership Challenge, whose programs highlight the difference between management and leadership, and include skill-building procedures.

- **The feedback approach** is utilized at the Center for Creative Leadership in Greensboro, North Carolina. Assuming that those who want to be effective leaders already possess certain skills, the program helps participants identify strengths to build on and weaknesses that need attention.
- **Skill building** is emphasized in the Forum Company's Leadership course, with the understanding that leadership can be broken into a set of behaviors that can be learned.

Conger's conclusion is that an effective leadership training approach must incorporate core elements of all four of these approaches. He contends that each of those elements builds upon the other, creating a synergistic outcome. He also sees the primary value of all these programs as awareness building and affirming that ultimately developing leadership depends upon the gifts and desire of the individual and the receptivity of the leader's organization.

Conger also advocates realism. Even if a leader changes for the better, that transformation may threaten superiors and followers who want stability. What he says about organizations applies equally to many churches: "Many organizations are simply not prepared for leadership. Conformity is more important to them than vision and risk-taking."[2]

HIGHLY PERSONALIZED LEADERSHIP DEVELOPMENT

In 1992, Leighton Ford Ministries launched the Arrow Leadership Program. It was conceived and developed by Tom Hawkes, our leadership development director. For several years we had done informal mentoring with younger leaders, and sponsored a variety of seminars on evangelism leadership, some in association with seminaries and some as peer forums among those engaged in similar evangelism ministries. These seemed to be having a positive effect. I had sensed during a quiet period of retreat, however, that the way to have the most profound influence was not by multiplying programs, but by investing in people. At the time, I noted in my journal that I felt led to bring together about a dozen key young leaders as a core group of partners through whom our small organization could link to a larger family.

This was a key decision through which our strategy began to develop more intentionally.

After forging a team of people who were skilled for and committed to this task, we began to work through the specifics of how to identify, encourage and nurture young leaders who had great potential. Our success to date is also deeply attributable to the prayer support group that daily upholds our efforts before God. Like all else we endeavor to do, this prayer emphasis is based on the model provided by Jesus. He prayed all night before selecting His inner core group; at the close of His earthly ministry, He prayed that their faith would not fail them.

It may be helpful if I tell the story of how we chose the arrow as our symbol and metaphor for the process we have created. Certainly we did not have everything thought out from the beginning. It happened step by step, as God directed and led us to those who would both challenge and help.

The vision was clear: We were to help develop emerging young leaders in evangelism. What did that mean, though? How could we picture it so it would grab people's minds and imaginations?

Early on we convened what came to be known as the Point Group. This is a special collection of young leaders who have vision and an outstanding track record of personal development in leadership, who partner with us in the conceptualization, development, application and critiquing of the Arrow program. At the initial meeting of this group, the thought of the arrow flashed back in my mind from the past. I once spoke at chapel at Duke Divinity School, and in the discussion following the session I was asked how I had seen Billy Graham change through the years. A picture came to my mind I had not thought of before.

"Billy Graham has been like an arrowhead," I suggested. "I don't venerate him, but I do admire him and he has been like an arrow. He has kept to the sharp, cutting edge of the gospel. He has never lost the focus on Christ. Wherever he goes he preaches John 3:16. But like the base of the arrowhead he has grown broader. Over the years he has seen the implications of the gospel whether for race relations or concern for poverty or the relationships between nations, or cooperation among believers."

The more I reflected on that metaphor, the more apt it seemed. Some leaders as they age grow broader but flatter. They are exposed to more, they know more, but they lose the sharp, cutting edge of their vision. Others become very, very narrow. They have one theme, one idea. They say it constantly until, like strumming on one string, it becomes very tiresome. The best leaders, though, are like arrowheads: they keep that sharp edge of their vision and they grow broader—and like the shaft on an arrowhead, they go deeper.

God's description of His servant as "a polished arrow" (Isa. 49:2) also became a formative part of my thinking. Young leaders are to be polished like arrowheads. These arrowheads are not to be mass produced, but hand shaped through personalized attention.

The arrow also becomes a symbol of leadership development. We want to help young leaders **sharpen their vision**—like the point of the arrow—and to understand clearly God's call to them. As Jesus in many ways would ask His disciples, "What do you see?" I developed the habit of asking every young potential leader, "What is your vision?" If the person was not sure, I would say, "If you did have one what would it be?"

The base of the arrow also has significance: **shaping their values**. As Jesus would ask His disciples, "Where is your heart?" we need to see that the leader's vision is carried forward only with solid Christlike values.

Finally, we are called to help young leaders by **sharing their ventures**. Like the shaft that helps the arrow fly forward, we need to encourage young leaders to act on the visions God gives. Jesus was constantly pushing His disciples beyond their depth and comfort zone, saying, "Where is your faith?" He also made them venture out. So our task is not to recruit young leaders for our cause and visions, but to stand with them and behind them—to invest "spiritual risk capital," so to speak, and give them a chance to go for the ventures God has put into their hearts.

Sharpening vision. Shaping values. Sharing ventures. This sums up the leadership development process.

VALUES TO PASS ON

Values are foundational to leadership. We could not have a complete developmental process unless we incorporated an understanding of core values into that mix. What are these values we want to pass on to the emerging cadre of leaders? In a nutshell, we want young leaders to:

- Have a heart for God (see Matt. 22:37);
- Love their neighbors and their families (see Matt. 22:39);
- Lead and serve like Jesus (see Mark 10:42-45);
- Be able to communicate the gospel effectively, have passion, thoughtfulness, creativity and integrity (see 2 Cor. 3:5,6);
- Live humane and holy lives that will make the gospel attractive (see 1 Tim. 4:12; Matt. 5:16);
- Be aware of their world and alert to their generation (see Acts 13:36, Eph. 5:15-17);
- Act compassionately for the lost and the needy (see Matt. 9:36-38);
- Be kingdom seekers, not empire builders (see Matt. 6:33);
- Long for the unity of Christ's people (see John 17:20-23);
- Learn to "pray the work" (see Matt. 9:35).

THE CHARACTER/COMPETENCY MODEL

If our goal is to help young leaders lead more **like** Jesus and lead more **to** Jesus, leadership development must emphasize both character and competency. The arrow is a symbol we have chosen and the Arrow Character/Competency Model is our attempt to flesh out Kingdom leadership with substance and clarity.

When we reached the point of creating a process that would enable young leaders to embrace these values and to lead people based on their character and their competencies, Tom Hawkes, our director of leadership development, began a process of consultation. He met with people from across the country who had focused on developing leaders, and talked with young leaders themselves about what they needed. He found they were saying in effect, "We want our character developed. We want our hearts to be deep. We want to be reminded that evangelism is the name of the game. And we want to know some of the new things that God is doing."

Tom then developed the design for our Character/Competency Leadership Model, of leading **like** and **to** Jesus. It covers four main areas:

- *Spirituality*—growing a leader's "heart for God";
- *Leadership* understanding and skills;

- *Evangelism* understanding and skills;
- *Kingdom Seeking*—commitment to the wider and global aspects of the Church.

Under each of the four main areas are thirteen characteristics of the called and effective young evangelism leader, characteristics such as having a heart for God, sensing a clear calling and vision from God, leading like Jesus, being a passionate and thoughtful evangelist, understanding the trends and views shaping his generation and devotion to God's kingdom rather than a personal empire. The characteristics are then expressed in sixty-four specific leadership qualities.

The Character/Competency Model forms our core curriculum. It integrates all our leadership programs, from the one-week seminars and forums through the lengthier Arrow Program to the Advanced Arrow Program now being developed.[3]

UNDERLYING ASSUMPTIONS

The Arrow Leadership Program as we have developed it operates on several key assumptions:

- That God is at work raising up and developing young leaders. When we seek to help them we are neither their creators or their producers; we are "mid-wives" who walk with them through the process God has started.
- That Jesus is the ultimate model for "transforming leadership"—of leading more **like** Jesus and leading more **to** Jesus.
- That emerging young leaders can benefit most from leadership programs when they are at transition points in their careers—growth spurts, times of stress and times when they face major change. Depending on the person and the circumstances, this often occurs in the early thirties.
- That leaders grow best in a highly personalized way. Relationships are more important than programs, and helping people to pursue God's call to them is more important than standardized content.
- That character and spiritual development are more important than competency. Making time for reflection,

prayer, study and accountability are key.
- That growth takes place best in a learning community, not a hierarchical structure. Every leader is also a learner, and in this community older and younger leaders learn together from God's Word and Spirit and from each other.
- That growth requires one-on-one mentoring to facilitate character development.
- That people can learn from their peers and more mature experienced leaders.
- That experience is necessary to fully learn any character trait or skill or knowledge. "Experience it, learn it."

How the Program Works

The Arrow Program took shape in a clear vision and articulated values, expressed in a Character/Competency Model. We had a clear idea of the expressed and perceived needs of younger leaders; we had some excellent counsel. Most important of all, we had the model of Jesus and the promise of His presence!

Based on all this, Tom Hawkes asked the question: What resources are available to help young leaders grow? He identified the following: the Bible; older leaders; peers in leadership; other books and materials; and, through and above them all, the Holy Spirit.

Interestingly, though we had not seen Conger's conclusions in *Learning to Lead*, the program that developed contained all four of the elements he identifies as important: personal development, conceptual understanding, feedback and skill building.

The Arrow Leadership Program emerged as a seventeen-month intensive nonresidential program, emphasizing both leadership and evangelism. A new class begins every fall (September or October) and graduates seventeen months later. Participants maintain their own residences and ministries or occupations, while coming to North Carolina four times during the program for weeklong seminars. In between these visits, regular contacts are made through meetings of peer clusters, with mentors and by contact with the staff.

The following key process elements describe the Arrow Program.

Recruiting and Qualifying
The program is not publicly advertised. Potential participants are

identified through a network consisting of former graduates, faculty, denominational and organizational leaders, pastors, lay leaders and key recommenders. Applicants must have demonstrated leadership, a heart for evangelism, strong character and growth potential. References are sought from those who know the applicants well.

Selection Process

From the pool of applications, we select a class of twenty-five. We aim to stay at that number to provide both for the sense of community and individual attention. A selection committee meets in the spring of each year to select those applicants who seem most qualified.

Pretesting and Assessment

We want to help the participants assess their own strengths and weaknesses and set their goals for growth. To help them, we have a careful assessment process. All participants take a battery of tests, which include:

1.   Spiritual Gifts Inventory;
2.   Lead;
3.   Arrow Leadership Questionnaire;
4.   16PF;
5.   Performax (DISC);
6.   Leadership Practices Inventory.

In addition, a "360 degree" evaluation is made of each participant based on the Character/Competency Model. The participant's spouse (if married), supervisor, a peer or close friend, and a follower express evaluation of the person in each of sixty-four areas.

At the first seminar, major attention is given to this assessment. A team of assessors—most of them mature lay leaders—attend the entire seminar to meet, observe and get to know the participants. A psychologist guides this process and is part of the assessment team. The team observes the class members in a variety of settings: presenting a vision statement to a small group, as part of an evangelistic outreach team, in an outdoor adventure experience, participating in the classroom setting and in informal times. Each participant is personally interviewed by an assessor.

At the end of the week, the entire assessor team meets and agrees upon an evaluation of each participant based on the psychological leadership tests, the observations and the personal interviews.

A summary of this feedback is given individually to each participant on the last day of the seminar, including encouragement to build on personal strengths and to make plans to grow in areas that are weaker. Almost without exception, the response is, "You are right on. I don't know how you knew me so well. This is exactly what I needed at this time in my life." The person is encouraged to use this material for personal reflection and attention in all the other aspects of the program.

Team Building

Leaders must work as team captains and members, and not as stars. From the beginning, the Arrow Program aims at creating the team spirit. When participants first introduce themselves, they are asked to do so not in terms of their work or their accomplishments, but in terms of something very human and personal.

On the first day of the first seminar, participants take part in a series of "soft and hard" team-building exercises, ranging from games and sharing groups to rappelling and rock climbing an 80-foot cliff. Professional and qualified guides lead these exercises. Rappelling and rock climbing is a new experience for many. Most are nervous if they have never done it before. Each participant is urged not necessarily to do the rappelling or climbing, but to go to the point where he will make the decision whether he will do it or not. Most do. Even those who do not, have learned something important about pushing their limits.

An additional plus comes in the help and encouragement of other team members. The pastor of a fast growing church may be a big person back home, but when he is going over the cliff backward for the first time, he realizes he is dependent on the young inner-city worker below who is belaying him with a rope and the woman church planter, who is shouting her encouragement.

Similar team-building exercises from white-water rafting to climbing mountain trails build personal insight, confidence and team spirit throughout the program. A young ministry leader who overcomes his fear of heights and scales to the top of Grandfather Mountain may both recognize his vulnerability and trust his instincts and courage more when he gets back to his challenging ministry situations. Those who decide not to go to the top are affirmed in deciding what is right for them, knowing they have climbed their own inner mountains.

Seminar Modules

Arrow participants attend four one-week seminars in the course of the seventeen-month program. During these seminars, one- or two-day modules are included on the following topics:

Empowering Relationships
Heart for God
Leadership Assessment
Vision for Ministry
Cultural Awareness
Focusing Your Life
Leadership Communication
Mobilizing Others for Evangelism
Evangelistic Preaching
The Leader's Family Life
Leading Like Jesus
Team Building
Living Compassionately
Prayer
Seeking Kingdom Growth
The Church Mobilized

We seek the best qualified faculty to lead these modules, and ask them to consider themselves more as consultants than as lecturers. Because adults learn better through interaction and involvement, we seek to use as many creative learning approaches as possible. Each instructor is given a planning sheet per module, which asks him to do three things: specifically describe what he wants the participants to know, feel and do as a result of the module; provide detailed explanations of how he plans to use time in his module; and describe a variety of learning activities and approaches he plans to use.

Wherever possible we use case studies, discovery approaches, group interaction and discussion. For example, when we teach about vision we may begin by telling a case study of a large church where the pastor's solitary vision that they become a seeker-oriented church seems to be accepted by everybody, works well at the beginning, but then falls apart. The participants critique what happened based on their knowledge of vision, the Bible and life experiences, and then are asked to think of their own creative alternatives.

We keep remembering that Jesus' disciples—His leaders in process—learned in a living classroom, that He used everything and every experience in His midst as His material for learning. We need to keep going back to Him.

Peer Clusters

Young leaders learn from each other as well as from the senior, experienced leaders, so an integral part of each Arrow class is the "peer clustering."

Whenever possible, participants who have some geographical proximity are recruited. During the first week, these peer clusters meet and get to know one another. At the end of the week, they form their own ongoing peer clusters based on geography or other affinities.

Between seminar gatherings, each peer cluster is requested to meet regularly. Many clusters spend a day together every six to eight weeks. If the participants are too distant to meet face-to-face, a cluster may "meet" through conference calls. This latter approach is decidedly a second best option, but it is used when necessary.

The agenda for these meetings is set within the group members according to their needs. It is understood that they will provide stimulation, encouragement and accountability to one another in their growth. This may happen in relation to the content of what they have heard, or in their personal character growth, or in their evangelism and leadership ministries. Many of these peer clusters delve deeply into personal and family concerns and form spiritual support teams. They provide wisdom for each other in maintaining balance in ministry, handling conflict, making decisions, facing temptations and struggles, and all the challenges young ministry leaders have in common.

We allow these clusters to be either gender specific or gender mixed. We have tried to think carefully and sensitively through the issues involved in having specific or mixed gender groups. Because we believe both women and men are called and gifted for leadership in evangelism, we do not want to handle the makeup of groups in a superficial manner.

Some of the groups want to talk in depth about areas of vulnerability, including sexual temptation and struggles and relationships with the opposite sex. Some men and women for that reason prefer gender specific groups so they are more free to talk without inhibitions.

For others, the central issue is learning to relate to each other as peers in ministry, whether it be men or women. They feel a great benefit in having a small group in which they can relate both to men and women in a helpful and mutually supportive context, which enables them to see each other as persons, not just in terms of gender.

The helpfulness of the peer cluster depends on the chemistry of the group, the ability to meet regularly and the honesty and commitment involved. We have seen many times that young leaders have helped each other more than the staff or senior leaders could have.

One of our Arrow participants was at a crisis point in his ministry. He called, urgently trying to talk to me, to Tom Hawkes, to anybody on our staff. None of us could be contacted swiftly. By the time we got back to him a day or so later, he laughed and said, "Oh, I just got my peer group on the phone. I talked it through with them. They gave me great advice. Problem solved. Thanks anyway!"

Mentoring

Mentoring has become a buzzword today. It really is an ancient concept, however, one exemplified by the wise, older guide who helps a younger protégé along the journey. Joshua had Moses as his mentor. Elisha had Elijah. Timothy had Paul. Earlier I spoke of the important place mentors had in my own life.

We have found that most younger leaders are hungry for an older person who will simply be available and interested, providing a listening ear and an understanding heart and whatever counsel the person can give from his own experience and knowledge of God, life and people.

For this reason, mentoring is another key ingredient of the Arrow Leadership Program. Each participant is asked after the first week either to pick a mentor of his own choosing or to link up with one we would recommend. We have a list of potential mentors who have agreed to serve, and we ask that mentor if he would work with this Arrow person for the next year and a half.

Mentors come in many shapes and sizes. Some are retired. Some are still working full-time. They are men and women. Some come from business backgrounds, others from the ministry, from the healing professions and some are homemakers. These mentors are expected to empower the Arrow participant by sharing God-given resources with them. Those resources may include wisdom, information, experience, confidence, insight, relationships and status.

Mentoring may take place at varying levels of involvement and different degrees of intensity. It may range from being very deliberate to being much more casual.

- **Intensive** mentoring would involve mentors who may be disciplers, spiritual guides and coaches.
- **Occasional** mentors could be counselors, teachers or sponsors.
- **Passive** mentors might include models, whether from history or contemporary life.[4]

Another slant on this process is provided by Edward Sellner, a Catholic lay theologian who wrote the book *Mentoring*. Sellner goes beyond the usual concept of one-on-one mentoring to point out other ways in which guidance may come. He wrote a chapter about C. S. Lewis who, as a literary figure, was a spiritual mentor from a distance for Sellner. He also discusses the Celtic historical concept of the "soul friend." He believes that dreams may be mentors of our souls, particularly at key transition periods of our lives, as God speaks from deep within.

Sellner lists characteristics that can help identify a contemporary mentor or soul friend:

- *Maturity*, the wisdom that comes only with age;
- *Compassion*, the ability to hear what another is attempting to put into words without judging;
- Genuine *respect* for others and their stories and their times—a respect that begins with reflection upon one's own story;
- The ability to *keep things confidential*;
- *Self-disclosure*, the willingness to share parts of one's own journey when appropriate and the willingness to be honest;
- To be something of *a scholar* who is continually reflecting on one's own experiences and relationships with God;
- The ability to *discern* the movements of the spirit and the heart.

Sellner describes the mentor as a "mid-wife, a person intimately involved in the process of helping another bring something to birth."

He also cautions that no one perfectly embodies all these characteristics, and that ultimately "one must look within one's heart and to the God who works through our strengths and weaknesses."[5]

The ministry of mentoring is often undervalued, not only for what it can mean to a younger person, but also for what it can mean to the mentor. I am convinced that many senior leaders hold on to power because they do not know what they will do if they step aside and let go. One of the marks of maturity, though, should be turning from the power mode to the wisdom mode, remembering that as the proverb says, "grey hair" speaks of wisdom (see Prov. 16:31). Personally, I have found tremendous fulfillment in the small group of young leaders I have had the privilege to mentor. They have kept me sharp and alert and growing. I have learned as much from them as I have been able to share with them.

Senior leaders are sometimes timid about being mentors. We wonder whether we really have much to share. We think we are out of touch with the younger generation. We may feel inadequate in our lives. Provided we are willing to take the risk, to be vulnerable and honest, to listen and to drop our own agendas, we may find the ministry of mentoring one of the most significant contributions of our lives.

Mentoring is not just for older people. I urge every person, young or old, lay or clergy: "You should be passing on what you know to someone at least ten years younger than you are. Who are you doing that with?"

The Word and the Work

According to Mark, Jesus chose His inner core of leaders both to be with Him and to send them out (see Mark 3:13ff.). His leadership development process had a rhythm to it.

First, His leaders-in-the-making were called to be close to Him, observing Him, watching Him and listening to Him. He taught them by example, by word, by question, by rebuke, by encouragement, by correction and by stories. His word was the seed of growth He planted in their minds and hearts. It is not an overstatement to say that Jesus created leaders by putting His mind in them and by changing their way of thinking.

He also sent them out by twos, by teams to preach and heal and to cast out evil spirits. After they had gone, they would report back to

Him for debriefing and for more teaching. His leaders did not develop in a classroom, but in real life. The rhythm of their growth was to listen and learn, to try and succeed or fail, to be corrected and strengthened, and then to keep that process going—all in the context of intimacy with Jesus and with a committed community.

When I talk with young leaders about developing their vision, I often put it in this simple paradigm: Observe - Reflect - Act.

- Observe—look carefully around at what God is doing, at the needs of the world, what you see happening, until you are attracted to some area of need and opportunity where you can make a difference.
- Reflect on that—prayerfully read Scripture and other pertinent literature related to what you have observed. Think about it, pray about it, journalize about it.
- Act—in small ways begin to act on what you observed and reflected and, in that way, your vision and your leadership will develop.

Based on this paradigm, we have structured the Arrow Program to allow for this process of observing, reflecting and acting. The participants learn from each other, from mentors, from faculty and from the Spirit speaking to their hearts during the weeklong seminars. They then go back to their places of ministry to observe carefully what is going on around them in their own lives, to reflect on a time with God, His Word and with their peers, and to put what they have learned into action. After a few months, they come back together to share what has been happening in their lives and ministry, to focus on other important areas and, again, to keep the process going of observing, reflecting and acting. I am convinced that this process of learning, doing, reflecting and relearning, in community and along with guidance and coaching, is absolutely essential to leadership growth.

THE VOICE AND THE TOUCH

Earlier in this chapter, I mentioned that leaders in growth may be like apprentices who learn a particular skill or artists who are able to use those skills in a project; but essentially leaders are in a lifelong growth process of becoming.

This is inherent in Jesus' words, "Follow Me, and I will make you"—not only fishers of men, but also leaders. Finally, leadership growth is a process in which God invests Himself through Jesus and His Spirit in the lives of leaders He is raising up. This involves not only forming them in terms of their skills, abilities and gifts, but also transforming them in terms of their persons and character.

Ultimately, the best we can do with leaders-in-the-making is not just to offer ourselves as their friends, but also to offer them to God for His transforming work to make them leaders like His Son Jesus.

My friend Max DePree, former chairman of Herman Miller, Inc. and author of *Leadership Is an Art*, tells a fascinating story. His daughter, a physician, was expecting a child, when her husband left her. A little bright baby boy was born three months prematurely. When Max went to see his little grandson for the first time in intensive care, he stood looking at the tiny figure hardly as long as his hand, wires running into his body.

The senior nurse came to him and said, "Mr. DePree, for the next three months you are going to be the surrogate father. Here's what I'd like you to do. When you come, put your hands in and rub his back and talk to him at the same time. It's very important that he get your voice and touch together. Premature babies especially need that for security." So Max would go day after day, put his hand in and gently rub the little back and, in his grandfather's voice, talk.

"That," says Max DePree, "is a good picture of what leadership is. Leadership involves getting the voice and the touch together."

If we want to raise up leaders like Jesus who have a clear voice and a strong and compelling touch, those of us who are called to develop them need to embody the same. We need to have a clear message of what leadership is. We also need to touch them with our prayers and time and character and involvement. This is a costly involvement, but one that will affirm them and help them become all God has called them to be.

Notes
1. Leighton Ford, *Transforming Leadership* (Downers Grove, Ill.: InterVarsity Press, 1991).

2.   J. A. Conger, *Learning to Lead: The Art of Transforming Managers into Leaders* (San Francisco: Jossey-Bass Publishers, 1992), p. 180.

3.   A copy of the Character/Competency Model can be obtained by contacting Leighton Ford Ministries, 6230 Fairview Road, Suite 300, Charlotte, NC 28210.

4.   Much of our thinking and practice related to mentoring is based on the work of Paul Stanley and Bobby Clinton. In addition to actively creating our mentoring process, they have written a book on the topic. For insight into this important area, see *Connecting* by Paul Stanley and J. Robert Clinton (Colorado Springs: NavPress, 1992).

5.   Edward Sellner, *Mentoring: The Ministry of a Spiritual Kinship* (Notre Dame, Ind.: Ave Maria Press, 1992), pp. 76-79.

THE LFM LEADERSHIP COMPETENCIES MODEL

These competency statements describe our goal for leadership development in three areas: being (values, character), thinking (attitudes, understanding) or doing (actions, skills). Taken together they describe a model toward which we are growing: to be, think and do like Christ in our character, leadership, evangelism and kingdom seeking.

| CHARACTER FORMATION | TOWARD GOD | **I. Character Formation**
A. Has a heart for God
1.   Longs to be in God's presence, through prayer, communes deeply with Him
2.   Intercession undergirds ministry and life
3.   Is pursuing personal Holiness and obedience
4.   Relies on God to minister through him/her
5.   Worships God with His people

B. Has a clear calling and vision from God
1.   Has a clear call from God to serve Him and His people
2.   Has a clear vision from God of what God wants him/her to accomplish
3.   Has a clear and integrated philosophy of life and ministry |
| | OTHERS | **C. Has a heart for people**
1.   Intercedes for, and prays with, others consistently
2.   Leads and shepherds his family well (married men)
3.   Follows husband's lead and nurtures family (married women)
4.   Demonstrates an active love for his/her neighbor
5.   Performs acts of compassion for those in need
6.   Enjoys people and relates effectively
7.   Is committed to accountability relationships |

CHARACTER FORMATION	SELF
LEADERSHIP	MODELED ON CHRIST / MANAGED WELL / MOVES PEOPLE
EVANGELISM	PERSONAL VISION

D. Is maturing personally
1. Has the mind of Christ/Biblical perspectives
2. The Bible is integrated in his life and ministry through active theologizing
3. Demonstrates integrity and consistency
4. Knows his/her personality, gifts and emotional strength and weakness
5. Maintains his/her physical vigor

II. Leadership
A. Leads like Jesus
1. Can articulate and demonstrates a Christ-centered leadership philosophy
2. Has a servant attitude toward others
3. Understands the importance of team ministry
4. Raises up leaders; a shepherd maker and discipler
5. Empowers followers
6. Develops strategies for ministry
7. Grasps the role of suffering in leadership
8. Communicates vision and purpose effectively

B. Can manage well
1. Can manage ministry priorities and self
2. Knows how to strategize, plan, organize, control and evaluate
3. Know how to staff, build a team, supervise
4. Able administratively to manage information systems
5. Can budget, raise funds, and control them responsibly

C. Leads people skillfully
1. Understands his/her leadership style and can adapt it for group's need
2. Can engage conflict constructively, and lead groups to reconciliation
3. Has an effective strategy for problem solving and decision making
4. Communicates well verbally and in writing throughout the organization
5. Continually questions followers and others for feedback

III. Evangelism
A. Is a passionate and thoughtful Evangelist
1. Reflects Biblically and theologically on evangelism
2. Has a passion for evangelism
3. Is a capable personal evangelist
4. Preaches well evangelistically
5. Can train and mobilize Christians for evangelism
6. Uses creative approaches to evangelism

EVANGELISM — WORLD VISION

B. Is aware of the world and sees trends in his/her generation

1. Aware of the community and culture around him/her, assesses people's needs
2. Understands trends occurring; observes, reflects and acts
3. Aware of the tensions between the gospel and culture
4. Aware of the global movements of God's people
5. Has a heart for people in other countries, a world vision
6. Participates in world missions

KINGDOM SEEKING — LOCAL CHURCH

IV. Kingdom Seeking

A. Has a heart for the growth of the church

1. Understands the Biblical vision of God's people
2. Understands what makes a church healthy and growing
3. Committed to equipping and mobilizing God's people for vocation/ministry
4. Effectively leads God's people in prayer and worship
5. Is committed to incorporating new believers in a church
6. Has a cross cultural appreciation of the church
7. Builds the church through excellent Bible preaching and teaching

KINGDOM SEEKING — UNIVERSAL CHURCH

B. Seeks the kingdom not his/her empire

1. Helps other Christ centered movements grow
2. Is not concerned to build his/her own reputation
3. Does not depend on ministry success to validate his/her worth
4. Understands the sovereignty of Christ's Kingdom over all spheres of life
5. Longs for the unity of God's people

EIGHT

THE LIFE CYCLE
OF A LEADER

J. ROBERT CLINTON AND
RICHARD W. CLINTON

We would like to tell you a brief story about an interaction between some leaders. They are leaders like you and us, people who are trying to make some sense out of their pilgrimage of faith and their development as leaders. Read the following story and imagine yourself in this situation. Ask God to speak to you.

YA GOTTA GET PERSPECTIVE

It had been an incredible time. Mike thought back to two weeks ago as he began to listen to the pile of tapes sitting on his desk. The scene came back to him. He was truly glad they had agreed to record the interaction that had occurred during the five days. There was so much rich insight and material that he could never have remembered all the things that went on. Twelve men and women had been gathered about the large round table in the room. One spoke gently, though sometimes raising his voice in animation to make a point. Eleven mainly listened. From time to time they questioned him. They had invited him to share his wisdom.

The place was a large six-bedroom home bordering Lake Gregory. As they sat around the table, from time to time they would peer out through the large plate-glass window and see the breathtaking view overlooking the green pines and the lake below. They had rented the place for five days, Monday through Friday. Those five days were intense—filled with interaction, sharing and teaching about leadership and leadership development. Now they were reaping the benefits.

Mike remembered how he had felt, sitting at the table, as Pastor Ray first started talking. Mike had thought, *Ray was finishing well.* A brief biographical sketch of Pastor Ray flitted through his thoughts. It was true that Pastor Ray was closing out fifty-one years of ministry, mostly pastoral—two extensive times in two different churches, and some odds and ends of ministry serving in two different parachurch groups.

Pastor Ray looked all seventy-four of his years. His face was lined. Every well-earned wrinkle spoke loudly of experience. He had probably seen it all. He had faced conflict. He had seen great successes. He had seen failure. He knew what it meant to have a heart broken by people suffering. He had lost parishioners to cancer. He had seen Christians die of AIDS. He had gone through physical suffering himself. He had seen church splits. He knew the electrifying elation of wonderful ministry breakthroughs. He had seen giants fall. Through it all—risks, successes, trials, major changes in society, heartbreaks, moments of joy, the varied experiences of the decades—he had been shaped by the loving hand of God. Now here he was—a gentle and wise leader who bridged that dynamic tension. He spoke the truth in love.

Mike knew that in his latter years Pastor Ray had emerged somewhat as a Christian celebrity. He had been invited to speak abroad. He had traveled the world and seen ministry on six continents. His counsel was invaluable. He was wanted everywhere. So it is with leaders who are finishing well. He had come here to Lake Gregory, on their retreat, to spend his precious time with them and to speak to them. So he spoke; and they listened. Mike remembered how his eyes had engaged each of them. They were eyes that bespoke love, care and concern. They were pastoral eyes. He wanted the best for each of these eleven. That message was sensed in turn by each as those eyes peered around the table. Mike was one of those.

Who were the eleven? Four of them were pastors and their wives—

Dan and Gloria and Gordon and Betty. One was a widower, Pastor Tom, whose wife had passed away after a long bout with cancer. One headed a large parachurch organization—Sam, whose wife, Alicia, was unable to attend. Four were missionaries—one (Rob, there with his wife, Cathy) was heading up a church-planting movement; Mike and his wife, Julie, were engaged in a missionary training enterprise. One single woman attended, Pastor Millie, who was in charge of small group ministries in a large church. The youngest of the group was Dan (at age thirty-six), the oldest was Gordon (forty-nine). They were all amazed that Pastor Ray had been willing to come and spend five days with just the eleven of them.

This group had stayed connected to each other for the past eight years. They tried to meet yearly in a retreat setting to exercise mutual accountability, stimulate each other's thinking and challenge each other to grow. At their last gathering, out of a clear blue sky, Millie had said, "What do you think about inviting Pastor Ray to come and be with us next year at our accountability time?" Each had sensed that divine tingling that comes when you know God is in something. So they had written to the revered pastor.

Mike, Gordon and Sam knew Ray personally. Years ago Gordon had ministered with him for two years as a youth pastor. All of them had read everything Ray had written. His personable writing style made you feel as though you knew him. Ray knew all of them, at least by reputation. He was a missions-minded pastor and kept up with the late-breaking ventures on the mission field as well as the current movements on the American scene. He knew that all these leaders were influencers. They were top leaders on the move. So there was mutual respect. They revered Ray. He knew of their potential.

Would he come? Mike was not convinced of it, but Gordon thought so. He was the one who had written to Ray. It was a personal appeal. So he came. Mike wondered why. After the retreat, Mike asked him that very thing as they were walking to the car to leave. Quick as a wink Ray rattled off five reasons. Mike had jotted them down to tell Julie.

First, Ray knew the setting would be conducive to renewal in his own life. Second, he fully expected to learn from them as he shared and interacted. Third, he knew that many of his ideas would influence these leaders. Fourth, he knew the value of personal interaction. People are deeply moved through direct personal contact. Fifth, he wanted to influence these up-and-coming leaders in such a way as to leave a legacy with them. His legacy included accomplishments in life and ministry as well as the critical lessons and values he had learned through the years. He believed these ideas were worth articulating and passing on to others. He had a desire to invest them in other leaders who wanted to learn. He wanted these ideas to live on incarnate in the leaders. So he came.

As Ray closed the car door and drove away, Mike had prayed, "God make me a rich and fertile field. I want to finish like Ray is finishing."

FINISHING WELL

Several of them stayed on an extra day after the session and chatted. They each remembered special things. Throughout the next day, they continued to discuss the issues that had been raised.

The opening session had jolted Dan. He was shocked when Ray opened with the words, "I have observed and studied leaders' lives for years, good leaders and poor leaders. And I have come to a sad conclusion. Few leaders finish well! And I would like one result of our five days together to be that you would go away determined in your heart to finish well. And I want you to have perspective on what that means."

All were challenged as Ray shared what it meant to finish well. He identified six characteristics. A leader who finishes well is one who:

1. Maintains a **personal vibrant relationship** with God right up to the end;
2. Maintains a **learning posture** and learns from various kinds of sources—but especially from life;
3. Gives evidence of **Christlikeness in character** through the fruit of the Spirit in his life;
4. Lives out truth in life such that his **convictions** and the **promises** of God are seen to be real;
5. Leaves behind one or more **ultimate contributions**— that is, a lasting legacy;
6. Walks with a growing awareness of a sense of destiny and sees some or all of it fulfilled.

They were sobered by the seven major barriers to finishing well. Ray listed them on a flip chart:

Barrier 1. **Finances**—their use and abuse;

Barrier 2. **Power**—its abuse;

Barrier 3. **Inordinate pride**—which leads to downfall;

Barrier 4. **Sex**—illicit relationships;

Barrier 5. **Family**—critical issues;

Barrier 6. **Plateauing**; and

Barrier 7. **Emotional** and **psychological wounding**.

Pastor Ray also shared five things a leader could do to enhance his chances of finishing well. The group was inspired to discover what had helped others finish well. Ray noted that not all five are evident in the life of every leader who finishes well, but most of them usually are in place. These enhancements include:

1. A broad **perspective** on a lifetime of ministry from which to interpret ongoing ministry;

2. An expectancy for **renewal**. All leaders should expectantly look for repeated times of renewal. Most leaders who have been effective over a lifetime have needed and welcomed renewal experiences from time to time in their lives;

3. The practice of **disciplines**. Leaders need discipline of all kinds. Especially is this true of spiritual disciplines;

4. Having a **learning posture**. The single most important antidote to plateauing is a well developed learning posture;

5. Having **mentors**. Ray had emphasized that leaders who were effective and finished well had from ten to fifteen significant people who came alongside at one time or another to help them. At that point he stopped and told them about a mentor who had shown interest in him when he was in the seventh grade. That man had forever changed his life.

Then he put this matter in context. "A simple awareness of these five enhancements can greatly encourage you as a leader to move more deliberately and proactively to experience them." These concepts struck home.

Although Dan was the youngest in the group, he had logged fourteen years of ministry experience, working primarily with youth and with young adults. He was on the staff of a megachurch. His ministry focus in those fourteen years had been narrow and directed almost exclusively to those to whom he ministered. He had never even thought about a lifetime perspective on ministry. He was somewhat overwhelmed to be thinking ahead. It was all he could do to keep up with day-to-day ministry.

To Dan it was clear that Ray spoke from experience. Real-life illustrations backed up every point. That first session had lasted nearly three hours. Lots of questions and much interaction took place. The closing prayer time was special for them all. They gave themselves to God afresh with a renewed desire to serve Him and hear those words, "Well done, good and faithful servant" (Matt. 25:21). They wanted to finish well.

EFFECTIVE LEADERS

God met Tom powerfully in the second session. His twenty years in ministry, the last six as a senior pastor of a large church, had allowed him to confirm firsthand each of the seven observations Ray shared about effective leaders. He was both affirmed in his own ministry by those thoughts and challenged anew to be an effective leader. Ray began with these words, "While it may be true that few leaders finish well, it has been my privilege over the years to see a number of Christian leaders who have been effective." He gave them each a handout listing seven lessons he had learned about effectiveness.

1. Effective leaders maintain a learning posture throughout life.
2. Effective leaders value spiritual authority as a primary power base.
3. Effective leaders have a dynamic (vital and changing) ministry philosophy.
4. Effective leaders view leadership selection and development as a priority function in their ministry.
5. Effective leaders see relational empowerment as both a means and a goal of ministry.
6. Effective leaders evince a growing awareness of their sense of destiny.

7.   Effective leaders view present ministry in terms of a life-
      long developmental perspective.

To Tom, the statements seemed both simple and profound. Once
they were stated they seemed almost obvious. Yet each carried powerful implications that were not so obvious. Some required considerable
background and explanations to be accurately understood. Ray was
up to the task; he brought these concepts alive. They spent the next
three days working in depth on each of them. They had concluded by
spending almost two days talking about the seventh one.

Tom remembered the two quotes Ray had used to introduce that
session about perspective. The first quote was an empirical observation
in which Ray intimated that leaders are people who think broadly.

The difference between leaders and followers is perspective.
The difference between leaders and effective leaders is better
perspective. Effective leaders have better perspective.

Tom knew the challenge was meant for him personally. Ray's
words rang in his ears. "I want to give you those kind of perspectives.
A lifelong developmental perspective is just such a watershed perspective. It can make the difference anywhere along the line as you
persevere over the long haul."

The second quote was from Jesus, taken from the Sermon on the
Mount. It highlighted the fact that Jesus continually trained those with
Him by giving broader perspectives from which to evaluate. Ray had
paraphrased it for emphasis. Tom had copied it down word for word.

Matthew 6:22,23:
"The eye is the lamp of the body. If your eyes are good, your
whole body will be full of light. But if your eyes are bad, your
whole body will be full of darkness. If then light within you is
darkness, how great is that darkness!"(NIV).

Ray's paraphrase of Matthew 6:22,23:
"How you see things is critical! Your perspectives filter what
you see. They allow you to see truth or not see it. You must
seek good perspectives or you will fail to see the truth you
need."

Then Ray said, "Folks, if you want a productive lifetime of ministry you gotta get perspective. Get perspective! Effective leaders view present ministry in terms of a lifelong developmental perspective."

Tom would never forget his own heartfelt response. "I need perspective."

A LIFELONG DEVELOPMENTAL PERSPECTIVE

At that point Mike had asked for clarification. "Ray, what do you mean by a lifelong developmental perspective?"

Ray gave a prolonged preliminary answer. "Let me preface my answer with some observations as I have watched God work with leaders. These observations, when fleshed out, will describe what I mean by a lifelong developmental perspective." Then he ticked off these observations:

1. God shapes or develops a leader over an entire lifetime.
2. God intends to develop a leader to reach the maximum potential and accomplish those things for which the leader has been gifted.
3. A time perspective provides many keys. When using a time perspective to analyze and overview a leader's development, the life can be seen in terms of several time periods, each yielding valuable informative lessons. Each leader has a unique time line describing his or her development.
4. Shaping processes can be identified, labeled and analyzed to contribute long-lasting lessons and values.
5. Patterns can be identified and are highly suggestive for anticipating future processing by God.

After presenting the list, Ray answered Mike's question more directly. "When a leader has a lifelong developmental perspective, that leader expects God to shape him over a lifetime. The leader views the things that happen to him as God's sovereign way of developing him. That leader recognizes that all of life, while being vital and true for the moment, is also used to prepare him for all of the rest of life.

Bad things happen. Good things happen. All things are used by God to shape the life and help the leader realize his maximum potential. A leader with this perspective views the events in his life in terms of the longer viewpoint. He asks such questions as: How is this incident shaping me to be more like Christ? How is it helping prepare me to do what God wants me to do? How will this help me reach my God-given potential?

"A leader with this perspective embraces and even anticipates the most positive response possible in the shaping processes. A learning posture pervades the whole experience. The leader recognizes that many of these shaping experiences have been part of God's way of shaping other leaders. Knowing this and knowing these kinds of things help a leader to persevere and profit from them. Off the top of my head I can think of at least fifteen common shaping experiences. Knowing them to be a developmental tool helps a leader to face them. Sometimes, without these experiences a leader would never be challenged to reach the potential that God placed in that individual."

At that point Ray turned to Mike. "Does that help explain what I mean by a lifelong developmental perspective?"

Mike was getting the picture. "I think so. You're saying that a leader with a developmental perspective views everything that happens in terms of a bigger picture of a lifetime of ministry and knows that God sovereignly uses many things to expand a leader in beingness. God also shapes that leader to influence with God-given giftedness. And God will continue this shaping activity until leadership potential is realized."

Ray affirmed, "You got it, Mike! But in addition I am saying that the leader has a knowledge of **what** kinds of things happen and sometimes **when** those kinds of things are most likely to happen. Forewarned is forearmed. Anticipating the timing of these shaping activities allows a proactive approach to handling them."

THE LIFE-CYCLE PERSPECTIVE

Sam piped in at this point, "Well Ray, you have given us a feel for what it means to be developmentally aware as we go through life. Could you explain a little more about the time perspective—the time line? It seems to me that knowing where you are on a developmental time line would help a leader be more proactive in having a lifelong perspective. What have you learned about the time perspective?"

Ray grinned. He knew that Sam, like all the rest around the table, was eager to find out where he was in his own lifelong development. "Well, as a matter of fact, I have learned a good deal about this. I have read secular works on developmental theory as well as related works by a few Christian writers.[1] Along with this, I have made it a practice to study Christian biographies for the past forty years.[2] About ten years into my ministry I discovered how important Christian biographies could be to my own personal development. I have made it a practice to study at least one fresh biography each year. Some years I have done two. At this point I have used biographies to analyze the lives of more than Christian leaders. And, of course, I have also observed many fellow Christian leaders over the years. From all of this study I have been able to piece together a life cycle of development in terms of a **ministry time line**. This ministry time line fits full-time Christian workers best, but with a little bit of adaptation it can be helpful for Christian lay leaders as well."

Rob interjected a question at this point. "I thought you said earlier that each leader has a unique time line. My gut level feeling is that the church planters I work with will have a time line that differs from pastors in regular pastoral ministry. Is a general ministry time line useful for all?" Millie piped in, "And what about women in ministry? Won't a woman's time line differ from a man's?"

Several recalled how Ray answered these questions. "A comparative study of many unique time lines of full-time Christian workers resulted in the creation of a generic time line, which I call the ministry time line. No one fits it exactly but all can be helped as they compare their own life to it. Church planters will differ slightly, especially in the Early Ministry portion, from pastors. Women in ministry will have some issues of development unique to them. But on the whole, the same general kinds of things happen because God is in the business of developing leaders. And He is consistent. And certain things must be there—like character, spiritual authority, relationships and giftedness. Bear with me. I'll give you more on this later."

Then Ray walked to the white board to introduce the ministry time line. He sketched the following diagram before explaining the various terms it contained. He continued with a lesson on the life cycle of leaders, which intrigued them all.

Figure 1. The Simplified Ministry Time Line

I. Ministry Foundations (16-26 years)	II. Early Ministry (5-12 years)	III. Middle Ministry (8-14 years)	IV. Latter Ministry (12+ years)	V. Finishing Well (?)

"This is a simplified diagram describing the life cycle of someone who finishes well and develops normally over a lifetime.[3] Many leaders run into one or more of the barriers and that retards their development. Many drop out altogether and never progress through the phases. But many also move all the way through the latter ministry stage. They may or may not finish as well as they could. And a few go all the way and finish well. With those caveats in mind we can use this time perspective." He then began to clarify each of the time divisions.

"First, let me give you three quick overall sweeps of what happens in the life cycle of a developing leader. In the first pass, I have talked about the general things that happen over the life cycle of a leader as God shapes that person toward accomplishing the unique purposes for which that leader was destined." Ray punctuated that thought by writing Ephesians 2:10 on the board. He then read and emphasized the phrase "created in Christ Jesus to do good works, which God prepared in advance for us to do," before continuing his monologue about how God shapes us toward this destiny.

Figure 2. The Ministry Time Line—Moving Toward the Focused Life

I. Ministry Foundations	II. Early Ministry	III. Middle Ministry	IV. Latter Ministry	V. Finishing Well
Basic character, personality and underlying values are shaped. Some destiny activities may occur though perhaps not recognized as such. The potential leader comes alive to God	A basic commitment to leadership is made. Basic leadership character is formed. Early experiences at ministering occur. Intimations of	Life purpose clarifies. Giftedness clarifies. Major role clarifies. Breakthrough insights for empowering people in ministry are learned.	There is lifetime movement toward an ideal role. Efficient ministry becomes effective ministry. Peak ministry occurs.	A lifetime of ministry is consolidated. Ultimate contributions are proactively developed. Important values are passed on to the rising

either through conversion or some major renewal experience if a heritage Christian.	life purpose appear. Hints of giftedness emerge.	Conflict is faced. Authority issues are faced. There is efficient ministry.	Ultimate contribution clarifies.	generations of leaders.

"Now let me make a second sweep. I have noticed that the end results of God's shaping activities can be described by three concepts: spiritual formation, ministerial formation and strategic formation. **Spiritual formation** has to do with those activities that shape the inner life. **Ministerial formation** has to do with shaping the leader to effectively lead. It has to do with skills, giftedness and ministry insights that help the leader to deliver efficient and effective ministry. **Strategic formation** has to do with destiny processing that guides a leader to a specific life purpose, and a major role through which life purpose can be realized. These result in what I call ultimate contributions—the lasting legacies we leave behind because we have fulfilled our life purpose. If we look at the time line again with these ideas in mind we can see the focus of formational activity for each time division. There are reasons for changes in priority of these three aspects of formation. God's shaping activity will be directed to reorder these aspects as He develops a leader over the lifetime."

Figure 3. The Formational Priorities Over Time

I. Ministry Foundations	II. Early Ministry	III. Middle Ministry	IV. Latter Ministry	V. Finishing Well
Basic character formation; after conversion or commitment: spiritual formation	1. Ministerial formation 2. Spiritual formation 3. (Strategic formation)	1. Spiritual formation 2. Ministerial formation 3. Strategic formation	1. Strategic formation 2. Spiritual formation 3. (Ministerial formation)	1. Spiritual formation 2. Strategic formation

"Earlier, I mentioned that I could point out some shaping activities. I have seen God repeatedly use certain things to move leaders along toward their unique Ephesians 2:10 life. I have noted the kinds of things He does to bring about spiritual formation, ministerial formation and strategic formation."

Figure 4. Some Major Shaping Processes Across the Time Line

I. Ministry Foundations	II. Early Ministry	III. Middle Ministry	IV. Latter Ministry	V. Finishing Well
• Character shaping	• Leadership committal	• Ministry insights	• Spiritual warfare	• Destiny fulfillment
	• Authority insights	• Leadership backlash	• Deep processing	
	• Conflict and crises	• Challenges	• Power processes	
	• Giftedness discovery	• Paradigm shifts		
	• Guidance			

Mike remembered how they felt at that point in the session. The looks on the eleven listener's faces showed tilt, overload, whoa, hold on, give us a break, let us catch up. So Gordon, who was facilitating the session, had the group take a thirty-minute break. As they walked around, they admired the beautiful scenery. What a place! What a touch from God! They knew that Ray was God's divine contact for them for this moment of time.

THE FOCUSED LIFE

After a break for refreshments, Ray stood at the flip chart and wrote down the questions his presentation had stimulated. Although he asked that the queries be related to his "first pass" (i.e., looking at how God focuses a leader toward an Ephesians 2:10 life, which Ray termed a "focused life"), the questions came at him fast and furious.[4] After recording their questions for a while, he interrupted the process and told them, "We've got enough to work on. Let me start with the final question. Its answer will shed light on many of these other questions. What is the focused life? And how does that relate to the life cycle of a leader? Once, about ten years ago, I took a yearlong sabbatical to study eight Christian leaders. Each had effective ministries. Each finished well. As I studied their lives, the notion of focus over a lifetime emerged. I define it as follows.

A focused life is:

- A life exclusively dedicated to carrying out God's unique purposes;
- By identifying four key concepts—the major role, life purpose, unique methodology or ultimate contribution—which allows

- An increasing prioritization of life's activities around these key concepts; and
- Results in a satisfying life of being—what you are, and doing—what you've accomplished.

"While this definition basically applies to full-time Christian workers, it can also fit strong lay leaders." Ray looked around the group, briefly engaging the eyes of each before asking, "How would you like to bring more focus into your life? How would you like to be assured that you are moving forward in your Ephesians 2:10 life? That's what the first pass at the time line is talking about." He then proceeded to address some of the other related questions that had been raised.

Ray turned and asked Julie to restate her inquiry. "You said that in the Ministry Phase our basic character, personality and values are shaped. Then you mentioned that 'destiny activities' may occur. What's a 'destiny activity'? Do all leaders have them?

"Julie, destiny activities relate to the Ministry Foundations time period. God sometimes gives hints of future life purpose during this time period. Destiny activities refer to those kind of shaping activities in which God hints at, reveals or fulfills previously revealed destiny in a leader's life. Early on it is usually a hint, like Joseph's unusual birth and his twofold repeated dream at age seventeen. Destiny activities will cumulatively build a sense of destiny in a life. A sense of destiny is an awareness of God's intervening hand in a life for His special purposes. These destiny activities will be part of God's means to divinely impart to a leader a life purpose."

Rob could not wait any longer and burst out, "That's how it has been with me! I knew from the time of that first church plant that God wanted me to catalyze many church plants around the world. I knew He had taken me through the experiences in order to help others plant churches more efficiently. That is a burden on my heart. It is my life purpose."

Rob's passionate outburst moved the group. Ray piggybacked on the emotion of the moment. "Folks, a *life purpose* is a burdenlike calling, a task or driving force or achievement, which motivates a leader to fulfill something or to see something done. Rob has just introduced you to the notion of a life purpose in a vivid way.

"Julie, I'll come back to your question more fully later when I talk about patterns. But for now, remember one of the observations I made about effective leaders: *Effective leaders evince a growing awareness of their sense of destiny.* Destiny activities are not always spectacular. There are the providential circumstances that God uses as well. More on this later when I introduce the notion of the destiny pattern that involves destiny preparation, destiny revelation and destiny fulfillment."

Ray turned to look at the chart and determine the next appropriate question to address. He circled the words "giftedness" and "major role" with his marker, then turned to face the group. Holding up his hand with four fingers showing, he gave the following definition and bent down one finger each time he made a point. "A leader is a person with a God-given capacity and a God-given responsibility who is influencing a specific group of God's people toward God's purposes for the group. Please note that *influencing* is the key concept of leadership.

"Now, with this definition in mind, let me come back to your question, Julie. When we talk about *giftedness* we are talking about a God-given capacity. When we talk about role we are relating to the central concept of the definition—influencing. We are talking about the platform from which a leader influences. All leaders have some sort of role, the formal part of which is usually specified by a job description. But frequently there is much in the job description that doesn't fit the leader. *Major role* is an ideal concept I use to describe a role that has been adapted to fit one's giftedness."

Gloria, Dan's partner in youth work, interjected this question: "Ray, when you speak of giftedness, do you mean spiritual gifts? We have done several studies with our youth on spiritual gifts and used some spiritual gifts tests. They usually are not too helpful."

"Gloria, teaching on spiritual gifts proves much more profitable later on in the development cycle. Let me explain. When I talk about giftedness I'm referring to three things: natural abilities, acquired skills and spiritual gifts. And any one of these three can dominate a life and become the linchpin of giftedness—the focal element of the giftedness set.[5] Natural abilities emerge first. Basic skills are picked up next. Some complement natural abilities. Others break new ground. During the first baby steps of the Early Ministry time period, an emerging leader begins to do ministry. Ministry experiences allow for hints of spiritual gifts. But it isn't until the Middle Ministry time period that a person's giftedness becomes clear. At that time the leader will know which spiritual gifts are consistently being used and which of the elements dominates in his life. That's why I say that teaching on spiritual gifts is best done after some ministry experience.

"Now you can see why knowing giftedness information helps a leader get a grasp on what kind of role best fits that leader. I call that role by the label of *major role*. Now most leaders do not naturally move into a situation that equates to a major role. They must adapt their assigned role and also live with some parts that do not fit. But wherever they can, and whenever they have a choice, they make decisions toward matching giftedness, major role and life purpose. They move toward focus."

Sensing that Ray was ready to move ahead, Cathy pushed Ray to cover the other key topics that were still on the flip chart. "Ray, you haven't said a word about ministry insights nor about ultimate contributions other than giving them to us in the definition of a focused life. I know they are key issues. But what are they? And when do they come in the life cycle?"

"Okay, let's complete our discussion by dealing with those items." He paused for a drink of water then launched into the material with a new energy. "Ministry insights represent breakthroughs in how we do our ministry. We learn effective methodologies for using our giftedness to deliver ministry to those we serve. Sometimes it takes paradigm shifts for us to see effective ways to influence those we lead. We get these throughout our Early and Middle Ministry time periods. Think of Campus Crusade's 'Four Spiritual Laws.' That evangelistic technique was a ministry insight for someone early on in Campus Crusade's ministry."

He then went around the table and asked each one to describe one or two of their most important breakthroughs in ministry. Each person was able to identify several such insights in their own ministries. Ray affirmed each one as they shared.

Then he went on to answer the other part of Cathy's question. "Ministry insights occur throughout the Early and Middle Ministry time periods. As we move on in ministry and become more focused, we learn to get much mileage out of these insights. That happens in the Latter Ministry time period.

"Young folks," Ray used this greeting to get their attention about ultimate contribution, "as you get older like me you become more and more concerned about three things. First, that you are not only doing things right—that is efficient ministry—but doing the right things right. That is effective ministry. Time is much shorter. You have to be focused. Strategic formation is important to help a leader make the shift from efficiency to effectiveness.

"Second, you are concerned about leaving a legacy behind. I use the term 'ultimate contributions' to sum up for me the whole notion of lasting legacies.[6] When life is over, each of us who has served faithfully would like to look back and see some lasting fruit from our ministry. Usually it is in a leader's sixties that he begins to proactively focus on leaving behind lasting legacies.

"And third, in the last part of the Latter Ministry time period or the Finishing Well time period, you will probably make a special effort to consolidate the labor of a lifetime. That will include not only focusing on ultimate contributions, but also doing such things as writing to capture ideas and values, encouraging the Timothys and Priscillas in your life to go on, going back and affirming those lives that have been touched over the years with a personal and special word of encouragement, passing the baton on to those who can run with it and thereby keep your values and ideas alive, helping out with leadership transitions and so on." Ray shrugged and with a sigh of frustration muttered, "Time! Time! I could speak on each of these items for longer than you could listen. But we must move on."

FORMATION

Betty, Gordon's wife, was confused about the whole notion of spiritual formation, ministerial formation and strategic formation. For twenty years she had concentrated on ministering to her children. Gordon had the up-front ministry. She had only recently begun to enter public ministry again. Mostly she was a supportive help for Gordon. She wondered how spiritual formation, ministerial formation and strategic formation applied to her. She posed a question, "Ray, could you give an overall explanation of the three formations? I have my chart here before me. But I don't exactly see how they fit me."

"Betty, I would say that this diagram applies more specifically to those who are involved in public ministry than those who have ministered in the home as you have. But its basic controlling idea relates just as much to you as it does to others. *Ministry essentially flows out of being.* God is concerned with who we are as persons. God first works in us and then through us. This applies to everyone. You are a case in point. Betty, in your situation, you first progressed in beingness. I remember when you dealt with some basic character issues of what it meant to be a wife and mother. Then I remember when you began to study about parenting. You became a skillful parent. I remember once you shared with me some major values God had given you which you wanted to impart to your family. If you think back you will realize that you had in mind a long-term strategic view—the release of your children into maturity, where they can each walk with God on their own.

"Now that is essentially what happens in the interplay of the formations along the time line. The pattern is the same for public leaders or those leading in the home: first, character; second, ability to do things; third, values underlying why we do things; fourth, a long-range goal that helps us integrate our character, abilities, values and goals."

Ray then turned to the diagram of the time line he had earlier drawn on the white board, and modified it as he explained the natural progression involved. (See Figure 5.) They were taking notes as Ray scribbled on the board.

Figure 5. The Formational Priorities over Time—Modified

I. Ministry Foundations	II. Early Ministry	III. Middle Ministry	IV. Latter Ministry	V. Finishing Well
Character—especially integrity is highlighted here.	We are concerned primarily with doing here (MF) but God is more concerned with being (SF). Strategic Formation (STF) is yet in the future.	After we become competent at doing (MF) we recognize that without God's presence and power it is meaningless thus (SF) becomes a priority with us. We are now also beginning to recognize a difference in efficiency and effectiveness.	Because we know the importance of (SF) as a priority, we can now focus on strategic formation (STF) as a major emphasis. Effectiveness now reigns over efficiency. We no longer worry about ministerial formation (MF). We are efficient doing things right and more important focusing on doing the right things right.	We know that our spiritual life will have major impact as a model. So it (SF) dominates this period of life. We also are highly focused on strategic formation (STF) because we want our lives to count.

Ray then went to the chart and added the following, commenting as he did, "These symbols represent critical incidents relating to formation that are important in the life of a developing leader."

Figure 6. The Formational Priorities over Time—Critical Incidents

I. Ministry Foundations	II. Early Ministry	III. Middle Ministry	IV. Latter Ministry	V. Finishing Well
		C1	C2	C3

He turned to the group. They sensed that it was challenge time again. There was something about that look in Ray's eyes. "I have three questions for you. Each question relates to one of those critical incidents." He then posed the questions listed in Table 1.

Table 1. Three Critical Formational Questions

Critical Incident	Label	Question
C1	Doing to Being Paradigm Shift	1. On what do you base your identity? What you are or what you do?
C2	Efficiency to Effectiveness Paradigm Shift	2. Have you made the shift from doing things right to doing the right things right? Do you have focus in your life?
C3	Finishing Well Burden	3. Are you proactively moving toward finishing well?

Ray then had them break up in twos and threes and discuss which of these critical incidents they had personally experienced. Here were the answers the group fed back to Ray:

Table 2. Three Critical Formational Questions: Who

Critical Incident	Label	Question	Answers
C1	Doing to Being Paradigm Shift	1. Which is the basis for your ministry, doing or being?	**doing**—Dan (36), Gloria (35), Mike (48), Millie (43), Rob (38), Sam (48) **being**—Julie (44), Gordon (49) and Betty (48), Cathy (37), Tom (42)
C2	Efficiency to Effectiveness Paradigm Shift	2. Have you made the shift from doing things right to doing the right things right? Do you have focus in your life?	**Yes**—Gordon (49), Sam (48) **No**—the rest were either no or didn't know
C3	Finishing Well Burden	3. Are you proactively moving toward finishing well?	**none**

The sharing was honest and most convicting. Ray closed the sharing by assigning each one to be alone with God for the next hour and reflect on these issues with a view toward understanding what God wanted for each of them.

SHAPING PROCESSES

When they returned, they were ready to listen to the description of the shaping processes. Their time alone with God had sensitized them to the whole notion of the usefulness of a time line to give them perspective. Ray built on this momentum.

Ray anticipated their questions and cut them off at the pass by giving them a handout that listed each of the shaping processes, including definitions and descriptions. His introductory story, however, was what got their attention. Through the story of Tim, they saw how important it was to know about these shaping processes.

This was Tim's story:

Tim had been a go-go enthusiastic youth worker from age twenty-two till age thirty-one. His enthusiasm was contagious. He inspired many young people to give their lives to Christ. Many also went into ministry because of his influence. He was considered a very successful youth worker. It was clear he had both evangelistic and exhortative spiritual gifts. He was also a strong leader and highly directive in his leadership style. He was a creative leader constantly finding innovative techniques that attracted youth.

His church decided to plant a daughter church in a suburban area about twenty miles from the mother church. Tim was challenged to be the founding pastor of this fledgling congregation. At age thirty-one he accepted the challenge and shifted ministry to do this church plant.

Eight months before the anticipated start of the new church plant, church leaders had tapped about eight young couples in their late twenties and early to mid-thirties, two older couples—one in their forties and one in their fifties—and six singles to be the core group of this new church plant. Only twelve people in this group lived in the actual target area. The rest would have to commute. They began to meet monthly during the Sunday School time.

Six months before the church plant, Tim attended a seminar run by a well-known church leader who advocated cell groups as the basis for developing a growing church. Tim was sold on the method.

Immediately he began to share these ideas with the group. His highly directive style overrode some of the more passively resistant folks. Apparently all were committed to using a cell group strategy as their basic approach even though none of them had ever been in a church that had cell groups.

The launch date came. The twenty-eight people began to meet in the new community in a school building. They started with three cell groups.

People gave it a real go for about eleven months. But problems began to arise. The commuters found it harder and harder to attend all the cell group meetings. Leaders also found it difficult to attend all the leaders' meetings. Several of the younger couples had babies. In the next year three of those couples became infrequent participants.

Tim exhorted and admonished these core group members. Techniques that had worked with youth groups did not work so well with adults who had many commitments. They did not react well to his badgering. He sensed he was losing it. Only a few new people in the community were participating in the church. Eventually the cell group model failed and half of the core group went back to the mother church. More than half of the original core group complained about Tim's leadership. Some even became bitter about it. Tim became discouraged as the small group gallantly tried to hold on. Eventually the church plant fizzled. Tim became disillusioned and, at age thirty-five, left full-time ministry. What had happened?

Having finished telling the story, Ray lowered his head and shook it in despair. "This is a classic case *of leadership backlash*. It will happen two or three times over a leader's lifetime. How a leader handles it can make or break the leader. Biblically you see a case of this in Exodus with Moses and God's people. They were with Moses as he attempted to get them out of slavery to freedom. Eventually they rebelled against Moses' leadership. But Moses persevered and there is much we can learn from his example.

"Sometimes a leader feels convinced about a course of action. That leader then convinces followers of that astuteness of that action, perhaps even demonstrating that it is from God. The group then takes the action and it brings unforeseen ramifications along with accomplishment of its major purposes. Because of the unexpected ramifications, the followers turn against the leader in a backlash action. This particular form of conflict processing can be difficult to take unless one is forewarned about it and responds properly. I call this shaping process 'leadership backlash.' Essentially, it refers to the reactions of followers, other leaders within a group and/or Christians outside the group. They react to a course of action taken by a leader because of various ramifications that arise due to the action taken. The situation tests perseverance, clarity of vision and faith in the leader's life." Ray paused, then confided, "I've gone through this process, have you?" Several affirmed that they had indeed faced that same kind of struggle.

Ray then took them into the Scriptures and showed them some key lessons from the Moses example he had alluded to earlier. "Exodus 5:20, where the people react to Moses' leadership when persecution comes, typifies this shaping process. The backlash cycle can be seen readily in this example. Again in Exodus 16:2,3 the backlash continues. Usually the unforeseen ramifications involve persecution or hard times of some kind. And though followers may have agreed originally that the course of action was proper, they now blame the leader for having taken it."

He then went to a new sheet of paper on the flip chart and wrote the eight stages of this shaping process. He told them, "The full cycle of this item includes the following:

> First, the leader gets a vision—that is, specific direction— from God.
> Second, the followers are convinced of the direction.
> Third, the group moves in the direction suggested.
> Fourth, comes persecution, hard times or attacks from Satan—spiritual warfare is common.
> Fifth, there is backlash from the group.
> Sixth, the leader is driven to God to reconfirm the action and get God's affirmation in spite of ramifications.
> Seventh, invariably, God reveals Himself further: who He is, what He intends to do. He makes it clear that it is God who is going to deliver.
> Eighth, finally, God vindicates Himself and the leader.

"Tim made it to stage five. The backlash from the group took him down eventually. Do you think it would have made a difference if he had been aware of these stages? I believe it would have," asserted Ray. "This is a common process. Knowing it and knowing that God uses it to test perseverance, clarity of vision and faith can make a difference.

Tim should have been committed to the church plant primarily and to the methodology more loosely.

"Now what I have just illustrated with Tim could be repeated over and over with many of the shaping activities of God," said Ray hoping to really get their attention. "The basic principle is *know the ways* God shapes; *recognize them* when they are happening to you, and *respond in them to learn* from them what God has for you. Many of the shaping activities follow stages and patterns. Knowing this can make a big difference as you face the confusion that often accompanies shaping activities.

"Take a look at this handout. It describes the fourteen categories of shaping activities I previously listed," said Ray as he handed out the following list.[7]

Handout on Shaping Activities

Name	Description	Use/Further Explanation
Character shaping	God tests and imparts integrity, obedience and sensitivity to His Word through various kinds of shaping activities.	1. To instill leadership character; leaders must be trustworthy to lead. 2. To ensure an obedient heart; leaders cannot expect followers to obey if they don't obey themselves. 3. To sensitize a leader to hearing God; to guide others, leaders must be able to hear God themselves.
Leadership committal	Each leader must come to a resolute decision to be used by God in leadership. This conscious committal is a major turning point. Both lay leaders and full-time leaders face this critical issue in life.	1. Frequently, this is a surrender experience in which the leader gives up other ambitions to serve God. 2. This does not necessarily mean full-time ministry, but it does mean that ministry effort in life will have a priority over secular vocation. 3. This is often a marker event accompanied by a sense of destiny. Such a marker event will carry one on through the difficult times that will come. 4. There is a sense of God's special intervention in this issue. 5. Such a real God-led committal will also be eventually recognized by others.
Authority issues	Submission to authority, the use of authority and learning to operate with spiritual authority are taught to a leader through many experiences.	1. To teach leaders how to follow, which is essential in order to lead others. 2. To teach leaders how to influence followers. 3. To instill the dynamic tension of *leading by serving and serving by leading*.

Name (cont.)	Description (cont.)	Use/Further Explanation (cont.)
Conflict and crises	Sometimes called deep processing, these kinds of activities develop the inner life of a leader by taking the leader through times that necessitate trusting God for deliverance.	1. Take away self-trust and self-confidence to lead. 2. Mellow character (i.e., develop fruit of Spirit) and reveal other inner life issues that must be dealt with. 3. Teach truth that could not be seen in any other way. 4. Open new doors that would not be seen otherwise. 5. Conflict can be personal or ministry oriented.
Giftedness discovery	God uses ministry experiences to show or impart or develop in a leader natural abilities, acquired skills and spiritual gifts.	1. To identify the basic means by which a leader will influence followers. 2. To develop the leader toward efficient leadership. 3. To focus the leader concerning decisions about ministry. 4. To focus the leader toward a major role.
Guidance	God teaches the leader to receive guidance through various means.	1. To show leaders personal guidance for their own lives. 2. To give leaders guidance for ministry. 3. To direct leaders toward vision. 4. To give a sense of divine presence in the leader's life and ministry.
Ministry insights	God opens the way for the leader to have break-throughs in ministry so that ministry has impact.	1. To give the leader methods for impacting those being ministered to. 2. To challenge to new ministry opportunities. 3. To bring God-given results that honor God. He is the One who has shown how to do it.
Leadership backlash	An experience in which followers initially are in agreement with a leader on some course of action but later as it unfolds and negative things happen, they rebel.	1. Tests perseverance. 2. Clarifies vision. 3. Instills faith in the leader. 4. Develops spiritual authority in the leader. 5. Vindicates God's direction of the leader. 6. This shaping activity is described by an eight-stage process. Recognition of these stages helps anticipation of them.
Challenges	God must often stretch a leader beyond a comfort zone in order for that leader to reach potential. Prayer, faith and sphere of influence are often aspects of challenges that God brings through many kinds of experiences.	1. To inspire vision. 2. To move a leader further along in strategic formation. 3. To bring further awareness of a sense of destiny. 4. To take a leader into deeper experiences with God, which add to spiritual authority. 5. To force a leader to model before followers so as to demonstrate the presence of the unseen God. 6. Results in major advances in the leader's

Name (cont.)	Description (cont.)	Use/Further Explanation (cont.)
		confidence and ability to influence and hence significant advance in competence. 7. Kinds of challenges include: faith challenges, prayer challenges, ministry expansion challenges, expansion of one's sphere of influence both in size and type.
Paradigm shifts	God uses new ideas and new experiences to give the leader new ways of perceiving self and ministry.	1. To change an inflexible leader into a much more flexible leader. 2. To bring about new thinking that will lead to efficient and effective ministry. 3. To allow a leader to see truth that previously was hidden. 4. To open up possibilities of wider vision.
Spiritual warfare	Satanic opposition will appear in many forms, some of which seem very human. God sensitizes a leader to these attacks of various kinds and to methods for combating them.	1. To gain victory over evil forces. 2. To vindicate God. 3. To reveal the glory of God. 4. To learn discernment. 5. To develop spiritual authority 6. To make major breakthroughs in the work of God. 7. To authenticate God in a new pioneer work.
Deep processing	Leaders move to new levels of depth in their relationships with God and their ministry for God when they go through difficult times. It is the turning to God and learning to trust Him in and through these experiences that develops the depth of spiritual formation that will take a leader on to a powerful Latter Ministry Time and a Finishing Well Time.	1. One form of this shaping is called isolation, in which the leader is set aside from normal ministry for usually an extended time by sickness, persecution, prison, conflict, personal relationships deteriorating, etc. Isolation shaping takes one deep with God alone. Spiritual authority is developed. Isolation sometimes is self-choice; a leader chooses to get alone with God for an extended time in order for God to meet that leader with renewal, affirmation, clear guidance, growth, a paradigm shift, etc. 2. Life-threatening crises form another kind of deep processing. 3. Intense ministry conflict often serves as another kind of deep processing. 4. A special kind of guidance, called negative preparation, uses very negative shaping activities to force a person to recognize that God is leading out of a situation. 5. A proper response to deep processing is to go deep with God. One who does so does not seek to get out of the deep shaping activities (see them cease), but seeks to get out of them that which God has in them. It is the heartbeat of 2 Corinthians 1:3,4 repeated in a life.

Name (cont.)	Description (cont.)	Use/Further Explanation (cont.)
Power processes	God has to often take a leader through a paradigm shift so that the leader recognizes the supernatural aspects of ministry: Spirit of God, spiritual warfare with demonic forces, supernatural power, etc.	1. Spiritual warfare from Ephesians 6:10ff. is one power process. 2. Power encounters in which the root issue in a ministry situation is seen to be that of the unseen world in which God's power is being tested against demonic power. 3. Prayer power in which a leader is tested to intervene in a leadership setting by seeing God answer prayer. Essentially the leader moves people by interceding with God. 4. Gifted power represents the leader's appropriation of God's power by the leader's giftedness. A subtle paradigm shift goes on here. The leader recognizes that efficient and effective use of personal resources essentially come from God. God is trusted, not self. And there is repeated demonstration of power. 5. Networking power is another form of power process. The leader recognizes the sovereign way God connects to people and resources and sees them used by God to multiply ministry.
Destiny activities (fulfill-ment)	This is the culminating effort of God to bring a sense of destiny to pass. It represents deep moments of God's intervening power and affirmation in a leader's life.	1. Early in the Ministry Foundations time period and the Early Ministry time period, God gives intimations, hints, of His sovereign plan for the leader. These are called destiny preparation shaping activities. 2. During the latter part of Early Ministry and especially in the Middle Ministry time period, God reveals further and clarifies a leader's destiny. Some of these shaping activities are highly supernatural and unusual; others are providential. 3. During the later part of the Latter Ministry time period and especially in the Finishing Well time period God brings to pass events and activities that fulfill His promises of destiny to the leader.

Ray had the group spend an entire day dissecting and discussing these shaping activities. He first took one of the shaping activities and illustrated it from his own life or from a Christian leader he knew well. Next, he showed how God imparted lasting values or other insights from the shaping that affected all the rest of the leader's ministry. Then he made the eleven break up into three groups and identify the various shaping activities in their lives and how their leadership had been shaped by it. Finally, he brought the group back together and debriefed what had been learned in the small groups. He followed this process for each of the fourteen shaping activities. At the close of the final debriefing session, there was a sense of awe. Each leader knew that God had intervened personally in his or her life repeatedly. They all knew personally of the sovereign activity of God in their lives—and they were absolutely convinced God would continue to do this over their lifetimes.

KEY PATTERNS IN LEADERSHIP DEVELOPMENT

Mike obviously had a question that was important to him. He began tentatively, "These concepts and ideas about leadership development are great, but I was wondering how you use them with other people. I'm involved in training young people for ministry and one of the major issues we run into again and again is how to recognize leadership potential and encourage it to develop. Are there particular things you look for?"

Ray thought for a moment. "You know, I don't know that there is a simple answer to your question. Each leadership situation is different. Different contexts and different types of followers require different types of leaders. You definitely can't have a cookie-cutter approach to recognizing and developing leaders. I have learned to look for certain patterns of thought, attitudes or behaviors in the lives of individuals. I have learned to recognize God's shaping activities in them."

"What do you mean by a pattern?" asked Mike.

Ray responded, "A pattern is something that is repetitive over time and is therefore recognizable. Sometimes it is made up of a combination of things like behaviors, attitudes or qualities that combine to become characteristics of a person or a shaping process. And then, after you have worked with enough leaders, you will recognize that the things which are repeated in many lives will probably show up in many others lives. Let me give one more pass through the time line and describe some common patterns. Then I'll talk about two of them, in particular.

"Now, even though I could talk about all of these patterns, let me describe two of the patterns that I believe are the most important ones for leaders who are just beginning to emerge. Mike, these patterns will help you recognize leadership potential. I call the first one the 'ministry foundation principle.' It relates to faithfulness. You see, leadership is all about serving. One of the key characteristics of service is faithfulness. God actively works to shape each leader by ensuring that he is faithful. Faithfulness is a critical characteristic of every leader. The principle for this pattern is found in Luke 16:10, which says, 'Whoever can be trusted with very little can also be trusted with much, and whoever is dishonest with very little will also be dishonest with much' (NIV). A pattern of faithfulness in little things is a prerequisite for me when I look for leadership potential."

"You make it sound easy to see this. But in practical terms, how do you recognize faithfulness?" asked Millie.

Ray smiled and responded, "Well, first of all, if you know what you are looking for and you are an observant person, it is easy to see faithfulness. But I have also learned that it helps to *test* that which seems to be faithfulness. I often create situations where people can demonstrate faithfulness if they want to. Then I sit back and watch. Some people only like to be "faithful" when there is recognition and visibility. Leaders with good potential will be faithful no matter what. They will respond to any ministry responsibilities or requests for help with an attitude of service whether they are recognized or not. God is interested in promoting these kind of leaders."

Figure 7. Five Developmental Patterns

I. Ministry Foundations	II. Early Ministry	III. Middle Ministry	IV. Latter Ministry	V. Finishing Well

1. The Destiny Pattern

Destiny preparation activities————>	Destiny revelation activities ————>	Destiny fulfillment activities ————>

2. The Ministry Faithfulness Pattern

A cyclical pattern occurring repetitively throughout every time period described briefly as faithfulness in ministry leads to expanded ministry and new tests of faithfulness at a new level. The pattern continues until potential is reached.

3. The Testing Patterns

	Positive Testing	Advanced forms ————>
	Negative Testing	

4. The Giftedness Development Pattern
Natural abilities,
      basic skills, early gifts
          acquired skills
               later gifts   Mature giftedness————->

5. Like-Attracts-Like Giftedness
      Gifted leaders ————————————->
      Attract emerging leaders who
      potentially are like gifted

Dan jumped in, "You mentioned that there are two patterns that are especially helpful in identifying potential leaders. Which of these you listed on the board is that second pattern?"

Ray leaned back and smiled. "You know, the second pattern is one that most people don't like to think about because it involves the notion of testing. In fact, I call it *the testing pattern*. I have observed that God likes to test His emerging leaders. In the earlier stages of their development, God uses many different kinds of situations to test their character. As they mature in ministry, the tests shift from primarily character tests to tests regarding faith—challenges, if you will.

"I have experienced testing both in my life and in my corporate ministry," Ray emphasized. "Let me describe it primarily for the individual, but keep in mind that it often happens for a corporate body as well. Here is how this *testing* occurs. There are three stages or parts of the pattern—the test, the response, the after effects. In the first part of the pattern, a situation or circumstance arises in which the person faces a test of some kind, usually a character issue. The test involves responding to the circumstances of the situation. The response of the leader will either honor God and His principles or will not honor God. Sometimes the person is aware that this is a test and other times the person doesn't recognize that God is involved in the situation. The response of the leader is the second part or stage of the testing pattern. The third stage of the test can go either of two directions, depending on how the person responds to the situation. If the person responds in a positive or God-honoring way, God brings expansion to the person. By expansion, I mean that He blesses the leader, takes the leader on, gives new opportunities, opens up ministry in some way or other. The person goes forward in his or her development."

Ray continued, "Let me point out that testing can involve integrity, obedience or sensing a God-given word. You see this in the lives of Daniel and Joseph. They are classic examples of being favored by God because they passed *tests*. If the person does not respond in a God-honoring way or *fails the test*, the third stage looks different. God usually takes the leader into what I call *remedial activity* or a *retesting*. In other words, God usually brings about another situation in which the leader gets tested in the same area or about the same issue.

"Jonah's story is certainly the most dramatic *retesting* situation in the Bible. If the leader continues to respond inappropriately to the circumstances, he may enter into the discipline of God in order to learn how to respond in a God-honoring way. If the person continues to respond negatively, then they may be cast aside from leadership and cut off from further participation. This happened to King Saul. King Saul's story is certainly a dramatic warning to all of us in leadership," Ray stated as a sad look appeared on his face.

"Are there any other patterns that you think are important for us to know about?" asked Gordon.

Ray chuckled and asked, "How much time do we have? I've only got about twenty other major patterns that I've identified. Do we have another four days? I'll tell you what. Let's take a break and if you want, I can mention some of the most important ones and give you some resources to follow up on. By the way, I think the destiny pattern, the first one listed on the board, is critical for someone at your stage of development. You are starting to think about the latter stages of ministry and want to make the next twenty years count. I believe the best years of ministry are yet ahead of you—if you can get focused. Let's take our break."

During the break, they continued to talk about sense of destiny and the destiny-shaping activities they had personally experienced. Several of them were surprised to hear of some unusual, almost mystical experiences the others had gone through. They had never shared these personal experiences before. In the context of sense of destiny and the notion of destiny activities, however, they felt free to do so. Finally, Ray said, "Lets get back together. I have a final exercise I want us to do for our last three hours together."

When they were gathered, Ray once again held center stage. "It is clear to me that God has been with us and has touched each of us. I want us to spend the next hour or so giving honor to God by sharing with one another what God has been saying. Answer this question for me. What one thing, the most important thing, has God impressed upon you personally in these sessions?" He then smiled, sat and waited for the group to respond.

After a period of reflection they opened up. It was a powerful time for each one in the group. They all had been struck by something different, and spent a few minutes talking about how they intended to make their most poignant lesson a reality in their life. Through it all, Ray whispered prayers of thanksgiving to God for His touch in their lives.

When they finished, the entire group thanked Ray for his ministry and gave him a lovely landscape picture of Lake Gregory and a beautiful card signed by all, each one writing encouraging words. Ray closed with a simple prayer, which touched the hearts of all: "Lord, let them finish well."

In the after session the next day, those present commissioned Mike to summarize in his usual clear and succinct way all they had learned from Ray about the life cycle of a leader. Mike spent several weeks preparing this summary. He carefully listened to the tapes, replaying some of them several times. He reviewed his notes. As a result, he developed a one-page summary of what they had learned.

Overview of the Life Cycle of a Leader

	I. Ministry Foundations (16-26 years)	II. Early Ministry (5-12 years)	III. Middle Ministry (8-14 years)	IV. Latter Ministry (12+ years)	V. Finishing Well (?)
Ephesians 2:10 Life Development	Basic character shaped. Some destiny hints.	Commitment to leadership. Leadership character formed. Learn by doing. Intimations of life purpose and giftedness emerge.	Life purpose and giftedness and major role firm up. Breakthrough insights for ministry occur. Conflict and authority issues occur. Efficient ministry.	Movement toward ideal role. Efficient Ministry becomes effective ministry. Peak ministry occurs. Ultimate contribution clarifies.	Life ministry consolidated. Ultimate contributions developed. Values passed on to rising generations of leaders.
Formational Development	Spiritual formation	1. Ministerial formation 2. Spiritual formation	1. Spiritual formation 2. Ministerial formation 3. Strategic formation	1. Strategic formation 2. Spiritual formation	1. Spiritual formation 2. Strategic formation
Shaping Activities God Uses	• Character shaping	• Leadership committal • Authority insights • Conflict and crises • Giftedness discovery • Guidance	• Ministry insights • Leadership backlash • Challenges • Paradigm shifts	• Spiritual warfare • Deep processing • Power processes	• Destiny fulfillment
Critical Incidents			C1 Doing to Being	C2 Efficiency to Effectiveness	C3 Finishing Well Mode
Patterns					
Destiny	Destiny preparation	Destiny revelation	Destiny revelation	Destiny revelation and fulfillment	Destiny fulfillment
Ministry Faithfulness	Small to more responsibility	More to larger responsibility	Continued faithfulness leads to maximum potential	Maximum potential	Reap the fruit of a life of faithfulness

Testing	Positive leads to expansion; negative leads to remedial shaping	Positive leads to expansion; negative leads to remedial shaping	Testing now moves toward faith challenges	Testing now toward reaching potential
Giftedness Natural Abilities; Basic Skills	Early spiritual gifts; further acquired skills	Confident identification of spiritual gifts and giftedness set	Later spiritual gifts; giftedness used efficiently	Very mature use of giftedness
Like Attracts Like Giftedness Pattern	Leader attracted to other leaders with like gifts	Leader attracts emerging leaders who are like gifted	Uses like attracts like pattern to help in leadership selection	Strong use of like attracts like pattern for leadership development

Notes

1. For Christian developmental writings, see: Evelyn Eaton Whitehead and James D. Whitehead, *Christian Life Patterns* (New York: Doubleday, 1992), Bobby Clinton, *The Making of a Leader* (Colorado Springs: NavPress, 1988). For secular writers, see Daniel J. Levinson, et al, *The Seasons of a Man's Life* (New York: Alfred A. Knopf, 1978); Gail Sheehy, *New Passages* (New York: Random House, 1995).

2. See the concept of Historical Mentors in chapter 10 of *The Mentor Handbook* by Drs. J. Robert and Richard W. Clinton. From Barnabas Publishers, 2175 N. Holliston Ave, Altadena, CA 91001.

3. For the more complicated diagram from which this simplified time line was derived, see page 40 in the 1993 position paper by Dr. J. Robert Clinton, "Getting Perspective—By Using Your Unique Time-Line," available from Barnabas Publishers, 2175 N. Holliston Ave, Altadena, CA 91001.

4. See *Focused Lives—Inspirational Life Changing Lessons from Eight Effective Christian Leaders Who Finished Well* written by Dr. J. Robert Clinton and published by Barnabas Publishers, 2175 N. Holliston Avenue, Altadena, CA 91001.

5. See Clinton and Clinton, 1994, *Developing Leadership Giftedness* for a full discussion of the giftedness set, its focal element and development over a lifetime. Available from Barnabas Publishers, 2175 N. Holliston Ave, Altadena, CA 91001.

6. See Dr. J. Robert Clinton, 1995, *Strategic Concepts—That Clarify a Focused Life*. Twelve types of ultimate contribution categories are described there. Available from Barnabas Publishers, 2175 N. Holliston Ave, Altadena, CA 91001.

7. Some fifty-one specific shaping activities have been identified and described. The list on this table has been generalized and simplified. For a detailed list of shaping activities see Bobby Clinton, *The Making of a Leader* (Colorado Springs: NavPress, 1988); and *Leadership Emergence Theory*, available through Barnabas Publishers, 2175 N. Holliston Ave, Altadena, CA 91001.

NINE

THE ROLE OF INNOVATION IN LEADERSHIP

ELMER L. TOWNS

A leader has been described as a person out front with people following. J. Oswald Sanders says in his book *Spiritual Leadership*,[1] "Leadership is influence." This means the more people following you, the greater your leadership, and the more deeply you influence people, the greater your leadership. In church circles, the pastor is out front influencing parishioners. In military circles, the sergeant is out front influencing soldiers. In the educational world of ideas, the teacher is out front influencing students.

The concept of leadership implies direction and movement. A leader takes followers from where they are located to where they should be. This implies change. Followers have to change the location, direction, thinking or attitude. If followers want to change, then leadership goes well. If they do not want to change, then leadership is difficult.

The idea of change implies innovation, alter, replace or transfer. Sometimes innovation has a positive meaning, as in regenerate, create or sculpture. At other times the word has a negative meaning, as in overthrow, exchange or rebel. All leaders confront change.

This chapter focuses on the role of the leader in bringing about innovation or change. Therefore, the chapter will examine the role of leadership in producing change, innovation and redirecting or reconstructing the organization within which they are ministering. The first law of leadership is called the "Law of Vision/Dreams."[2] It is expressed in the slogan, "When followers buy into your vision, they buy into your leadership." As long as the followers buy into the leader's dream, usually little resistance is expressed to his leadership or to the fact of change itself. So innovation is easy when the followers and the leader have the same dream of a preferable future, and they both agree on the methods to achieve the desired outcome.

Problems arise for leaders, however, because they are imperfect, and exercise imperfect communication to followers who have imperfect powers of observation; thus arriving at imperfect interpretation and imperfect understanding of the task at hand. When an imperfect relationship exists between leaders and followers, the less than perfect situation creates a barrier to change or innovation. Tension results to both leader and follower. This tension works out in distrust, lack of confidence, second-guessing the motives of leadership, undermining the attempts of leadership or out-right rebellion to leadership. This list of problems is not exhaustive. Many other problems can occur as a result of imperfect communication between leadership and followership.

EXAMPLES OF RESISTANCE TO INNOVATION AND LEADERSHIP

Pastors confront resistance when they try to implement another worship service other than a worship service at the traditional hour. Even if the traditional Sunday morning worship service is filled to capacity, the congregants usually have such deep loyalty to the traditional time that any change is questioned and resisted.

In one church, the board had difficulty trying to eliminate the position of youth pastor. All the young people had grown into adulthood and the board wanted to employ a young adult minister to coordinate their activities.

Still another church experienced difficulty attempting to shift a morning Vacation Bible School to an evening time slot.

In another setting, a youth pastor found that parents were opposed to a shift in location of the high school Sunday School class from the second floor of the educational building to the basement of his home. The parents complained that the youth stayed away from the church service on Sunday morning because they were not in the church building.

An east coast church heavily committed to supporting foreign missionaries experienced trauma when the new pastor suggested that foreign mission's money newly available by a retiring foreign missionary be shifted to plant an inner-city church among a minority group.

UNDERSTANDING PRESUPPOSITIONS

The following are a few basic presuppositions leaders should understand when attempting change or innovation.

Change/Innovation Usually Begins with the Leader

Technically, any growth in the church or in the leader equals change. You cannot grow unless you change, therefore all physical growth, social growth, mental growth or spiritual growth involves a change in life. The opposite, however, is not true; all change is not growth. Many people do not change things for the better, but for the worse. John Maxwell, former pastor of Skyline Wesleyan Church, has noted, "All change does not represent progress, but if we do not change there will be no progress."[3]

To put it another way, change and innovation is the price tag that hangs on the item called growth. Many people want a new building, a new evangelistic outreach, they want their Sunday School to be successful or they want their foreign missions program to be effective; but they do not want to make any changes that will cause it to grow. Change, however, is progress along with growth. Rick Warren, pastor of Saddleback Church, Mission Viejo, California, explained recently in a sermon titled "Why People Fight Change": "All growth is change, all change is loss, all loss is pain."

To be a leader is to be a change agent. Every pastor who leads a church must understand that leading people is asking them to change something. The same can be said of a church board; it is a change agent. A Sunday School teacher who wants pupils to grow, and every youth minister attempting to lead adolescents to Christ, is a change agent. A leader is attempting change when he tries to change programs, upgrade buildings, communicate new thoughts, convince people of a new strategy or implement a new outreach ministry.

Therefore, the first thing a leader must change is himself. To change a church, the pastor must face three truths: (1) he has been changed in the past, (2) he must be willing to change as the followers are changed and (3) he must be willing to face the problems of leading people through change. The first change is that the leader must grow in his understanding and in spiritual life. Rick Warren, pastor of Saddleback Church, states, "Leaders are learners. Because they are constantly leading people into change, a leader must be constantly learning, which is another way of saying they must be constantly growing."

Followers Must Be Prepared for Change

When leading people through change, leaders must communicate several assumptions about change to followers. First, followers need to know that we live in an era of change. Everything around us is changing, from the information network to work habits to styles of dress to television viewing preferences. Approximately 20 percent of Americans move their primary households each year from one residence to another. When a high schooler graduates to face the marketplace, he cannot expect to hold one job for the rest of his life the way his grandfather did; rather, he must be prepared to hold an average of five jobs in the next fifteen years.

The second assumption about change is that when people are going through significant change, they look for leadership to help them get through transition. Children look to parents for leadership; soldiers look to their officers; and workers look to management. When it comes to church circles, pastors and boards have a great responsibility to lead people through change and innovation. Those leaders who can successfully "sell" the vision of change are those who will be successful ministering to people. Those leaders who cannot handle change will be ineffective in ministry.

The third assumption is that people will follow leaders who have an effective ministry in other areas of their lives. People follow a pastor who is effective in teaching the Bible, in counseling, in leading worship or in some other ministry dimension. Actually, the roles of ministry and leadership have a reciprocal interaction: each supports the other. When a pastor can effectively lead his people through change from former patterns and traditions into new methods of doing things, that pastor will be most effective in ministry.

The Leader Must Know What to Change

Many pastors see change as threats because they have not analyzed the substantive aspects of change. When pastors know what and what not to change, they can better lead people through the process. But what should a leader change?

We should never change our doctrine, because doctrinal truth comes from God's Word and that truth is eternal. Pastors who try to change the belief of people will find resistance. The Word of God is eternal and Jesus Christ is the same, yesterday, today and forever. Because biblical principles come out of truth, we should not change principles. The principles of evangelism, teaching, ministry, fasting and holiness remain the same; but our *methods* must be modernized. A method is applying the principle of truth to culture.[4] When our culture changes, we have to change our methods to be more effective in applying the principle.

> Methods are many,
>   Principles are few.
> Methods may change
>   But principles never do.

As an illustration, we may change Vacation Bible School from the morning to the evening, but we never change our commitment to the principle of teaching and winning children to Christ. We may change our worship service from Sunday morning to Saturday evening "because 23 percent of America's workforce are employed on Sunday morning," but we never change our commitment to the principles of worship, preaching or evangelism.

When the average layperson thinks a pastor is pulling him away from God because of the changes that are going on in his church, the layperson will resist change. Some may even try to undermine the pastor's leadership. On the other hand, when changes are pushing people closer to God, the people will probably endorse the changes wholeheartedly. Usually, when a person understands what is being changed, he will buy into the vision of change.

The problems leaders have in relation to changing methods is compounded by the very nature of most leaders. Many leaders tenaciously hold to the methods that first gave them success and credibility in their leadership. As the times and the culture change, however, the degree of success achieved by applying those antiquated methods diminishes. Their methods are no longer relevant. With the passing of time, many leaders refuse to look for newer methods or innovations to enhance their ministry. As their work becomes stale, or as culture changes around them, these leaders have failed to keep pace and grow. Consequently, they become saddled with programs they introduced into the church with success some years earlier, but that are no longer effective.

For instance, Vacation Bible School is not an eternal principle mandated in the Word of God. It was introduced more than one hundred years ago and its past success was dependent upon the time children had available when they were on summer vacation. But times have changed. The growing urban population of America has produced many children who no longer have free time in the summer. They are enrolled in sports leagues, take extended vacations, live in second homes (cottages at the lake) or are involved in community recreation programs. Children are not as available for Vacation Bible School as they were in the past, so in many places Vacation Bible School can be moved to the evening schedule to be successful.

Adapting to the Changing Times
When leaders look at the very nature of today's innovation, they must realize the future will not be the same as the past. Leaders have learned too much to go back to the old methods. Because the natural inclination of true leaders is to strive for improvement, they will do things better and they will do things differently.

Today, leaders must realize that change is coming faster than ever before. Someone noticed that as many pages were written about the war in Vietnam as the total number of pages written in all the books published prior to 1900.

The future will not be what leaders expect, and it will arrive here faster than leaders expect. When this nation was founded, more than 90 percent of the people were farmers living on self-contained farms: they provided for their whole livelihood on their farms. No one ever expected America to be anything other than a nation of farmers. Today, however, only 2 percent of Americans work in agriculture, providing food for the other 98 percent of Americans. The rate of change is faster today than it was in the past, the content of change is not what we expected and we cannot go back.

UNDERSTANDING WHY FOLLOWERS RESIST CHANGE[5]

People do not want to change for many reasons. It is the duty of a leader to know his followers and what they want in life (i.e., their visions and dreams). It is also mandatory, however, that a leader know why followers resist change. If people vote against change or growth, they may be voting against his leadership. At other times, they love their leader and want to follow him, but vote against the suggested change.

One of John Maxwell's favorite stories about resistance to change is about a person celebrating his one hundredth birthday. A reporter interviewing him said, "I bet you've seen a lot of changes in your life!"

"Yes," the man said, "and I've been against every one of them."

When leaders are able to answer the barriers to change, they will be more successful in leadership. When the leaders can develop a strategy that incorporates people into the change process, leaders can answer problems before they arise, they can change their approach or strategy, or they may learn from their insight and not attempt the project.

Misunderstanding
Rick Warren says when people are "down on" any projects they are not "up on." This means the leader must communicate vital information, solve problems and paint the vision.

Lack of Ownership in the Project
At times followers feel that projects are being forced upon them. They feel change or innovation is coming from the pastor or the church board and they are not a part of the process. To answer this problem, leaders must involve as many of the followers as possible in the process and the project. When people are involved in the planning stages—the implementation stage and the delivery stage—they will reduce their opposition to the project. Basically, when followers do not have ownership of a new project (i.e., they don't buy into the dream or vision) they will fight the new project.

Habit Patterns
Sometimes people perceive a new program as a threat to their estab-

lished way of doing things. They do not want to change their place, their routine or their comfort level; the status quo is what they know and they prefer to stick with it. People are creatures of habit, so they are against anything that displaces their habits.

The Perceived Price Is Not Worth It
Basically, people resist change when they think the payoff is too small for the price they may have to pay. The leader must remember the Law of Rewards: That which gets rewarded, gets done. When people feel a proposed change offers them the rewards they seek, they will support that innovation.

The Loss of Something Valuable
Within any church or ministry constituency, a range of comfort levels are related to potential change. A person's comfort level relates to his position, prestige, relationships or even attachment to physical things such as a seat in the sanctuary. Any transition in the way things are done, whether it be a new service or a new procedure, will threaten people to varying degrees. They feel they are losing control, or maybe losing their security or, even worse, they feel it will cost them too much (financially, emotionally or reputationally).

"Satisfaction" Level with the Existing Way of Doing Things
These situations occur because the leader has not properly initiated his people into the dream/vision. Leaders should recognize that when people resist an innovative idea, it is not the people who are at fault, but the leader who has not done a proper job of communicating the vision/dream of where the ministry is headed—and why.

Negative Attitudes Toward Change in General
Some people are maintenance oriented: they want to maintain the status quo. These people have a tendency to resist anything new, whether it is a new idea, a new program or a new way of doing things. The leader should be sure to communicate the biblical basis or principles of any innovative plans. The people need to see that their higher calling is to serve God and be obedient to Him.

Lack of Respect for the Leader
Many times people do not have a negative reaction to an idea or new

project; it is just that the people do not have faith in leadership. Perhaps the leader has failed them before, and has not regained sufficient credibility. Perhaps the leader's life is not deeply rooted in the Lord Jesus Christ or the leader has demonstrated bad choices, indiscretion or even a lack of Christian testimony.

Favoring Tradition
This is perhaps the most common barrier to innovation. The old adage is often quoted, "We've never done it that way before." Therefore people are not open to change.

THE PRESUPPOSITION OF CHANGE

When introducing any change, a leader should understand that the task of guiding followers is the same as the task of introducing change. Therefore, to initiate change is to apply the laws of leadership.[6] The following list provides an overview of those laws.

Law One: The Law of Vision/Dream
People follow a leader who directs them to a desirable objective.

Law Two: The Law of Reward
People follow a leader who provides them rewards from their chosen goals.

Law Three: The Law of Credibility
People follow a leader when they have confidence in his plans.

Law Four: The Law of Communication
People follow a leader who effectively communicates his plans to reach the objective.

Law Five: The Law of Accountability
People follow a leader who involves them in reaching a goal.

Law Six: The Law of Motivation
People follow a leader who gives compelling reasons to reach the objective.

Law Seven: The Law of Problem Solving
People follow a leader who gives solutions to problems that
hinder them from reaching the objective.

Law Eight: The Law of Decision Making
People follow a leader who gives answers to the decisions
involving the objective.

When leaders are introducing a change, their first step is to give the
people a vision of the change. When followers buy into the vision of
any innovation, they will buy into leadership and the objective will
probably be accomplished with little resistance or controversy.

The second law reminds us that when followers are able to see
what is in it for them, they are much more prone to move toward the
goal. They should understand their rewards and the probability of
receiving rewards as a result of the change they are going through.

The Law of Credibility underscores the importance of the people's
belief in their leader—and the power of a leader who has similar confidence in his followers.

Obviously, communication (the heart of the fourth Law of
Leadership) is necessary for any change or innovation to make head-
way. Many times innovation is resisted simply because the people do
not know what is coming.

The Law of Accountability cautions a leader to involve followers in
the process of change, not just the end product. People will not do
what the leader expects (his vision or dream), but followers will
accomplish what the leader inspects.

None of the innovation will be implemented unless the leader can
motivate the people to embrace and initiate the changes in mind. Too
often motivation is viewed as telling funny stories, touching people's
emotions (such as sympathy or fear) or even using tools such as videos
to get the message across. But motivation is simply giving people a
compelling reason to make the change and be innovative in their
approach to ministry.

No matter how good the leader, how loyal the followers, how
strategic the proposed change or how airtight the action plan, there
will always be problems when a new idea is introduced.

The Seventh Law of Leadership notes that leadership must solve
the problems that keep people from moving into new frontiers.

Therefore, the leader must understand the whole process of problem solving before he introduces innovation.

Finally, the Law of Decision Making suggests that excellence in decision making is at the heart of leadership. Leaders who can make the proper decisions are those who can effectively lead followers through change.

Pastor Paul Walker, of Mt. Paran Church of God in metropolitan Atlanta, Georgia, has been effective in beginning many new ministries within his church. Although his list of Eight Principles of Innovation are not identical with the Eight Laws of Leadership, they are similar in strategy and focus. When Walker was asked his strategy for introducing new programs into his church, he outlined the following eight-fold strategy.[7]

1. *New ministries must be built on the longevity of the pastor.* People have to trust leadership before they follow leadership.

2. *A leader must share his vision of a new ministry, and the people must buy into the vision.*

3. *A leader must develop a reputation for integrity.* People must be able to believe what the leader is saying, before they will follow him.

4. *Always try to test a new program before implementing it churchwide.* "I do this and find that this way I am not locked into a new program that may not work. Usually the church tries a program for three to six months before going public or making a permanent commitment."

5. *Get a few people to buy into a new ministry, but recognize that not everyone will buy into it.* One of the secrets of Dr. Walker's success is realizing that not everyone in his church will become involved in every ministry, and not everyone will be at the church building every day.

6. *Give everyone a loophole.* This means giving everyone the opportunity not to take part in a program, without feeling guilty. "Guilt," Walker says, "is an accusatory sense of failure. It is one of the diseases that kills spirituality and hinders programs.

   "By giving people a loophole, they can accept the existence of a program without feeling obliged to get

involved or attend. When people do not feel an obliga-
tion to a new program they will not attack it or try to kill
new ideas. But if they are not given a loophole they will
feel guilty and intimidated and will try to kill the new
ministry."

7.   *Don't fear failure.* Fear of failure, Walker believes, "kills
innovation more than any other cancer."

8.   *Never be afraid to try something, but at the same time be willing to recognize when it is not working.* "I drank at that cup
and learned valuable lessons."

A Strategy for Ministry and Change[8]

John Maxwell gave the following strategy described as five circles,
each circle within another circle. His illustration appears similar to a
rock thrown into still water. The circles closest to the center splash
highest, and those people in the church who are closest to the change
agent are the most important people in the church to make change take
place effectively.

It takes more than just a good attitude on the part of a change agent
to influence the decisions of a church or to instill a desire for innovation. The following strategy by Maxwell indicates that the change
agent works in each of the five circles of ministry activity, beginning
with those closest to him (because they are the most influential people), then adjusting his methods according to the nature of each group
with which he works.

Maxwell was quick to point out that a change will not automatically happen just because a minister applies the following strategy for
change. At the very heart of the change agent's relationship to each
person in each circle is ministry. First, the minister wants to build up
the spiritual maturity of the followers and to communicate the gospel
to them at their points of concern. When the minister does this first, he
earns the right to bring innovation into the church.

Circle One: The Change Agent
The first person to be changed is the change agent, who stands at the
center of all change. "The innermost circle is myself," Maxwell says.
"We must always remember that change does not begin with followers, nor does change begin with workers. Change always begins with

the leader, and the pastor is the shepherd of the flock, the leader of God's people." When Maxwell was pastoring a church, he customarily asked himself five questions before trying to change something in his church.

1. Is this idea mine, or God's?

2. Am I willing to pay the price this change will require? (The price may be a commitment to stay at the church, physical energy, a spiritual commitment to fast and pray or time out of a busy schedule to visit or minister to people.)

3. Who will I lose by instituting this change? (If you have heard Maxwell speak, you may have heard him say, "Choose who you lose." By this, he indicates that some people will automatically quit when you put innovative programs into place. Maxwell indicates that some people will not be satisfied, and cannot be placated. They have made up their minds to leave the church if progress takes place.)

4. How long will it take?

5. Will I be around after the change is made? (Sometimes, when the change backfires, the church will ask the pastor to leave. At other times, a change is necessary and is not done properly, so the church feels the pastor has to leave.)

Maxwell asserts that these questions must be faced honestly and answered accurately. If not, the leader will not be settled in his approach to change, and his leadership will not be bold and courageous.

Jerry Falwell has often said, "Make a decision, and make it work." After a leader has asked these questions, he then can make the decision for change, and move on in confidence.

Circle Two: The Main Person

Every organization has crucial people who will influence the multitude of followers. Some call these people "the main man" or the "key lady." This main person can influence other people's ideas, and without his or her help any innovative change will fail. Sometimes this main person has responsibility because of the office he holds; other times this person may not have an office but still influences the opinions of others.

Maxwell says the leader should communicate four things to the main person. First, the main person must understand the leader's vision and commitment as well as the sacrifices the leader will make for innovation. Second, the main person must be given ownership for the change. More than just understanding the change, the main person must buy into the change to make it happen. Third, the leader must give support to the main person as he influences others in the group. This support must be reciprocal: the main person must also support the leader. The fourth thing is element. The leader must give the main person enough time to work through the proposed innovation to ensure that the two of them can move forward together. Together, they must come to the place where they say, "This change is our idea."

Circle Three: Decision Makers

When the leader moves into this circle of people within the organization, he is among the movers and the shakers. These people are more than position holders and elected officials: they are decision makers. These are the men and women within the Body who help the majority form their opinions and ideas. This group may be the board of a church, the finance committee, the music committee or a denominational council.

The leader will spend time with decision makers so he can know them. This is one of the prices the leader must pay to be successful in his position. This involves knowing what "floats that boat" of each decision maker. In this process of discovery, the most important meeting is not always the group meeting. The senior leader may have to meet individually with his decision makers before meeting with a group to give them input and background material.

Maxwell's rule is: "When you've got it going for you, bring them together. When it's going against you, deal with them separately."

In summary, when the main person becomes convinced that an innovation is needed, and when the decision makers on the committee are convinced innovation is needed, the leader will probably be successful in introducing the innovation.

Circle Four: Those Most Affected

The people who will be most affected are probably the workers, servants and fellow laborers. In a church, this will be Sunday School teachers, ushers, the leaders of women's ministries and so on. When the leader enters this circle, he is looking for those who will be most affected by the innovation to become involved in its workings. Therefore, the leader will attempt three things at this level: ask for input, appeal to their interest and make concessions whenever possible.

When the leader arrives at this level, he does not have all the answers about implementing the innovation, because the people of Circle Four are involved in implementation. Many times the vision/dream is broad based and the leader is operating at a general level. Those in this circle must apply the vision to their task. "What about getting my children to the bathroom?" Or, "Both of us want to use the kitchen at the same time." The leader must recognize that these people have genuine concerns. They see problems the leader does not see, and they can solve problems the leader cannot solve. Thus, when working with those from Circle Four, the leader is looking to fine-tune and implement the dream.

Circle Five: The Members

This circle comprises those who attend the church or those who are church members. These are followers; few of them are actively involved in ministry or the organization. The leader is not always looking for a vote of approval from the members; often, the leader is seeking to understand their inclination or intention. The question he must answer is: Will they follow their leader? If the first four circles are positively inclined, the people in the fifth circle usually will say yes. This is why business meetings in most large churches are easy to conduct. They take care of the problems in smaller meetings before bringing issues to the congregation. This is another way of saying: churches that are large have learned how to solve problems and overcome barriers. Therefore, the ability to solve problems contributes to the church's growth, which then makes it a large church. On the other hand, some small churches always take their problems to circle five and try to solve those problems en masse. Because of the inevitable hostilities and misunderstandings that occur, those churches seldom grow. The inefficiency of their problem-solving process, and their inept approach to introducing innovative change, prevents them from growing.

TWO KEYS TO INNOVATIVE CHANGE

The entire process of innovative change involves two critical factors. The first is timing. When it comes to making a change, remember: People resist change they do not expect. Maxwell says, "Resistance is always greatest when change comes as a surprise." Therefore, his experience has led him to the following rules:

The Maxwell Rule of Timing:

- The wrong decision at the wrong time is a *disaster*.
- The wrong decision at the right time is a *mistake*.
- The right decision at the wrong time is *unacceptable*.
- The right decision at the right time leads to *success*.

The second factor is having the courage to make innovative changes. This is not blind courage, where a person jumps off the diving board hoping there is water in the pool. Some leaders call themselves courageous in innovation, but in reality, they are simply foolhardy because they do not understand the process of change, the implications of change and how to get people to follow them throughout the implementation of the change.

What is a courageous decision related to making an innovative change? When a leader knows where he is going, how to get there and how to involve followers in the change process. When a leader knows the change is right, the timing is right and the motives are right, then the leader can be bold and courageous.

Notes
1. J. Oswald Sanders, *Spiritual Leadership* (Chicago: Moody Press, 1972), p. 7.
2. Elmer Towns, *The Eight Laws of Leadership* (Lynchburg, Va.: Church Growth Institute, 1992), p. 21.
3. Elmer Towns, *An Inside Look at 10 of Today's Most Innovative Churches* (Ventura, Calif.: Regal Books, 1990), p. 27 ff. Much of the information in this section is taken from an interview with John Maxwell and published in the analysis section of the book. The author believes Maxwell has one of the clearest strategies for innovation evident among pastors. The ten churches examined in the book are themselves case studies of change and innovation to help understand the role successful leaders follow in introducing new ideas, ministries and programs to a church.
4. Ibid., p. 22.
5. Ibid., pp. 30-31.
6. Towns, *The Eight Laws of Leadership*, pp. 17-18.
7. Towns, *10 Innovative Churches*, pp. 171-172.
8. Ibid., pp. 35-41. The strategy for leading a church through change is reflective of the methods used by John Maxwell in leading Skyline Wesleyan Church into several innovative new programs. The quotations in this section by John Maxwell come from the interviews cited in the book.

TEN

THE LEADER AS
CHANGE AGENT

DOUG MURREN

Let's talk about change that is encouraged, inspired, enforced or directed by an agent. Particularly, let's focus upon leaders who engage in being agents of change.

I like the phrase "leaders—agents of change." It provides a fascinating picture. An agent is a person who represents someone else. So a leader who serves as a change agent is representing either the change itself or the one who wants the change. Change agents serving in ministry capacities are those who represent the cause of the Lord by bringing about the change.

CHANGE IS BIBLICAL

"Change" is a common word in the Bible. The apostle Paul, when talking in 2 Corinthians 3 about the work of the Holy Spirit in our lives, offered a prediction. He said we would be changed as from glory to glory, meaning we would be in the process of constant change.

The Bible places a great deal more confidence in leaders than it does in the democratic processes of humankind. Some would say this is a cultural reality of the biblical era, a time when dictators—either destructive or benevolent in nature—ruled the world. The Bible refers to those dictators as kings. They were leaders who clearly exerted a strong influence upon the people and their lives.

From the many biblical accounts of how leaders interact with their followers, I believe God enjoys seeing leaders in front of followers, changing things for the better. Many passages of Scripture proclaim the importance of change agents in fulfilling God's sovereign plan.

Take the prophet Jeremiah, for example. He was not widely loved in his time. Why? Because he was more comfortable with change than others were. He was the one who said, "Surrender to the Babylonians." The patriots and the spiritual leaders of the land considered that statement both heretical and an act of treason. How could they ever be comfortable with the godless idols of the Babylonians? How could they possibly live under the political regime of Nebuchadnezzar?

Jeremiah was able to see beyond the past and present and envision a way the Jews could prosper in Babylon. He saw that being Jewish was meant to be a blessing in all the earth. It also meant that it was possible to be a Jew even if not present in Jerusalem. If a person was a Jew at heart, he could be a Jew in Babylon. Jews had never been described this way before; but Jeremiah was a biblical change agent.

Joshua and Caleb were also change agents. In Numbers 13:25,26, we are told they had a different heart and a different spirit. They realized that an Israelite could work effectively, even in the midst of the Egyptians. The rest of the Israelites could only imagine widespread incarceration and imprisonment. Thankfully, these leader-change agents bridged the world of the Jews in Egypt, thus experienced reaching the Promised Land. Without Joshua's ability to serve as an agent of change, our Messiah would not have appeared in the Promised Land centuries later.

In the New Testament we see the great change agent, the apostle Paul. In Acts 9 and in Acts 13 we are introduced to his seminal perspective that some churches could consist of only Jews, but churches could also consist of both Jews and Gentiles. Paul also went so far as to suggest that churches consisting solely of Gentiles could worship the God of Israel through Jesus Christ. These were unheard of notions in his time. Without Paul's commitment to change, unless you and I were Jewish, we would not be proclaiming the glories of Christ today.

THE ATTRIBUTES OF CHANGE AGENTS

You would be hard pressed to argue convincingly that a person can be a leader without being a change agent. In the course of my own career as a leader, I have come to recognize the critical characteristics a strong leader who is creating positive change must possess. An effective change agent must have the following:

- The innovative urge;
- An above-average passion for principle;
- A need for affirmation that is much lower than average;
- A high level of curiosity;
- A track record of mastering failure.

These attributes are essential for a person who wants to change things.

Perhaps what enables one person possessing strong skills and vast experience to succeed while others of similar background fail is the manner in which these attributes are deployed in the leadership change context. A leader is more of an artist than a scientist or a politician; leadership itself is an art form. Great leadership requires a great deal of intuition mixed with a high appreciation for the facts, ultimately coordinating these disparate inputs into an intelligible output upon which followers may strategically act.

Skilled artists react well to change. Recognizing the leadership value of this ability, I recently started the hobby of painting in acrylics. My goal was to stimulate some of my thinking through a more intentional involvement with colors. As soon as I got into this hobby, I began to notice colors in the world I had lived in for a long time that I had never seen before. I began to perceive with an artist's eye. I supplemented my initial explorations by reading several books about the artistic approach, and learned how to develop an artistic vision and how to focus.

Then I added to my venture into painting with a foray into photography. Once again, the conscious decision to invade my world from a different angle enabled me to see things everywhere—things that had always been there, but that I had never noticed. For example, I was walking through the woods one afternoon when, in my mind's eye, I saw a giant gorilla in one of the massive trees alongside the path. I suppose some might say no gorilla was perched up there, but in my evolving artist's eye, I could not imagine the tree without that gorilla. I carefully took a photo of that tree, and the gorilla actually appeared in the picture. Now, I know that gorilla does not live there, but if you would look closely, you, too, might see it sitting in the tree.

Leaders are this way. They see things no one else sees, and they find ways to present them to other people. They see colors in the church and in life that others may not perceive or recognize. A good leader creates a masterpiece that is not only intelligible, but also brings a sense of delight and joy about it to those who share the experience.

Change-oriented leadership is neither simple for the leader nor comforting to the masses. Thus it is essential we find ways to allow change agents to express their creativity in their leadership efforts. This cannot be done without accountability and process. Yet we must be careful that the systems and procedures we embrace do not squelch the spirit of the change agent. In other words, ministries should create a change-friendly environment, places that allow leaders who champion positive change to be who they are and to lead.

STIMULATING CHANGE

Without the change agent-leader, change rarely occurs. I tremble sometimes when we identify aberrant events from church history or unusually successful pastors and make them normative.

Good ministry does not happen accidentally. Prayer is essential in having a life-changing ministry. In the last twenty-five years, I have seen a lot of prayer and a lot of leadership. However, I have never seen prayer, alone, be as effective as prayer combined with true leadership in bringing about positive change in a ministry setting.

Creating Harmony out of Dissonance

Leaders initiate change by being voices of discomfort. Let me get a little musical with you here. One of my favorite forms of musical expression is the blues. This is based on what musicians know as a 1-4-5 chord pattern. If you are not musically inclined, that probably does not mean much to you, but bear with me for a minute and I think it will begin to make sense.

In a blues tune, normally two or three chords are played in a "major" tonality. For our purposes, let's consider a major chord is one that fits smoothly into its place—when you hear it, it just seems right, it makes sense to your ear. Hearing a major chord is like having a warm cup of soup on a winter day in your mom's kitchen.

What makes the blues distinctive, though, is inserting into a chord pattern a different kind of sound, what is known as a seventh. That's what turns a song into the blues. Without that seventh chord, it would be a song, but it would not have that familiar, heart-grabbing sound you know as a blues tune.

A good blues player will keep inserting that seventh every once in a while. Sometimes he will also throw in what is called a flatted fifth, which is like someone walking up and scratching a chalkboard with finger nails. Putting all these unusual elements together creates a sort of dissonant, or bluesy feeling.

I think good leaders are like great blues players. They know how to create a feeling of dissonance so that change will work. They create something outside of the common and comfortable that keeps unsettling people, persistently communicating information designed to move people toward positive change. They add comments in their sermons, insert notes in bulletins—whatever the forum, change agents invariably find positive, fun-loving ways to stimulate people's thoughts and actions by building creative tension while challenging them to realize that what has been can be no longer.

Great change agents are also like skilled jazz musicians. The distinguishing mark of great jazz players is that they can take familiar themes and do things with it that no one has ever thought of doing. These transformations of the familiar into something totally new and exciting can be complex, or very simple. Miles Davis, the jazz musician, was noted for using simplicity in improvising major themes.

Like the great jazz players, a great leader is one who creates positive change by translating common knowledge or existing conditions into something new through introducing innovation. A leader-change agent, therefore, is skillful at both the blues (i.e., dissonance) and jazz (i.e,. transformation) forms.

Discovering Things on the Horizon

Let me use another analogy. A change agent is also like a telescope or set of binoculars. He keeps discovering things on the horizon that might otherwise go unseen. This function became real to me the first time my father took me deer hunting. He played the role of leader-change agent. He scrutinized the fields and hills around us, using his pair of high-powered binoculars to spot the prey. He was determined to help me learn to hunt. My problem was that as I stood next to him and looked out over the fields, I could not see any deer. Dad would point here, there and everywhere, but all I saw were brown bushes and trees. I was standing almost in his shoes, straining my eyes to catch a glimpse of the large animals he claimed were in our midst, but I was not getting it. Everything that appeared to me to be a deer wasn't.

Eventually, through my father's guidance and help—and the assistance of those wonderful binoculars—the deer came into focus. After a few more hunting trips with him, my eye was trained to spot the elusive prey. Well into that hunting season I was so sufficiently capable of finding deer in the fields that I was able to take a few shots at those deer.

At first I did not believe my father when he told me the deer were really there. I did not know he was telling me the truth until he showed me again and again how to see something I had not seen before. Once I had been trained to recognize our quarry, making the transition from simply seeing the omnipresent bushes and trees to locating the camouflaged deer, I saw them regularly.

THE INGREDIENTS NEEDED FOR CHANGE

Arnold Mitchell, a social psychologist from Stanford, has spent years studying the attitudes and behaviors of Americans. He contends that three ingredients are necessary for change to occur.[1]

First, Mitchell notes that *change comes from dissatisfaction.* At the time a person receives Christ as Savior, the individual is likely to be experiencing a high level of dissatisfaction in life. Researchers have discovered that people who are not highly dissatisfied with life at the time they receive Christ rarely continue to develop a relationship with Him. The mature believers in a congregation are likely to understand that dissatisfaction and disappointment are part of the process of maturing spiritually. Effective change agents assess the chances for change by evaluating the level of dissatisfaction within the group. If dissatisfaction is strong, the potential for change exists.

Second, *change takes energy.* Altering the existing conditions experienced by a group consumes a terrific amount of emotional and physical energy. Americans these days are facing toxic levels of change both at work and in their families. To effect change, we must have a change-friendly environment. Without such a setting, an extraordinary degree of energy is spent fighting for or against the change process rather than investing that energy in establishing the change. Often, especially in ministry contexts, change fails to occur because the leader had not paved the way for change to happen. Consequently, not enough energy was available to effect the desired or necessary change.

Finally, *change requires insight*. A group considering the acceptance of change requires a leader who is credible and trustworthy. If the followers believe that their leader has created a workable plan, the chances of that leader seeing the change through to implementation are greatly improved. The people, however, are not likely to give permission to make a significant change unless they first have hard evidence of a well-conceived strategy for making things better.

THE PITFALLS OF CHANGE

These insights alert us to several pitfalls that could easily and quickly undermine the change process.

Effective change agents develop and nurture the energy required to carry out their plans for the future. Instituting change is a draining process, even under the best of circumstances. Change agents who are best poised to succeed are those who protect their energy reserves, using their energy sparingly and efficiently.

To be effective, a leader must also *deliberately* develop dissatisfaction. As a leader, I have often intentionally developed dissatisfaction within my church. On several occasions I needed to persuade key, recalcitrant church leaders that we were not living up to our potential in various dimensions of ministry. Simply expressing my perceived need for change did not penetrate their comfort zones. To make an impression upon them, we went as a group to visit churches that were doing a far better job in the ministry dimensions of concern to me. My fellow leaders needed to buy my perspective about the need for change and the potential for improvement before I could push ahead. Our team visits to see more effective churches almost always created dissatisfaction with our own performance of our ministry duties. That common sense of dissatisfaction enabled me to lead forward, without unnecessarily expending precious resources.

Preparing people for change sometimes takes what seems like forever. On occasion I took as much as five months to gradually and gently get a foundational point across to the congregation through my sermons. I shared startling or even embarrassing statistics about where we were as a church Body and where we needed to be, seeking to create the right level of dissatisfaction.

Additionally, strategic thinking needs to be a part of the process of change. An outgrowth of such thinking is plans. The plans that work best tend to be conservative. Because change agents are always somewhat suspect—you know, we never are content to leave things the way they are—it is wise to propose plans for change that are "doable"; in this way, you won't lose credibility with those who will implement, experience and (ultimately) benefit from the changes instituted.

Realize that sometimes you may have one or even two of the three elements required for change, but without the third factor in place, the prospects for positive change are diminished. For instance, some ministries have coalesced a group of dissatisfied individuals who possess the necessary energy to create change, but they lack the insight to channel their dissatisfaction and energy into positive outcomes. They tend to expend their energy on a wild goose chase, wearing out themselves and their leaders in the process.

Other ministries have developed the healthy sense of dissatisfaction and have great ideas for converting their discomforts into better scenarios. However, they are held back by lack of energy. They sit back and complain, they imagine all kinds of potential solutions to their collective dilemma, but they fail to rise to the occasion they have created. Another possibility are ministries in which there is insight and energy but not widespread sense of dissatisfaction. These entities simply lack the motivation to make positive change happen.

APPLYING INNOVATION

Positive change rarely intimates "returning to the way it used to be." Most positive change I have witnessed has been about creating a better future rather than returning to a cherished past. This forward-looking perspective requires a healthy dose of innovative thinking and action. Along my journey, I have developed a few notions that might serve as guidelines for innovators. Consider how adequately you have introduced these elements into your own efforts at change-oriented leadership.

- Ministries seem to do their best work when they encourage innovators and innovation. This is not a natural tendency. Apply yourself to the task of identifying, nurturing and giving opportunities to those who have the ability to be creative.

- As a leader, separate your reaction to ideas from your reaction to the people expressing those ideas. Too often, a valuable innovator is emotionally decimated by a negative reaction to the individual, rather than being redirected by a well-deserved rejection of the person's hairbrained idea.

- Conscientiously thank God that He brings into ministry settings people who look under rocks previously left unturned. Many of the great changes that enhance our ministries are not born of incremental thinking but "off-the-wall" ideas generated by those who have pursued unusual and unique lines of thought.

- Avoid the copycat syndrome above all things. The world needs more originals and fewer mimics. Allow God to create something new through you.

- Count the cost of leadership, change and ministry. This does not mean you should avoid any of these worthy pursuits because of the cost. Rather, it simply cautions you to move forward with your eyes open, knowing what to expect in terms of the toll that leadership and change in ministry will take upon you.

- Honor present commitments. Great change agents always build bridges from their present to the future.

- Be humble. Don't be a know-it-all. Granted, a leader must have confidence in the plans proposed, but a truly great leader acknowledges that he does not know everything and cannot perfectly predict the outcomes of new strategies. Sometimes the best thing you can do in response to those who are harshly critical of your own innovative ideas is to ask them to allow your idea a chance to fail. Rather than boldly predicting a smashing success, simply say, "Let's see if it'll work."

- Give people permission to pay part of the price with you. Too often, innovators want to pay the entire price. Gain ownership from others by allowing them to become full partners in the process.

- Be a nondefensive learner. The more open you are to discovering insights from unexpected people or places, the better off your efforts at innovation are likely to be.
- Budget for change carefully. You are seeking to create the unknown. The unexpected often occurs in such scenarios. Do not budget yourself into a corner.
- Anticipate change and its necessity before it arrives. Otherwise, you will be seeking to rewrite history rather than determine the course of history.
- Develop a life philosophy that views change as having the potential to make things far better. There is no value to change for the sake of change, or innovation for its own sake. For everything there is a season, even for stability. When change is introduced, it should be for the purpose of creating a better world.
- Celebrate variety.
- Stay young in your thinking. One way of doing this is to spend time with young people.
- Be decisive. A leader is a decision maker, not a consensus seeker. If you are going to introduce significant innovations, know that you will have to make some tough calls and will probably offend some good people by virtue of your decisions. Be sensitive and flexible, yes, but be firm in pursuing your convictions.
- Appreciate those who help you create positive change. Such change never happens in a vacuum. Those who assist you in developing and implementing your innovations are a special blessing from God. Always strive to show them your gratitude for their belief in you, their support of your ideas and their investment in a shared purpose or vision.

INEVITABLE CHANGE

Thus far we have talked about change as if it will happen only if you recognize a great idea and commit to its implementation. On occasion, however, positive change is virtually inevitable. In those situations, a leader's best bet is to recognize that change is coming and to provide direction to that process.

One of the most difficult tasks for many churches is to grow to a size that enables them to foster continued numerical growth. Church-growth experts call that point the "200 barrier." When a congregation exceeds roughly 200 people, tremendous changes happen in the group. The geometry and psychology of the group are remarkable. The pace of change multiplies and the church requires a leader who is guiding the continued expansion of the ministry.

Another condition in which a change agent must exert leadership, whether planned or not, is when the community within which the church is located experiences major demographic, social or economic changes. Those changes in the composition of the community mandate that the church respond in an intelligent, sensitive and strategic way. In my area, several logging towns lost hundreds and thousands of jobs, changing communities and their churches immensely. The churches that were comfortable with radical community change and that had leaders serving as change agents survived the upheaval and remain viable churches today. Those churches that were either uncomfortable with the necessity of change, or that lacked change agents to spearhead the transformational activity did not survive.

Change may be necessary for long-term stability and growth, but that does not make the act of changing any easier. New opportunities for influential ministry always seem to cause substantial, often unforeseen, change when those opportunities are exploited. I have also realized that every time someone has a new, big idea for our ministry, the effect is usually about ten times greater than expected. Those ideas also seem to demand about 100 percent more change in myself and others than I usually expect!

INTENTIONAL CHANGE

As the senior leader of a large and growing ministry organization, I have had to make many choices. One choice was whether I wanted to devote my resources to being a deliberate change agent or a victimized change agent. Toward that end, it was imperative to develop a strategic plan and to then marshal the resources needed to implement that plan in light of new opportunities for change that faced our church.

Yet, while deciding to create change rather than be recreated by change, it has been readily apparent to me that change sometimes demands an entirely new paradigm to solve existing problems or to take advantage of emerging opportunities. In my mind, this process can be illustrated as follows:[2]

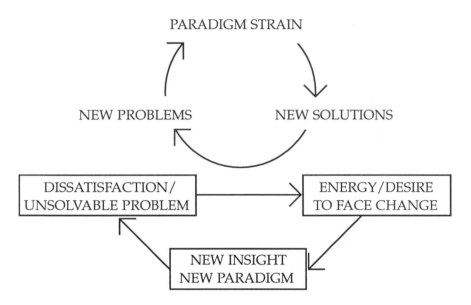

Although most of my experience with these realities has been in a church setting, I believe these dynamics are constant, whether they occur within churches, movements or countries. When the old ways no longer work—whether it is the way in which we communicate God's truth, methods of organizing people to express dissatisfaction, means of raising funds for good works—new solutions must be sought. When these new solutions are applied, change occurs in profound and sometimes unexpected ways.

CONCLUSION

If there has ever been a time for leaders to be change agents, it is now. Today's climate, from the national down to the neighborhood level, works against cookie-cutter, predictable, imitative leaders. Being a change agent is similar to living in the womb, being courageously willing to take the steps necessary to move into light, while being uncertain of what the future holds. It reminds me of the parable of the twins.

Once upon a time, twin boys were conceived in their mother's womb. Weeks passed and the twins developed. As their awareness grew, they laughed for joy: "Isn't it great that we were conceived? Isn't it great to be alive?"

Together the twins explored their world. When they found that the umbilical cord passed life along to them from their mother, they sang for joy: "How great is our mother's love, that she shares her own life with us."

As the weeks stretched into months, the twins noticed how much each was changing. "What does it mean?" asked one twin.

"It means that our stay in this world is drawing to an end," said the other.

"But I don't want to go. I want to stay here always."

"We have no choice," said the other. "And maybe there is life after birth!"

"But how can there be? We will shed our life-cord, and how is life possible without it? Besides, no one has ever returned to the womb to tell us that there is life after birth. No, this is the end."

And so the one twin fell into despair: "If conception ends in birth, what is the purpose of life in the womb? It is meaningless! Maybe there is no mother at all."

"But there *has* to be," protested the other. "How else did we get here? How do we remain alive?"

"Have you ever actually seen our mother?" said the one. "Maybe she lives only in our minds. Maybe we made her up, because the idea made us feel good."

And so the last days in the womb were filled with deep questioning and fear. Finally, the moment of birth arrived. And when the twins had passed from their world, they opened their eyes. They cried with joy, for what they saw exceeded their fondest dreams.

"No eye has seen, no ear has heard, no mind has conceived what God has prepared for those who love him" (1 Cor. 2:9, *NIV*).

Notes

1. As reprinted in *Leadershift*, Doug Murren (Ventura, Calif.: Regal Books, 1995), pp. 79-80. Taken from Arnold Mitchell, *Nine American Lifestyles* (New York: Warner Books, 1983).
2. Ibid., p. 98.

ELEVEN

BUILDING A TEAM
TO GET THE JOB
DONE

TOM PHILLIPS

"I've got a gal in Baton Rouge; she ain't rich, but she sure is cute. Sound off, 1, 2, 3, 4, 1, 2, 3, 4."

Even in my days as a college student, I was involved in team building. You are probably involved in team building, too, whether it is through ministry, sports, scouting, family or formal education. The refrain listed above was one we chanted when I was part of the Air Force ROTC drill team at the University of Mississippi. Interestingly, though it was not a Christian environment per se, many principles of team building were formulated in the simple development of that small ROTC drill team. Among other things, the ROTC team:

- Was led by a capable leader;
- Recruited qualified individuals;
- Shared a common purpose;
- Focused upon a singular task;
- Was committed to completing the task together;

- Stressed that members must die to self for the sake of the whole team;
- Made a commitment to excellence;
- Recognized and accepted discipline;
- Removed those who were either unfit or uncommitted.

Teamwork—working together toward the fulfillment of a desired outcome without the loss of one's individuality—has been a major factor in my growth since adolescence. My family, my Boy Scout Troop, various sports teams on which I played, the ROTC drill team—all these helped to lay a foundation for a lifetime of involvement in teamwork.

While in seminary in Louisville, Kentucky, I worked with a team of skilled maintenance men who cared for fifteen hundred apartment units in six complexes. I could paint a two-bedroom apartment—ceilings, walls, bathroom and kitchen—in three and a half hours. At that pace, I was a real profit maker for my employer. One day a young lad eight or nine years old walked over to me as I was picking up trash after completing painting an apartment. He said, "Mister, what are you doing?" When I replied that I was just picking up trash, he decisively noted that he had bigger plans: "Mister, when I grow up, I'm not going to be a trash collector."

Granted, picking up trash was not a glamorous task. Some might have been stung by the boy's innocent put-down, but I was confident that this job was what God had given me to do for a season. I also wanted to be the very best trash collector I possibly could be. The Bible says a faithful man (or woman) is difficult to find (see Prov. 20:6). A team is made up of just that—faithful men and women who work at whatever job God, in His sovereignty, has given them to do.

One bright Saturday in August, just before the beginning of my third year of seminary, my boss, Mr. Boyles, drove up in his big gold Cadillac to the paint room at the apartment complex. One of the youngest deacons of the Southern Baptist church in Louisville, this man had grown in wisdom and economic stature. As he got out of the car, I noticed that he came toward me with purpose. The maintenance foreman on our crew had been with Mr. Boyles for twelve years. Until recently, he had been doing an outstanding job, but something had changed. As he pulled me aside, Mr. Boyles confided in me that the reason for the foreman's reduced production was that he was turning in his work forms without completing the jobs because he was visiting his mistresses in the various apartments in the housing complex.

As Mr. Boyles talked to me, I became aware that I was splattered with paint from head to foot. That is how I was able to paint a two-bedroom apartment so rapidly: When I painted, a lot of paint flew—on the walls, on the ceilings and on me. Yet in spite of my youthfulness, my lack of experience and my paint-speckled appearance, this man had come to offer me the position of foreman. Older men on the crew who had much more experience and skill were being bypassed for the sake of the youngest and lowest man on the totem pole, the kid who was merely the painter and trash collector. I was shocked and overwhelmed.

The Bible says in Psalm 75:6,7 *(KJV)*:

> For promotion cometh neither from the east, nor from the west, nor from the south. But God is the judge: he putteth down one, and setteth up another.

That was exactly what God was doing that day. Mr. Boyles's presence and offer was an answer to my prayers. My wife and I were new parents, and I wanted my wife to be able to stay home with our baby daughter. I did not know how that could happen, especially with the start of the new seminary year just two weeks away.

I told Mr. Boyles I would love to be the foreman of that team, but I wanted to complete my seminary degree. He was concerned about my education as well, so he offered me an attractive deal: If I could give him forty hours a week from Monday morning until Saturday night, I had the job. That would also allow me to finish school and to continue pastoring my country church on Wednesday nights and Sundays. Although I did not know how I could possibly work full-time, carry a full academic load at seminary, pastor the church and care for my family, I knew God was at work.

I still had to solve the Phillips's family financial crunch. Even as we spoke, the Scripture passed through my mind that "a laborer is worthy of his wages" (1 Tim. 5:18). Boldly, I told Mr. Boyles that I could not work for what I was making as a painter and trash collector. He reflected on my words for a moment then said, "Let me take care of that." A few days later, he offered me a raise that would put my pay at only $40 a month less than the combined salaries of me (as a part-time maintenance man) and my wife (as a school teacher). Later he gave me an additional $5 a day travel money. God's care is always sufficient.

Thus began my journey as a supervisor of men in their forties and fifties who were much more mature, experienced and capable than I. Yet, I never sensed any jealousy or bitterness from them.

I believe the reason is that they knew I lived for them. I made sure they had their work orders on time, that I had purchased all the supplies they would need and had covered all the necessary bases to ensure they could do their jobs well. We worked together; there was unity. We were committed to excellence in the business at hand. My boss was happy, his company was making money and my team and I had the wonderful experience of performing just about every home maintenance task known to humankind, including the war against cockroaches in apartments after less-than-tidy people had moved out.

THE TIMOTHY EXPERIENCE

God allowed me to finish seminary and begin working on a doctorate. Through a series of incredible circumstances, He placed me with the Billy Graham Team for a six-month internship under the supervision of Charlie Riggs, the Director of Counseling and Follow-Up for the Billy Graham Evangelistic Association.

When I met Mr. Riggs, he was directing the Crusade in Jackson, Mississippi, and at the same time directing all of Counseling and Follow-up. On the first morning with him in a devotional, Mr. Riggs shared a portion of Scripture and then quoted several to complement it. I had never been so close to such a powerful man of God. The Word of God literally permeated the man and flowed throughout all of us listening to him. By the end of that five-minute devotional time, I knew I wanted to be discipled by him. Although I had never been exposed to the concept of a Paul-Timothy relationship, I still knew I wanted to be a man of God like Mr. Riggs.

A few days later, I asked Mr. Riggs to invest an hour a week in my life. He responded that he was a very busy man, but would work with me under three conditions:

- That I would always do the assignments he would give me from the Word of God;

- That I would memorize the Scriptures he would give me each week;
- That I would accomplish the practical exercises.

Having just graduated from seminary, these expectations did not seem overwhelming, so I accepted his offer. For the next six years, one hour a week, Mr. Riggs met with me. In the sixteen years that followed, Mr. Riggs has never stopped being my spiritual guide and mentor as we labored together with the Graham team. I doubt if he will ever be able to let go of his concern for the growth of his Timothys. What an honor to be one of them!

LESSONS FROM THE GRAHAM MINISTRY

Amazingly, the six months of my internship flew by, and without realizing it, I lost all desire to finish the doctorate degree (though I eventually did). I wanted to be a part of what I had stumbled into: the Billy Graham team. Inadvertently, I had become a part of the family of God in an encapsulated form. Never before had I been a part of anything so focused as this group of men and women from all denominations and several countries. They wanted only to see a spiritual harvest (i.e., the proclamation of Jesus Christ as Lord and Savior and the maturing of men and women in salvation).

In twenty years of ministry with the Billy Graham team—from the lowest rung of the ladder to some of the highest—I have never seen anything but unity in mission. This team was never "buckshot" coming out of a gun and simply headed in the same direction. It was an arrow that pierces darkness.

This cohesiveness is unusual these days, especially in organizations that work globally, operate with large budgets and have hundreds of people directly involved in the operations. The secret to the influence of the Graham team is no secret at all; it is simply following the guidance of the Holy Spirit and using basic team principles.

Let me be more specific. People do not question Mr. Graham's *focus*. You never wonder what he said to a member of the politburo before communism fell, or to a vagrant he speaks to at a rescue mission. Regardless of the conversation or the topic of the message, one thing always flows through him—the gospel of Jesus Christ for salvation and life.

Behind this tremendous leader is a team of men and women who follow, regardless of the sacrifice, to see the ministry work in partnership with the local church. The goal is to produce men and women who have a personal relationship with Jesus Christ as Lord and Savior, to see them grow in that relationship so that they develop the ability to reproduce the life of Christ in others. There is no internal debate about the mission, or the nature of our leadership.

THE TEAM-BUILDING CONCEPT

When I started with the Billy Graham Evangelistic Association, all the leaders on the team had come through World War II. They had experienced the effect of the military in focusing individuals on a common objective. The followers within the Graham team needed to hear direction only once. Respectfully, one could question any directive, but implementation of that directive followed. Each person knew his leaders to be godly, committed, sincere, hard working and wise. Those leaders would never ask colleagues to do something they were not also willing to do. In those early days, few job descriptions were used. Each person's role came from an oral tradition. Therefore, the attitude of the team was *familial.*

> ### "HE WAS MADE WHAT WE ARE THAT HE MIGHT MAKE US WHAT HE IS HIMSELF."
> **IRENAEUS**

Without a lot of written job descriptions, policies or manuals, you may wonder how in the world anything was accomplished. How did a team member know the direction, parameters and procedures? Purpose, which is always vital in the development of a team, was without question. Because of the focused leader—Billy Graham—we knew the direction we were going. We also had an incredible guidebook called the Bible. It gave us the principles we used for evangelism, unity, discipline and team growth. We never doubted that our help would come from Scripture if a problem arose between members of the family. A more experienced team member could quickly tell the new member of the family when he had overstepped the boundaries of individual responsibilities. Everyone was a self-starter.

The history of the Graham team provides a clear understanding of what God had done to ensure its development:

- Called a servant-leader who was focused, not on kingdom building, but *Kingdom* building;
- Called a servant-leader who wanted to do only one portion of the ministry and trusted others to come alongside and pick up the various elements that make up the whole;
- Called a servant-leader who could delegate without abdicating;
- Called a servant-leader who was an encourager as well as an exhorter;
- Called a group of men and women around the servant-leader who were a holy "band of men, [and women] whose hearts God had touched" (1 Sam. 10:26, *KJV*);
- Called a group of men and women who allowed God to use their disparate gifts to accomplish a unified mission;
- Called a group of men and women who were "as iron sharpens iron" (Prov. 27:17, *NIV*). When strong, self-willed, courageous, adventurous, spiritual entrepreneurs who are servant-leaders come together, there are bound to be clashes. If that clashing is in love, however, sparks will fly, honing will occur and the arrow will be fashioned with a point so sharp that it pierces the darkness;
- Called others with spiritual leadership gifts to the fore. They "sit at the gate" of the team and judge the problems that develop between individuals. Then, those individuals, rightly judged, accept the results and go on their way for the sake of the mission. Every person's energy is applied to push this arrow farther into darkness and to see more hearts touched for Christ.

As Mr. Graham once said, "When I have preached the gospel with authority on every continent of the world, God the Holy Spirit has driven it into the human heart." That was the goal of the Billy Graham team. There was no other.

Each person had a clear understanding of the purpose of the ministry, of its leadership, of the Guidebook and of the objective truth that fashioned the ministry. The ministry could be measured against these principles at anytime. This allowed gifted and committed individuals to work together productively.

Interestingly, the doctrinal stance of the various team members was always secondary. It is not that doctrine, denominational ties or church affiliations are unimportant, but this particular team had one focus. Nothing was as important as seeing people come to Christ. Therefore, I personally never had, nor heard an argument about doctrine in the Billy Graham team, although the team consisted of people from many countries of the world, both genders, various denominations and all stripes of theological affiliation. The singular focus of the servant-leader permeated the entire organization.

TEAM-BUILDING PRINCIPLES

Several key principles helped all of us see the value of what we were accomplishing, to accept the roles into which God had sovereignly placed us and to work together. Shakespeare expressed this profound truth in the words of Wolsey:

> Cromwell, I charge thee, fling away ambitions,
> By that sin fell the angels; how can man then,
> The image of his Maker, hope to profit by it?[1]

This unique development of a very specialized team literally saw God's hand lift up people. No one jockeyed for position. J. Oswald Sanders says in *Spiritual Leadership*:

> Our word ambition derives from a Latin word meaning "canvassing for promotion." A variety of ingredients may be present in ambition—to be seen and approved by men, to be popular, to stand well among one's contemporaries, to exercise control over others. Ambitious men enjoy the power that money or authority brings. Such carnal ambitions were roundly rebuked by the Lord. *The true spiritual leader will never canvass for promotion.*[2]

> To aspire to leadership is an honorable ambition (1 Tim. 3:1, *NEB*).

You seek great things for yourself. Leave off seeking them (Jer. 45:5, *NEB*).

My life experiences have shown me the following principles of building a team:

1. **A team must have a gifted and committed leader.**
Leaders are those who serve the vision. To accomplish it, they serve their team. Some leaders are visionaries who have very little administrative skill, and others are well balanced and have the ability to work administratively as well. A team, however, will do well to assist the leader in as many administrative areas as possible so that he can continue to be the tip of the arrow, forging the future as others develop the present.

2. **A team must bring together a holy "band of men, [and women] whose hearts God had touched"** (1 Sam. 10:26, *KJV*).
Because a ministry team needs people through whom the Holy Spirit can easily flow, it is vital that each person work diligently to maintain his own personal walk with Christ through Bible study, Scripture memory, prayer and service to others. Whatever the vision, team members must all play some vital part in the actual ministry, never becoming aloof and only managing others or purely doing administration.

3. **A team is a group of people who are united under the Lordship of Jesus Christ.**
These are people who recognize that "kurios" is not an employer but our owner. As Paul has said, we are "slaves of Christ" (Eph. 6:6, *NIV*). The Owner does not give us options; He gives us a calling, a commissioning.

4. **A team has a focus that is so easily discernible that the devil, who is the author of confusion, can never interrupt the direction of ministry.**
Recognizing the adversary is essential to the team. Ministry teams are engaged in spiritual warfare. Certainly, people can create confusion. But if Christ is the center of all things, everything will fall into place (see Col. 1:17). If not, confusion, distrust and disunity

will occur. "Focus on Christ" must be the theme of every ministry team for that team to be successful.

The team must be very conscious of the role of the adversary. In the midst of the "me" generation, the "we" generation must be fashioned. Christ's model moves us from self-centeredness to selflessness.

5. **Gifted people on the team are chosen to get specific jobs done.**

    Fred Smith states in *Learning to Lead*:

    > One of the most important aspects of successful leadership is putting together a group of people to carry out the mission. Great athletic coaches know they must have talent to win, and therefore they take an active part in choosing players. Teams that just happen get happanstance results.[3]

    The placement of each person in a team is vital. As the Body of Christ, no member of the team is less important than another, or more important than another. People are gifted for specific kinds of service and usually grow through experience in ability, discernment and wisdom for future and greater levels of service.

"GOD HAS PLACED SOME MEN ABOVE KINGS AS HE HAS GIVEN THEM A MISSION TO FULFILL RATHER THAN A POSITION TO OCCUPY."[4]
ALEXANDRE DUMAS

6. **A team needs people who have "*Nike* hearts."**
    Most of the great CEOs and businessmen I have known operate in concert with the famous Nike slogan, "Just Do It!" This does not mean they don't do their homework and get the facts. They live in the midst of the facts. When the need for decisions arises, they can usually make them rapidly. They are constantly on the edge of decision making, continually assimilating facts in preparation for those decisions. A good team operates with adequate and accurate communication, constantly feeding the team leader necessary information so that

he will be sufficiently informed for decision making. Each team member, on the other hand, should know his respective area better than the team leader.

Sometimes people get so focused on planning that they never get around to doing. Teams that function best are those that devise strategic plans, and quickly turn them into tactical plans they implement. A plan not implemented is of limited, if any, value.

7. **A gifted team strategically trains its people, but most of the time, these capable and godly people are trained on the job.**
    I have worked with many pastors who prefer to develop their team members from within their own congregations rather than hire from the outside or from seminaries. To them it is more important to have someone who is already fervently witnessing as a lifestyle than to have a person who has a degree in evangelism but no enthusiasm for it. Academic and practical training can come later.

    Ability is less important than availability, but ideally both qualities are in place. In a team, I have seen God favor those who were less than adequate, including myself, and give them adequacy beyond their wildest imagination. Ephesians 3:20 states that our God is able to do "exceeding abundantly above all that we ask or think," because it is His power that works in us. This is true when people obediently follow. As we look at the great servant-leaders of the Church today, most of them have not come from positions of power and authority within their family or academic structures, but God has promoted them according to their obedience.

8. **Great teams use "participative management."**
    This is a relatively recent term. Yet it is the way we have seen God work most dramatically in teams. Authority still exists, and everyone recognizes it. Participative management is synergism at its best. The people involved realize that it is not a pure democracy. They know that they are expected to communicate at various levels within the team structure to accomplish the

desired end. They keep in mind that those in authority above them must be clearly shown the picture as it develops, and that each one must receive approval at every point of development.

9.   **Service is more important than position.**

But so shall it not be among you: but whosoever will be great among you, shall be your minister: and whosoever of you will be the chiefest, shall be servant of all (Mark 10:43,44, *KJV*).

The words "serve" and "servant" are listed in the Bible fourteen hundred and fifty-two times. Our model is Jesus Christ, the greatest Servant-Leader of all. Robert Greenleaf, a serving executive with AT&T, states in *Servant Leadership*:

In a radical fashion Jesus, by example and word, establishes servanthood as the way in which His men are to lead others. He expressly repudiates every secular model of leadership in favor of servanthood....It was the form of servanthood that the Son of God chose to pour His divine life into. And the Father didn't break the mold when He sent Him.[5]

J. Oswald Sanders expressed the leader-as-servant principle this way:

Because we children of Adam want to become great, He became small.

Because we will not stoop, He humbled Himself.

Because we want to rule, He came to serve.[6]

10.   **Team members must show respect for the leader and for other team members.**

Send men...every one a leader among them (Num. 13:2). As General Colin Powell has said, team members "respect leaders who hold them to a high standard and take them to the limit—as long as they see a worthwhile objective."[7]

A great team is usually an organization made up of as many (or more) followers as there are leaders. Within an excellent team are also several people who are capable of stepping into the slot of the leader if unfortunate circumstances remove him. Each person must have complete loyalty to the leader. In this way, the harmony in the team is consistent regardless of the challenges or sacrifices.

Though personalities will vary within the team, from the most relaxed to the most impulsive, the balance comes from the interaction of these. Everyone's strengths should complement the others' weaknesses. Anyone's strengths, however, can become his weaknesses if undisciplined. Therefore, the team members must respect each other enough to confront in love. Wise confrontation is always a growth process for everyone within the team.

Not every team is perfect. Even Jesus Christ had His Judas.

11. **A team is only as strong as it is disciplined.**
An effective ministry team exhibits discipline on three planes: spiritual, physical and mental. Discipline also operates on two organizational levels: personal and corporate. Discipline is vital. A physically unkempt team is normally undisciplined in other ways. Physical discipline, however, is secondary to spiritual. It is mandatory that every person in the team be responsible for scriptural intake, communion with God and his own personal intimacy with Christ and others. As Billy Graham has often said regarding early mornings, "No Bread, no bread." In my life, it is my goal to have a daily quiet time, exercise physically every day (even when traveling) and to read something to refresh my mind and help me to grow in knowledge.

12. **Effective teams realize that failure may be a step toward success.**
Failure is a part of success. One of the most successful people I know is the former Congressman, Bob McEwen, from Ohio. While in Congress, he served his constituents well and was positioned to become a major leader in the House of Representatives. When the boundaries of his congressional district changed, however, he lost his seat by a mere 2 percent of the vote. For an elected official, that is failure. Although failure is

always emotionally depleting, the way this man worked through his situation was an example of growth through defeat. His demeanor, honesty regarding the struggle, faith in God and attitude have made him more a man of success than ever before.

Likewise, great teams do not view failures as terminal outcomes, nor as paralyzing defeat, but as part of God's refining process. Failure represents a lesson that may facilitate a better future performance by the team. You would be hard pressed to find any team of influence that has not suffered serious setbacks along its path to influence.

13. **Teams must achieve a significant comfort level within the familial organization scheme.**

    When it comes to handling change and addressing opportunities, family units are poised to move quickly; bureaucracies are legendary for their inability to respond in a timely fashion. For a family to fully exploit its options, however, every member of the family must be comfortable with the intimacy of that close-knit relationship. In this way, each person will be able to confide, exhort, encourage and apply themselves for spiritual production.

14. **Communication is crucial.**

    In an era of significant change such as ours, there is no substitute for effective communication within the team. An effective team is well organized and well informed. Without the cohesiveness that comes from complete trust and clear communication, the buckshot will be headed in the same direction toward the target, but in the spaces in between, the adversary can work and cause division and disharmony.

15. **Great teams respond to change by remaining flexible.**

    In 1988, the Billy Graham team had plans for reaching the whole world with the gospel simultaneously through satellite. We secured offices in London, moved staff there and began training. After several months of preparation, we realized that the technology necessary to accomplish this worldwide was simply not available yet.

The decision was made to scrap the initial idea and to reach the world in quadrants from London, Hong Kong, Buenos Aires and Essen, Germany. Eventually, a major global effort would be attempted in 1994, if the requisite technology was in place—which it was.

This strategic change meant an upheaval in the lives of many families, individuals and tactical plans that had already been implemented. It was the right thing to do, though. A team must never be so locked into a plan that it cannot be flexible to the realities of the situation—and those realities change!

16. **Team leaders delegate; they do not abdicate.**
Gene Warr, a tremendous businessman and developer from Oklahoma City, has a saying that I love: "The best fertilizer for the job is the footprint of the boss." A team leader must recognize the spiritual gifts of those within his team and delegate the team's tasks accordingly. Of course, each team member's ability to persist, attitude toward the job and work performance, in addition to personal spiritual gifts, determines who is given which task. Then, though, the leader must allow the team members and/or the team as a whole to complete the task without unnecessary interference. Each team operates differently, and people within a team may use different approaches than might be used by other team members. Effective leaders allow for personal creativity and individuality in accomplishing assignments.

I learned the importance of delegation with the Billy Graham team. Working in three or more crusade cities with different teams each year for twenty years, I realized that different styles accomplish the tasks in different ways, but they do accomplish it. The team leader's job is to plan, delegate, oversee, control and encourage.

Allow your team to grow. Give team members tasks that are within their giftings and abilities, but beyond their previous experience. Stretch them, but be available to assist. Encourage, exhort, challenge or correct as needed.

17. **Attitude matters. Great teams exhibit sincerity, transparency and vulnerability.**

Maintaining and modeling these qualities is difficult for leaders, and it is made more difficult by public scrutiny. It has been said that only the strongest survive, and many people interpret that to mean that leaders are those people who step on others to get ahead. A vulnerable leader is one who is wounded not only in combat, but one who has also had his pride punctured by colleagues who love the leader enough to offer constructive challenge or correction.

18. **Within familial organizations, there is recourse.**

In an effective team, as in a functional family, everyone has access to all other people in the unit, regardless of the levels of responsibility held by each. This access is a privilege and must be used wisely, demonstrating respect for those being challenged or critiqued. In the Billy Graham team, we had an unwritten rule that if your supervisor was not functioning in a way you thought was appropriate, or decisions were not being made that would be acceptable, you would go to your supervisor twice for resolution. If resolution was not forthcoming, you could go to his superior. Though this was certainly humbling for the supervisor, it was not without precedent and was accepted throughout the team.

19. **Unity drives impact.**

It is vital for a team to be focused in direction. You never see a good football team, after the ball is snapped to the quarterback, run in eleven different directions on the field. To be effective, the team must move in a coordinated manner, in the same direction. Players from the opposing team strive to break through the offensive line to create chaos and destroy the play. The greater the common vision, shared purpose, joint understanding and togetherness the team with the ball displays on each play, the more likely they are to score touchdowns and win the game.

Similarly, God's teams must not give Satan any opportunity to invade their territory and wreak havoc. Ministry teams must unite to become a darkness-piercing arrow, eliminating all the spiritual space or gaps between members. A house divided against itself cannot stand. The hearts, wills and energy of team members must be knit together with common purpose and direction.

20. **Each person within the team is a coach and/or player/coach for those around and below.**

The leader of any team can fall, die or be removed at anytime. Therefore, each person in the team must be developing as a leader. Though particular people may never rise to become the primary leader of the team, the team itself can only progress if each member's personal growth is constant. For this to occur, each person must not only be actively involved in the game, but he must also be vulnerable with others and consciously building up the others through encouragement or exhortation.

In my experience, only 5 to 8 percent of people appear to be naturally gifted leaders. Perhaps another 6 to 8 percent can be trained as leaders. Eighty percent of people are excellent followers and appreciate that position. Even as followers, sometimes there are one or two levels below them to which they are giving leadership.

Often a few people at the far end of the spectrum are rebellious. They could be leaders, but they are so independent that they do not take into account the needs of the team as a whole, and decide to do their own thing. They are usually unilateral decision makers who head off in their own direction without communicating with others to achieve consensus. Often they look back, thinking they are leaders, and to their chagrin they discover that no one is following. These kind of team members tend to be draining to the others. These people are "high maintenance" in terms of time invested in them compared to what they produce for the team.

21. **Nonparticipatory team members could and should be removed.**

Process is vital in developing a team; knowing, communicating, supporting, encouraging and exhorting one another is necessary. Product is also vital. If the team has as its goal evangelism, that should be the ultimate return on investment. If the team has as its goal social concern, the number of mouths fed, bodies clothed and nights of sleep prepared is the product. If a person is not producing, he is "treading water." One cannot do this in ministry. The adversarial currents are too strong to allow team members to be treading water. That person is going backward and pulling the team in the wrong direction.

I have found that the following steps need to be involved in redirecting the efforts of unproductive or nonparticipatory team members.

• The person must be confronted in love by the person who sees the flaw.

• If no change occurs, that person must be lovingly exhorted by a couple of members of the team.

• If still no evidence of satisfactory progress is shown, the team must implement an established procedure for either adherence or removal of the person.

The best approach is a loving but firm confrontation. Unfortunately, this step is often avoided by Christian organizations. After the confrontation, a written contract between the team leader and the person should be created to establish the agreed-upon details of process, product and time allotment designed to facilitate developing the person who is letting down the team. Both the team leader and the person must sign that agreement.

• At a specified review date, if the contract has been fulfilled by the person, and satisfactory progress has been made, the development of the person can be furthered by establishing yet another contract, again designed to enable the person to continue on the growth track. This process is continued until he has reached a point of development that merits being removed from the probationary system and being restored to full participation on the team.

If the person does not meet the specified standards or is otherwise not able to be restored to full participation, he should be given a chance to resign, and be allowed to save face. If the requested resignation is not forthcoming, the person should be removed by the team leader. In the event of a dismissal, it is important for the leader to inform the remaining team members what has transpired so that they understand the process that has occurred, the justice of it and the recalcitrant position of the person being removed. Energy should not be wasted in focusing on internal conflicts. A leader must handle such matters quickly and justly.

22. **Stay focused on the goal; accept nothing less.** Relationships are important to accomplish a team's ultimate goal. Great relationships, however, are not the ultimate purpose or goal of the team's efforts. Such relationships are vessels through which God the Holy Spirit works to accomplish His task in individual lives and community.

    For example, a ministry that emphasizes friendship evangelism can easily degenerate into just friendship if the people on the team do not have passion, gifting and an action plan for evangelism. Because saving faith is developed by hearing the Word of God, the Word of God must be shared, the gospel must be understood by the person and a respectful invitation given. Otherwise our adversary has control of the situation and constantly removes the person from the ultimate decision. Certainly, grace theology is at work during all this; but at a certain point decision theology is necessary.

DEVELOPING YOUR TEAM

Teams usually develop in response to a desire to accomplish a task and the realization that it requires more than one person. If a person is involved in completing a task within an ongoing function or goal, it is best that this kind of development begin with an experienced and trained point person. This person usually becomes the servant-leader, but not always.

Then development of a team usually ensues. Initially, it is brought together by one or two people at a time as the ministry grows. Charlie

Riggs has often reminded me, "You always grow into ministry; never go into ministry."

Ministries that try to start too big often collapse. As I have looked back at the twenty years with Mr. Graham, I have seen many young evangelists who wanted to be the "next Billy Graham." More often than not, they moved too quickly, built their own kingdom and saw their ministry collapse financially.

The Billy Graham team started on its knees, without funding or endorsements. Mr. Graham was the one God called and anointed as leader. God gave him the vision of doing a task that was historically a vital part of the Church. Others who had the same heart for evangelism, but different gifts, joined him. They died to their own ambitions, taking pieces of the work so that Mr. Graham was free to do that to which God had called him. They became, in the power of the Holy Spirit, "the evangelist" together. One person's name was synonymous with the movement at that time, but they all worked in harmony.

A good example of this today is a group of twenty-one young itinerants in Denver, Colorado, called Kingdom Building Ministries. Begun by a young, focused evangelist, Dwight Robertson, this group of twenty-one young people has banded together to accomplish a common task. Some are itinerant evangelists, some are teachers, some disciplers and others perform the clerical and backup support. They have developed this team during approximately eight years, growing into ministry, but always remaining driven by a vision, led by a team-building leader, and accepting accountability to each other for the common good of the mission.

"FIND WAYS TO REACH DOWN AND TOUCH EVERYONE IN A UNIT. MAKE INDIVIDUALS FEEL IMPORTANT AND PART OF SOMETHING LARGER THAN THEMSELVES."[8]
COLIN POWELL

It is the task of the servant-leader to continue to restate the mission of the team so that everyone can clearly view the final goal from his perception. It is the prerogative and the purview of the leader of the team to establish the vision of the team. The Bible says, "Where there is no vision, the people perish" (Prov. 29:18, *KJV*). Experience shows that when people have a vision from God, they excel. Jesus saw things clearly—He had a steady vision, and the disciples could easily follow.

FUNDING THE TEAM

One of the outstanding guiding tools God the Holy Spirit uses is funding. By beginning in prayer and allowing God the Holy Spirit to guide interested people who want to see such a ministry funded, the ministry usually grows according to God's provision.

Potential dangers exist among ministries that start with strong funding. Many of them grow so quickly that the ministry team does not adequately mature as the levels of responsibility and the potential for influence increase. Such well-funded ministries often discover that they harbor people who want a position, but are not sold out to the mission. Sometimes these ministries are the design of men and women rather than the outcome of a direction anointed by the Holy Spirit.

Of course, having the necessary funds to perform the desired ministry is not always or necessarily bad. It just means that those in charge of the "design team" for the ministry must truly be men and women of God, wholly committed to the Holy Spirit and as pure as possible before Him so they can be adequate vessels through whom He can flow.

In 2 Timothy 2:21, Paul instructs us that God utilizes holy vessels prepared for His work. Relying on present resources and a personal game plan is not always blessed of the Lord. New works that are not of God will not succeed. A team must develop according to a true calling and mission of the Lord.

DEVOLUTION

Perhaps this sounds harsh, but I have seen it many times: People who want their positions to continue conspire to carry on the ministry so that they can have security. The ministry function may be worthwhile, and maybe God could use it. Without the proper motive, however, selfishness can creep into a team, dividing strong relationships, exalting individuals rather than the team and building a political system rather than a family for God.

In my opinion, the flow of organizational evolutionary degeneration is as follows:

- A few people in the initial team, who have a heart for God and a calling, bond together sacrificially to see God's will in this particular ministry.

- As the family of ministry develops, the entity becomes somewhat more organized. People allow their spiritual gifts to be utilized in specific areas. During this stage, those who have an entrepreneurial flair blossom. Having only unwritten guidelines in place, it can be one of the strongest ministry development periods. It is also the most fun kind of organization in which to work for those who love to try new things and work closely with a team of people.

  An example of an organization that flourished during this phase of development was Apple Computer. In its early days, the organization attracted a wealth of young men and women who were inspired by the vision of the company's founders, excited by the challenge of creating something revolutionary, and who reveled in the creative environment at Apple. Legend has it that many of the innovators at Apple during those days gathered regularly in a Jacuzzi to brainstorm. The company encouraged unusual creative endeavors toward developing a novel product. Eventually, they developed the most user-friendly tool in a new field of personal computers.

- As the ministry grows, more "managers" are usually brought into the picture. This does not necessarily represent a problem. After all, good management enables a ministry to respond quickly to opportunities, to organize efficiently for change, be flexible and to encourage creative thinking.

- Next comes the more formal organization of the players. This structuring is often necessitated by an organism growing in size and complexity beyond its ability to work from an unwritten framework. If godly leadership is in place, the ministry can continue to blossom, just as the organized class meetings in early Methodism did. If carnal, ungodly, selfish or political leadership is in place, however, this becomes less than an appropriate venue for people who want to address the contemporary needs of society. As society changes, organizations often fail to keep up with the dynamics of social change because the ministry is too static.

IBM is a fitting example of this phenomenon. In the sixties and seventies, this multibillion-dollar global giant felt its prestigious status in the computer marketplace was unassailable. The corporation had a singular focus: to produce large main frame computers. As the market changed around them, though, they realized that to survive they had to enter the personal computer market. They eventually organized a creative, entrepreneurial team to design a personal computer and compete with Apple and others.

- The final—and most frightening—phase is when the team becomes part of an institution. Organizational analysts describe this as the fourth and final stage of an organization going from birth to death, passing from man to movement, to machine, to monument. At this point, the activity of the entity has become so routinized that the entity has outlived its ability to maximize its potential. The monument will continue to sleepwalk through life unless a person of vision enters the scene and revitalizes the organization through the power of vision and strong leadership.

Aleksandr Solzhenitsyn stated in an address to the graduating class of Harvard in 1978:

A society based on the letter of the law and never reaching any higher, fails to take advantage of the full range of human possibilities. The letter of the law is too cold and formal to have a beneficial influence on society. Whenever the tissue of life is woven of legalistic relationships, this creates an atmosphere of spiritual mediocrity that paralyzes men's noblest impulses.

After a certain level of the problem has been reached, legalistic thinking induces paralysis; it prevents one from seeing the scale and the meaning of events.[9]

That theme is taken further by Alonzo McDonald, who reminds us that a bureaucracy is not immortal—not even a ministry bureaucracy. Team development within a ministry context, regardless of its focus, must operate with three priorities in mind:

1. All that is done is for the beneficiary. In ministry, the service is for those people who will benefit by the ministry and also God Himself who is honored by our selflessly responding to His calling.

2. The organism itself is the second priority. As we live to fulfill the needs of the beneficiary, we realize that the best way to accomplish this is through a team together. As the team is lifted up, focus maintained and internal strife minimized, the organism is honored before others and before the Lord. He in turn empowers it.

3. The employee is third. In the "me" generation, we have seen in many parachurch organizations and church staffs that "me" wants to be lifted up above "we." This is the death knell of an organization. When the employees live for themselves, they destroy the reputation of the ministry and literally suck it dry in a variety of ways.[10]

When people are more concerned about their positions than the mission, degenerative forces are at work. In contrast, I am reminded again of Billy Graham. During his decades of public ministry, Mr. Graham received many attractive offers of alternative employment, ranging from ambassadorships to the presidencies of major corporations. Without hesitation he rejected all of his suitors, noting that to accept any of those offers would be a "demotion." He could not step down from the highest calling of all, that of telling others about Jesus Christ.

MAINTAINING A TEAM

Effective team building requires more than vision, a called leader, a committed group of people who share a passion and complimentary gifts, adequate funding and a good plan of action. Those elements are indispensable, of course. Often the excitement of building a great team overwhelms the recognition that a great leader must not only build, but also maintain the team.

What does it take to maintain a team? Many of the same qualities that it took to develop the team in the first place, but applying the principles in ways that recognize the maturation of the team. To maintain the intensity of commitment and the sharpness of focus, the leader must creatively recast the vision and identify the team's priorities; establish fluid lines of communication; address conflict quickly and decisively, with the context of the ministry's vision and values; facilitate trust among members; deploy team members in areas of giftedness; encourage and exhort the members to retain a zeal for their cause; and model the very character traits the leader must possess to influence his people (vulnerability, accessibility, transparency, listening and so on).

One of the keys to effective maintenance—as opposed to survival maintenance—is for the leader to be so in love with the team that he will sacrifice his precious time for the sake of individual members, to weep when the team weeps and to share tough love whenever necessary. The leader is a steward of the complex web of relationships that comprise the heartbeat of the team. As A. W. Tozer noted:

> A true and safe leader is likely to be one who has no desire to lead, but is forced into a position of leadership by the inward pressure of the Holy Spirit and the press of external situations. Such were Moses and David and the Old Testament prophets. I think there was hardly a great leader from Paul to the present day but was drafted by the Holy Spirit for the task, and commissioned by the Lord of the Church to fill a position he had little heart for. I believe it might be accepted as a fairly reliable rule of thumb that the man who is ambitious to lead is disqualified as a leader. The true leader will have no desire to lord it over God's heritage, but will be humble, gentle, self-sacrificing and altogether *as ready to follow as to lead, when the Spirit makes it clear that a wiser and more gifted man than himself has appeared.*[11]

General Colin Powell has been through many tough battles—both in the field and behind the doors in decision-making capacities. His perspective is realistic and compassionate regarding the importance of maintaining the team through a balance of hard discipline and tender support. "Nobody every got to the top without slipping up. When someone stumbles, I don't believe in stomping on him. My philosophy is: pick 'em up, dust 'em off and get 'em moving again."[12] This is the same team-building philosophy used by Jesus Christ during His work on earth.

THE REWARDS OF TEAM DEVELOPMENT

For those who are truly leaders, building a team and maintaining it is indisputably one of the most fulfilling tasks imaginable. It allows a leader to exercise his gifts by drawing the most out of each participant, invest in those individuals and discover the joys of dying to self for the benefit of others. Jesus modeled it for us. For what more could we ask?

Notes
1. As quoted by J. Oswald Sanders, *Spiritual Leadership* (Chicago: Moody Press, 1980), p. 11.
2. Ibid., p. 14.
3. Fred Smith, "Learning to Lead" *Christianity Today* (1986): 93.
4. Alexandre Dumas, *The Count of Monte Cristo* (New York: Bantam Books, 1956), p. 176.
5. Robert Greenleaf, *Servant Leadership* (New York: Paulist Press, 1977), p. 3.
6. Sanders, *Spiritual Leadership*, p. 16.
7. Colin Powell, "Learning to Lead," condensed from *My American Journey* in *Reader's Digest* (October 1995): 148.
8. Ibid., p. 147.
9. Aleksandr Solzhenitsyn, *A World Split Apart* (New York: Harper & Row, 1978), pp. 17-19, 39.
10. Alonzo McDonald, *Book of Essays*, ed. Os Guinness and John Seel (Chicago: Moody Press, 1992), pp. 139-141.
11. A. W. Tozer, *The Reaper* (February 1962): 459.
12. Powell, "Learning to Lead," p. 146.

TWELVE

CONFLICT: THE REFINING FIRE OF LEADERSHIP

JIM VAN YPEREN

Two images come immediately to mind whenever someone asks me to describe leadership and conflict—Moses and Nehemiah. Edwin Moses and Rinaldo Nehemiah, that is.

Do you remember these men? Edwin Moses was the greatest 400-meter hurdler in the world. For more than a decade, he never lost. In 1976, he won a gold medal in the Montreal Olympics. Rinaldo Nehemiah was a world-class 110-meter hurdler. Interestingly, both men were strong runners, but many runners were stronger. Both were fast, yet many were faster.

So why did Moses and Nehemiah always win? They had the unique ability to anticipate, approach and overcome obstacles—the hurdles. Moses and Nehemiah were great runners, like their ancient namesakes were great leaders, *because of the obstacles*.

In other words, the hurdles made them great. As hurdles make the runner, conflict defines the leader. To define leadership, we must first understand the nature of conflict.

A great problem in the Church today is that we define leadership much too broadly and almost always disregard the role of conflict in the performance of leadership functions. Leaders are necessary, though, *because* of conflict. In America, Christians have embraced two mistaken views about conflict that negatively effect how we understand leadership. The first view sees conflict in terms of sin. The second sees conflict in terms of power. These views are seldom verbalized, but each is based upon a set of deeply held, often unconscious assumptions that guide behavior.

Those who view conflict as sin focus on the emotional pain generated by conflict. Afraid to hurt others, conflict is avoided like, well, sin. People are extremely reluctant to confront, to rebuke, to disagree or to offend. They are like runners who come upon a hurdle and stop, hoping the hurdle will go away, or who go around the hurdle, instead of over it, disrupting all the other runners in the process.

The irony, of course, is that this promotes what they are seeking most to avoid. Unresolved conflict does not go away. It becomes more divisive, resulting in deeper hurt. A "leader" who will not confront is not a leader.

At the opposite extreme are those who view conflict as a way to establish power and position—to show who is boss. Where the first view is passive and accommodating, this view is aggressive and authoritarian. People who hold this view are like runners who attack and knock down every hurdle, tripping themselves and disrupting everyone in their wake. Every problem and disagreement is spiritualized to prove "I am right" and "you are wrong." The smallest differences become tests of orthodoxy. This view creates a culture of confrontation where fear and guilt control behavior. It is a kind of Phariseeism that celebrates loyalty and autonomy, rather than servanthood and community. A "leader" who will not serve is not a leader.

Both views have some basis in truth. Conflict is often the result of sin, the consequence of living in a fallen world. Not all conflict, though, *is* sin. Rather, sin makes conflict necessary, and resolving conflict requires Spirit-directed leadership. The key, of course, is spiritual authority, not human power. Spiritual authority is different in nature and substance from the kind of power and control we commonly think of, and too often rely upon, for leadership in the Church.

CONFLICT IN SCRIPTURE

Conflict, in biblical understanding, is a place of contest, the arena where adversaries compete. The Greek word for conflict is *agon*, from which we derive our English word "agony." The apostle Paul writes, "The sinful nature desires what is contrary to the Spirit, and the Spirit what is contrary to the sinful nature. They are in conflict [literally, in competition] with each other, so that you do not do what you want" (Gal 5:17, *NIV*). Life, Paul says, is a spiritual contest. "Our struggle is not against flesh and blood, but against the rulers, against the authorities, against the powers of this dark world and against the spiritual forces of evil in the heavenly realms" (Eph 6:12, *NIV*).

For Paul, conflict is the collision between God's truth and the world's wisdom, between spiritual authority and human strength. This idea turns the common view of power on its head. The Cross, "a stumbling block to Jews and foolishness to Gentiles" (1 Cor. 1:23, *NIV*), becomes the turning point of history and the axis of true authority. So Paul's message to the Corinthians comes "not with wise and persuasive words, but with a demonstration of the Spirit's power, so that your faith might not rest on men's wisdom, but on God's power" (1 Cor. 2:4,5, *NIV*). This echoes what the Lord says to Zerubbabel, "'Not by might nor by power, but by my Spirit'" (Zech. 4:6, *NIV*).

In Scripture, conflict is the very stuff of faith. It is the creative tension between law and grace, sin and forgiveness, justice and mercy. It begins and ends the salvation story, from the garden of Eden to Golgotha, from the destruction of the Temple to the New Jerusalem.

This understanding changes our perspective. Now conflict is an opportunity to demonstrate a new reality in Christ. Leadership, it follows, becomes a process, not a position; it is learning and serving, not controlling.

Conflict offers us the chance to grow, to change our minds and to create new commitments based upon the truth God reveals. This opens the door for a whole new set of assumptions[1] and principles for spiritual leadership, including two assumptions that form the basis of this chapter. The first assumption is that conflict is necessary. The second is that leadership is a call and gifting.

CONFLICT IS NECESSARY

If death and taxes are the first two certainties of life, conflict is the third. Life *requires* conflict. It is the essential part of God's redeeming plan. Through conflict we know our need, acknowledge sin, recognize truth and test our faith.

Think about where we would be, for example, if Noah had not built an ark in "holy fear"; if Abraham had refused to sacrifice Isaac; if Moses had not challenged Pharaoh, or pled before God to preserve stiff-necked Israel; if Joshua had not marched around Jericho, or Rahab had not hidden the spies; if Gideon, Samson, Samuel, David, Jesus and followers of Christ throughout the two thousand years of history since calvary had regarded human opinion more than the will of God. The narrative of our faith requires conflict. By it we learn and grow.

Only by trusting God through pain, uncertainty and opposition do we prove His will and demonstrate His power. Spiritual leadership means making decisions that both cause and resolve conflict. A leader's decision to do one thing or to go one way must be a decision not to do another thing or to go the opposite way.

A biblical understanding of conflict changes our perspective. Danger turns into opportunity. Leadership becomes the art of discovering truth and obeying Christ.

This, in turn, changes the way we approach conflict. Conflict becomes a learning process. Confrontation and avoidance are replaced by discovery and dialogue. Instead of asking how to get out of conflict, we can ask a deeper, more relevant question, "what does it mean to follow Christ through conflict?"[2]

Before we answer this question, let me ask what you think about conflict.

- Are you the kind of person who is energized by change?
- Can you live with questions, without immediate answers?
- When there is conflict, do you address it openly and directly, or wait to see if it will go away?
- Have you recently looked a brother or sister in the eye and lovingly confronted their sins, admonishing them to change?
- Can you hear criticism or unfair personal accusations against your leadership and still keep your eye on the vision?
- Are you the kind of person who can make a Spirit-led decision, against vocal opposition?
- Can you stand firm in God's direction without any tangible proof or human certainty that you are right?

- Are you quick and ready to say "I don't know" or "I was wrong," when these are true?

If you answer no to some or most of these questions, you need to prayerfully examine your call and gifting to *lead*. Without a call and gifting you will certainly fail, because you will attempt to do in your own strength what only God's enabling can accomplish.

This leads to the second fundamental assumption: Leadership is a spiritual call and gifting.

LEADERSHIP IS A CALL AND GIFTING

Leadership is not a title, talent or interest. It is not a degree you earn or a position you hold. The principles in this and other books may make you more knowledgeable about leadership, but they will not make you a leader. Only God can do that. Leadership is a spiritual gift, a supernatural enabling. You cannot make yourself something God has not called or equipped you to be. Nowhere is this more important to understand, and more sadly demonstrated, than in church conflict.

Satan is having a field day in the American Church by dividing and preoccupying believers with issues that many pastors and lay leaders are ill-equipped to handle, because they have no spiritual gift to discern or lead. The call and gifting to lead is distinct from the call and gifting to pastor or to teach. Not understanding this difference has led many pastors and churches to fail.

The spiritual gift of leadership involves hearing and seeing God's vision, motivating and guiding people to follow the vision, making decisions and resolving conflicts on the basis of God's revealed plan. A gift to pastor does not automatically mean a gift to lead. Conflict reveals the line between the two. It is the refining fire of leadership. Conflict is where leaders are proved, or better, where God's enabling is confirmed.

From these assumptions we can draw many principles that begin to answer our question: What does it mean to follow Christ through conflict?

FOCUS ON PATTERNS, NOT EVENTS

The role of leadership is to see, *and to keep in view*, the big picture. In conflict, this means seeing the battle from God's perspective. That is, looking beyond what is immediately seen, to understand what comes before and after. Leaders focus on patterns, not events.

The ploy of Satan is to preoccupy the leader and the Church with the small picture—people and events. If the leader is caught in this web by reacting to events, emotions and behaviors, instead of looking for underlying truths, the ploy succeeds and the crisis deepens.

When the king of Aram ordered horses and chariots to capture Elisha, the human view looked bleak. Early the next morning the servant of Elisha looked up and saw the enemy surrounding their camp. He ran to Elisha, crying, "Oh, my lord, what shall we do?"

"Don't be afraid," Elisha answered. "Those who are with us are more than those who are with them." Then Elisha prayed, "O Lord, open his eyes so that he may see." The Lord opened the servant's eyes, and he looked and saw the hills full of horses and chariots of fire, all around Elisha (see 2 Kings 6:14-17).

Everything depends upon what you are looking at. The servant looked at the immediate event. Elisha saw the pattern of God's sovereignty. If you look at the small picture, your vision is shortsighted. If you fix your eyes on Jesus, you have hope in what cannot be seen.

Leaders who focus on events become part of the problem, not the solution. The issue becomes a political struggle with resolution dependent upon a human's ability, experience or knowledge.

Leaders who look for patterns see the spiritual truths behind the conflict. Spiritual truth, not human strength, opens up opportunities for God's power to be revealed and real growth to result. At issue is what occupies the focus—the Lordship of Jesus Christ, or man's opinions.

CONFRONT POWER WITH TRUTH, NOT POWER

The first instinct of most leaders is to respond defensively when challenged. It is always the worst response. In conflict, never confront power with power. Always confront power with truth.

Power hinders learning and growth. It polarizes the issue into sides, for and against. Resolution is linked to pride, personality and persuasion. Someone has to win, someone has to lose; someone has to be right, someone has to be wrong. The incentive is to win, not to learn and grow. The conflict takes on a life of its own, driven by self-protection, saving face and defending reputations. Honest disagreements suddenly become personal attacks. Emotions rise, feeding a cycle of insecurity and growing distrust, what system thinkers call the "dynamic of escalation."[3]

Escalation can occur when two sides are mutually threatened, each by the other. When this happens, every action requires a counter action, further polarizing the sides.

The dynamics of escalation enter into most church conflicts. A leader's attempt to "solve the problem" often exacerbates it.

Recently, I was called into a church that was experiencing sharp division between the leadership and members. Many issues fed the crisis, but issues soon became irrelevant. Members were convinced the pastor and board were manipulative and controlling, unwilling to hear or act on any member concerns. The pastor and board, in turn, viewed members as rebellious and singled out key members as "troublemakers."

Sides were formed, each side convinced that it alone was acting on God's behalf to save "our" church. Each new issue, however small, fed the division as if throwing fuel on a fire. The following diagram illustrates the cycle:

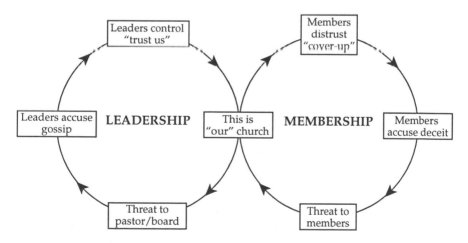

Both leaders and members believe "This is our church." Both sides want conformity to their perspective. Each side sees the other as a threat to achieving the kind of church they want.

Members accuse the leadership of not listening. Leaders accuse members of gossip. Each side becomes more entrenched. Leaders become secretive, giving out less information, reinforcing the members' view that leadership is "covering up."

To fill the vacuum of information, members rely on hearsay and their own interpretation of events to describe what is happening. These "educated guesses" are often wrong, reinforcing the leadership's position that members are "troublemakers." The cycle spins on and on.

Stepping back from the battle, you can appreciate the good intentions and intense frustration of each side. Members and leaders responded in a way they believed to be "biblical" and right, failing to see that their responses were becoming the problem. Each side believed God was calling them to stop the attacks of Satan. Each assumed they knew why the other was responding and attributed it to sin. This reinforced the "rightness" of their position, and the "wrongness" of the other. In reality, Satan was using their perceptions and assumptions to escalate the tension, deepen the division and hide the core spiritual deception.

Interestingly, the dynamic of escalation can work the other way as well. Either party can break the cycle simply by not responding to the perceived threat. If one side does not respond, it eliminates the threat to the other side and opens up a path of understanding.

This should sound familiar. Jesus tells us to "turn the other cheek," to "do good" and to "pray for" those who hate us. Refusing to react defensively can actually reverse the cycle so that the energy is given to listening, learning and serving others rather than protecting self. This is the essence of "considering others more important than yourself." It is the fulfillment of the Great Command, to love God with all your heart and your neighbor as yourself.

Affirm Truth in Community

Nearly all of Scripture is written to and for groups of people, not individuals. We must learn to read our Bibles this way. Instead of asking, "What is God saying to me?" we need to ask "What is God saying to *us*?" We are a Body. As believers, we have the mind of Christ. This is important to remember, because most conflict in the church is between brothers and sisters, people with whom we will spend eternity, people in whom the Holy Spirit resides. This means we have a way, by God's grace, to resolve conflict together. Why behave like people without the Spirit when we have access to the God of all truth?

Responding to power with truth places Christ at the center and builds bridges with our brothers and sisters. It acknowledges that no one person knows the truth completely,[4] so we need each other. It opens up the opportunity to own our assumptions honestly, state our convictions directly and allow others to give perspective openly.

By separating truth from emotion, the Body may examine the issue collectively, adding and subtracting ideas as the problem is seen from new and different angles. This gets individuals out of the way so the Holy Spirit can work. The resolution comes by affirmation in the Body as the Spirit reveals truth, exposes sin and convicts hearts.

Not long ago I was working with an established church of about two hundred and fifty people. The best solution to their crisis meant recommending that we cancel all regular church services and programs for a period of two months. In effect, the proposal was to shut down the church for sixty days. In place of the regular programs, special meetings would be held to address the specific issues this church needed to face.

This is not the kind of recommendation one makes lightly. It meant a huge inconvenience and no small disappointment for everyone. The youth retreat would be canceled, corporate evangelism efforts ceased, a women's weekly program stopped, everything suspended. Still, prayer seemed to confirm this was from the Lord. As you might expect, the recommendation raised many questions and complaints. My response was to acknowledge each concern, restate the evidence supporting the decision and advise people to test the idea before God in prayer.

During the next several weeks many people said to me, "You know, your recommendation made me angry, but when I prayed about it, God affirmed it was the right thing to do." Some people left the church, angry. Most stayed, went through the two-month period, and now look back on it as a spiritual turning point in the church's life.

The idea did not work: God did. The point is not the method, it is the process of allowing God to affirm and achieve the result. Resolving conflict is about discernment and obedience. If an idea or decision is from God, why are we afraid to allow the Spirit room to confirm it? We need to get out of God's way.

POINT TO CHRIST, AND GET OUT OF THE WAY

The contradiction of leadership is that you are called to lead in such a way as to make the leader irrelevant!

Leaders point to Christ. As David Hansen writes: a leader is "a parable of Jesus."[5] We are a temporary picture; never a lasting symbol.

This helps us understand conflict for what it is, not a challenge to our human power, but a test of God's kingly rule. Check yourself. Do your actions reflect a desire for people to like you, praise you or feel sorry for you? Or are you pointing people to truth revealed in Christ? You are not the issue; God is.

When Samuel was old, the elders of Israel gathered together and demanded that Samuel appoint a king so they could be like other nations. Samuel was grieved by this and prayed. The Lord answered, saying: "Listen Sam, this is not about you, they are rejecting *Me* as their king."

Conflict is ultimately a choice to follow or reject God's sovereignty. A leader who demands sympathy or loyalty to himself rather than the lordship of Jesus Christ is rebelling, not leading. Any "resolution" that comes merely by a leader's charisma, not God's *charismata* (Spirit gifting), does not resolve the real conflict.

Placing self at center always leads away from the Spirit, asks the wrong questions, seeks the wrong advantages and becomes preoccupied with the wrong events. Self leans on what is merely understood or seen. Conflict, by nature, concerns the unseen, often involving spiritual blindness and deception, dimensions no leader can fully understand alone.

Resolving conflict, therefore, requires a spiritual perspective. Leaders must have God's eyes—a spiritual vision, insight and discernment—attributes not possible without God's gifting.

Leadership is not knowing the right answers. It is a divine enabling to ask the right questions.

BE THE FIRST TO OWN YOUR PART IN THE PROBLEM

I ask three questions of any church seeking help out of a crisis. How they answer tells me if they will change, whether or not I can help them and how open they will be to hearing and obeying the Holy Spirit. The questions are:

1. Do you want to be well?
2. Are you willing to place absolutely everything on the table for evaluation?

3. Are you willing to identify and to own your part in the problem?

Beneath these questions lie critical assumptions about the nature of church crisis:

1. The cause of conflict is internal, not external (and so is God's solution).
2. The immediate crisis is likely not the fundamental problem, but is symptomatic of a deeper, systemic conflict. (Healing requires seeing the underlying structures of the conflict and learning new ways to trust God through change.)
3. A leader does not know all the answers, nor is he the solution. (God does and is.)

The easiest mistake a church leader can make is to resolve conflict too quickly. We think we know what the problem is, so we believe the remedy is simple.

Some church leaders see the devil in every detail. For these, the conflict is the result of secularism, or liberalism, or legalism or any other "ism" people love to hate. Although Satan surely is attacking the Church and looking to gain a foothold though all these issues and more, we may give him too much credit. Most problems start with us and are exploited by Satan. Conflict is always complex.

This requires a leader to look deeper, to acknowledge uncertainty and to live with pain. We don't like this. Most of our lives are spent trying to convince people we know the answers, minimize uncertainty and avoid pain. Scripture paints a different picture. Living in a fallen world means living with conflict. Faith is being sure of what we hope for and certain of what we cannot see. We follow a Savior who empties Himself and becomes obedient to death, even death on a cross, "for the joy set before him" (Heb. 12:2, *NIV*). Jesus tells His disciples to expect trials and tribulations. He prays *not* for God to remove us from the world, but to protect us from the evil one. James reminds us to "consider it pure joy" (Jas. 1:2, *NIV*) when we face trials.

Faith, and leadership, is a risky business. There is no cheap grace or quick fix, no formula or guarantee for resolving conflict. God wants to teach us *through* the process. It starts by asking questions about ourselves.

WHAT IS IT ABOUT ME?

A leader must be the first to own the problem. He must ask, What is it about me that is causing this event to happen?

Starting with this question opens windows of understanding that our nature wants to close. It offers us the opportunity to resolve conflict at the source, not simply to address the symptom.

If the origin of most conflict is internal, not external, the leader cannot separate himself from the problem.

For instance, let's suppose you want to end your traditional Sunday night service and replace it with informal home gatherings. You announce the change and immediately face opposition. Senior saints protest, reminding you that Sunday evening services are such a long-standing institution that not a single service has been canceled for twenty-five years: "Not even during the blizzard of '78."

You expected opposition. You knew Mrs. Smith would be the first to complain. So when she does, you immediately conclude that the problem is people like Mrs. Smith "who will never change." The problem is traditionalism. The remedy is to preach about stiff-necked people.

Mrs. Smith, however, does not believe in traditionalism any more than she believes in change. She believes in Jesus, whom she meets with brothers and sisters every Sunday evening. She is not stiff-necked, she is scared. What's more, you are the one scaring her by taking away her time to meet Jesus. She does not hear your sermons because you are not speaking to her concerns. You are preaching about your assumptions, not the real problem. Missing this, and seeing no change in Mrs. Smith, you give her the ultimatum: either accept this change, or leave the church.

Symptomatic problems and superficial solutions keep you from learning the fundamental problem—Mrs. Smith's fear and your failure to address it. You, and Mrs. Smith, are trapped by your assumptions.

If a leader is eager to fix the problem, instead of living, learning and growing through it, the conflict may go away for a while but it will always return—usually bigger and with greater fallout. (Today it is Mrs. Smith; tomorrow it may be teenagers, or couples or some other group who feel alienated.)

The alternative is to start with the assumption that you may be part of the problem. By asking the question, What is it about me that is making Mrs. Smith react this way? you can uncover her needs and learn ways you can grow. Before jumping to conclusions, or better, before you even announce the change, talk to Mrs. Smith.

You might say: "I see you are uncomfortable with our plans to change. I want to understand this more. The elders and I have spent a lot of time thinking and praying about this step, and we believe it is the right decision. But perhaps you see something we have missed. Can you help me understand what you are feeling?"

By giving Mrs. Smith the opportunity to express her feelings, you tell her that she is important and that her concerns have been heard. Most conflict arises not because people disagree, but because they feel left out of the decision-making process. By listening, you enroll her into the process of change. You open up the opportunity to keep Mrs. Smith as an honored member of your church while helping her through change, and making you a better leader as well.

Eliminate Blaming

Assuming that you are part of the problem has another benefit. It eliminates blaming. Assigning blame is one of the greatest obstacles to real learning and resolution. Blame is Satan's tool to divide and conquer. That is why Scripture exhorts believers not to judge, but to discover the "log in your own eye before removing the dust in another" (see Luke 6:42), and to consider the needs of others before your own. Even when clear-cut sin is involved, the admonition of Scripture is for Spirit-filled people to restore the sinner gently.[6] The goal of confrontation is always gentle restoration, always for health, never for harm. Blame is man's way, not God's.

By resisting the urge to blame, you can remove people and events from focus. You can uncover the underlying issues and correct the patterns of behavior to which the whole church contributes.

For example, suppose a man in your church named Peter is caught lying. If all you do is blame the sinner, you have missed the other half of the lesson. Why did Peter lie? Ask yourself, What is it about me or our church that Peter feels compelled to lie? Christians usually do not want, or intend, to sin. They have reasons. Learn to look for the problem underneath the problem and you will prevent greater conflicts down the road.

Similarly, when a leader faces some false accusation, no matter how far-fetched, attacking the accuser inhibits learning. Suppose someone accuses you of being a drunkard. You don't drink, but brother Bob sees you joining a toast at a wedding (mistaking your ginger ale for champagne) and questions your spirituality. Before you address the facts, stop and think. Ask yourself, What is happening in our church, or my ministry, or Bob's life, that he would assume the worst? This can get to the real problem.

Assigning blame to others may address the sin, but it often ignores how we contribute to the stumbling.

The church is a Body, not a machine. You can break down a machine into isolated parts, fix it and put the machine back together. Each part stands on its own. If a part breaks, just throw it out and get a new one. But you can't throw people out of church any more than the eye can tell the ear, "You are not important." As leaders, our goal is not to "fix" anything. It is to learn and grow like the living, interconnected organism God created the Church to be.

ASK WHY, FOUR TIMES

The purpose of asking questions is to clarify the issue in order to discover the solution. For this reason, it is important to keep asking. Don't stop at the first answer. A good exercise is to ask yourself "why" at least four times.

Suppose the conflict in your church is a question about responsibility between the elders and the paid pastoral staff. The conflict surfaces when John, a staff member, suddenly stands up in a meeting and states angrily, "You don't care about the staff," then storms out. As chairman of the elders, your first inclination may be to call John in for discipline, to tell him he is being selfish, even silly. You think of all those times you said "thank you" to John yourself, and how others have told John they love him. Of course people appreciate John! But wait. Instead of reacting, ask yourself, "Is being appreciated the real issue, or is it a symptom of something deeper?" The only way to know is to probe further.

You ask the "What is it about me?" question and realize something underneath John's outburst may require more insight. Now ask why, four times:

Go to John and ask him...

1. Why do you feel the elders don't care?
    This opens up the issue. John might respond defensive-
    ly at first, but if you listen and give him opportunity to
    air his feelings you can get to some specifics. In fact,
    John gives you many examples of how decisions were
    made without his input. He interprets this as intention-
    al and states emphatically, "The staff needs more power
    and control." Again, the temptation will be to end the
    inquiry here with some acknowledgment of neglect, or
    a promise to involve John in more decisions. But is this
    all there is to learn? Is power the real issue?
       After telling John you are committed to learn and serve
    together, you might ask yourself why a few more times.
2. Why does the staff need more power and control? What
    is it about the relationship the staff has with the elders
    or with the congregation that makes them feel power-
    less and want control?
3. Why is our relationship like this? Is there something
    about our structure, our form of governance, that
    threatens the staff, invites distrust or impedes good
    communication?
4. Why are we structured so? What is the spiritual belief,
    doctrinal position or theological understanding behind
    this structure? Is it biblical? Is it what we really believe?

This process of probing deeper often uncovers the systemic or fundamental problems beneath the surface response and emotional reaction. Most problems have little or nothing to do with the event that
reveals them.

DIG FOR THE THEOLOGICAL ROOT

Digging deeper for the roots of conflict will reveal that theology drives structure, structure drives relationships and relationships drive
behavior.[7]

In the example on the next page, John storms out of the meeting
(behavior) because he feels underappreciated and threatened by the
elders (relationship). He feels threatened because elders are making
decisions without his input (structure). John wants more control

because he equates position with power, not ministry, and power with importance, not servanthood (theology).

Theology ——▶ Structure ——▶ Relationships ——▶ Behavior

It does not matter whether John's assessment of the elders is accurate or not. What matters is that the root issue is revealed so that it can be explored in dialogue. What do we believe about power? What does position have to do with power? What does Scripture teach? Is our structure, and the relationships formed by our structure, consistent with biblical teaching?

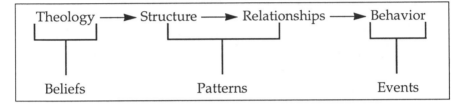

This drives us back to core values and beliefs. How is this issue described in Scripture? What values and principles are expressed? What would that look like here?

These questions, and others like them, form a picture of what could be Seeing this, we can then form new commitments based upon the truth of Scripture.

As long as we look at the behavior only, never asking what relationships and structures may be contributing to the behavior, only partial learning takes place. Real solutions are not found. The behavior is destined to repeat itself.

When a leader arrives too early at "the answer," it is usually by focusing on parts of the problem or individual events instead of the deeper issues underlying the conflict. This hides the real problem, the way trees hide the forest. Real learning is sacrificed to assigning blame and punishing the guilty. The "cause" is attributed to some irrelevant source. "John is having a bad day, he'll calm down."

THINK IN WHOLES, NOT IN PARTS

Most crises have internal, spiritual origins to which the whole community contributes. God views sin as a community responsibility.

When one person in the community sins, the whole community bears the guilt (see Lev. 4:22,27; Josh. 7:1). God judges whole nations for the sins (behavior or event) of a few. The whole community is accountable. When the apostle Paul writes to the Corinthians about a man who has had relations with his stepmother, his focus is on the character of the Church, not merely the man. "What is wrong with you [church] that you could tolerate such a thing?" Paul exclaims.

Thinking in wholes, not in parts, allows leadership to catch and correct a drifting away from core beliefs.

Church crises do not happen overnight. Like personal sin, corporate conflict comes gradually, step by step. The pastor who commits adultery or the elder who embezzles money does not wake up one day deciding to sin. A pattern of small compromises leads to bigger concessions until he can rationalize today what he would never have thought possible just a few months earlier.

When a church asks me for help out of crisis, my first step is to trace back and put together events that precipitated the conflict. This process always reveals early warning signs that were missed or only superficially addressed. In most instances, the crisis could have been avoided if leaders simply recognized the patterns and asked the right questions. Instead, blaming or superficial remedies created a whole new set of problems, thereby delaying real solutions. This dynamic is called "shifting the burden."[8]

Shifting the burden is a temporary, inadequate solution that makes the symptomatic problem "go away" and creates another problem in the process. Peter Senge uses this model to explain addictive behaviors such as alcoholism.[9] A businessman faces stress at work, so he stops for a drink before coming home. The stress "goes away." But tomorrow the stress comes back, so he stops for another drink. He starts drinking more and more. Before long he is drinking on the job and keeping a bottle in his briefcase. His "solution" creates new problems. Meanwhile, the problem does not go away. It remains, temporarily dormant, to return at a later date.

It might happen this way in a church...

Sin in the life of a prominent church leader raises calls for his dismissal. The leader responds first by defending himself, then, as evidence mounts and questions persist, he attacks his accusers. The burden "shifts" away from the fundamental problem of sin in the leader's life to the loyalty of leaders and parishioners. The solution becomes electing loyal leaders and disciplining anyone who asks questions.

This exact scenario nearly destroyed one church. The leader was asked by the elders to resign. He would not, and without a two-thirds majority, the elders could not force out the leader. Frustrated, several elders resigned. The leader appointed new elders who were loyal to him.

The "solution" to questioning the leader became stacking the board with loyal followers and attacking all dissenters. The message was stated clearly: All who cannot support our leaders should leave the church. Many did. The problem "went away."

Within a year, evidence of the real problem surfaced again. This time the burden was shifted to "outsiders" (members who left) gossiping and spreading rumors, and to "insiders" who believed them. Leadership responded, as they did before, not by opening up dialogue or looking for a pattern, but by suppressing dissent. This cycle repeated itself again and again for the next two years. Each new crisis caused more people to leave the church. Attendance dropped from four hundred to less than two hundred people. The one constant: the problem always came back.

Ironically, the people needed most to solve the problem were the people forced to leave. The conflict was difficult and sensitive, requiring discernment and leadership. Not surprisingly, people who had these gifts were the first to see the problem and to bring it out into the open. Forcing these people to leave further delayed the opportunity to establish open and discerning leadership.

The negative side effects were many, including:

1. Creating the illusion that there was no problem;
2. Accusing and hurting those who were not the source of the problem;
3. Keeping the leader in sin, and the Body blinded to the deception;
4. Presenting a negative witness to Christ's name in the region;
5. Delaying the opportunity to learn, grow and fulfill God's vision.

Leaders must be willing to see and own their part in the problem before they can help the church.

STAND FIRM, IN FAITH

Up until this point, we have talked about conflict as a learning process. This approach both avoids and resolves most issues before they reach a crisis. Some conflict, however, cannot be resolved in process. Honest differences remain, or sin prevents resolution. Here, a leader must make the decision and take a stand.

Scripture is clear: Obedience is what God is after in our lives. The role of a leader is not to please people, make them happy or comfortable. A leader is called to hear, obey and stand firm on what God reveals.

When honest differences exist after the process has clarified the issues, a leader must make the call by faith. This may result in one of at least three positive outcomes if a leader acts wisely and humbly:

1. The two sides may separate peaceably, as did Paul and Barnabas.
2. The two sides may reach a compromise, agreeing to disagree on nonessential matters, or each giving up some area of concern for the sake of unity while respecting the other's convictions.
3. One side may voluntarily remove its protest, allowing the other to move ahead.

(Note: The resolution should be explained clearly to the Body. Confessions of sin and reconciliation should be stated in direct proportion to the public nature of the sin.)

The rule of thumb is to allow the Spirit to work in such a way that the result declares the lordship of Jesus Christ.

When conflict results in a deadlock between two sides and one side refuses to peaceably disagree, it is sin. When this or any other sin is involved, it must be exposed. Discipline should be applied, the aim being gentle restoration. If the believer refuses to acknowledge sin, the principles of Scripture must be applied.

Matthew 18 allows for just two possible reactions to an accusation of sin:

1. Listening, with sincere action taken to repent and/or right the offense; or

2. Not listening, denying or taking defensive action to protect self.

Scripture calls a defensive, reactive posture being "stiff-necked." It is sin. Sin in the life of a believer grieves the Holy Spirit, disrupts the unity and fellowship of the community and weakens the witness of the Body. Unconfessed sin can destroy a church.

Leaders must lovingly confront when there is evidence of sin or a forsaking of the fellowship, following biblical guidelines such as these:

1. Upon discovery of ongoing sin in the life of a fellow believer, go promptly to lovingly confront the member in private (see Matt. 18:15).
2. If the believer confesses and renounces sin, grant forgiveness in Jesus' name.
3. If there is no expression of repentance, return to admonish the believer again in the presence of one or two witnesses (see v. 16).
4. If there is no repentance, the matter should be brought before the elders or your church leaders (see v. 17). The leaders should investigate the matter carefully and thoroughly, discussing the specific charges with the believer.
5. If there is no evidence of repentance, or if the believer refuses to cooperate in the process, the church Body should be made aware of sin (see v. 17).
6. If there is still no evidence of repentance, fellowship with this believer should be broken until there is repentance (see 1 Cor. 15:11; 2 Thess. 3:6,14; Titus 3:10,11).

RUN WITH PERSEVERANCE

A call to lead is a call to anticipate, approach and overcome hurdles. One thing is certain: there will be hurdles. The promise of Scripture is that God will equip you to meet each one.

In Acts 20:23-31 the apostle Paul gives instructions to leaders after stating his own resolve:

"I only know that in every city the Holy Spirit warns me that prison and hardships are facing me. However, I consider my life worth nothing to me, if only I may finish the race and complete the task the Lord Jesus has given me—the task of testifying to the gospel of God's grace....Keep watch over yourselves and all the flock of which the Holy Spirit has made you overseers. Be shepherds of the church of God, which he bought with his own blood. I know that after I leave, savage wolves will come in among you and will not spare the flock. Even from your own number men will arise and distort the truth in order to draw away disciples after them. So be on your guard!" (NIV).

Leadership is being faithful to finish well, to keep watch and to meet each hurdle as an opportunity to prove God's truth, through the power of the Holy Spirit. Lead by following Christ, so that you may say with Paul, "I have fought the good fight, I have finished the race, I have kept the faith" (2 Tim. 4:7, NIV).

Notes

1. You may choose to accept or challenge either point, but the principles that follow grow out of these two fundamental assumptions. This is critical to understand for this chapter, as the strengths and weaknesses of a person with the gift of leadership are almost directly opposite to those without a gifting. Whereas people without a gifting usually need a strong dose of "stand up and be counted," people who are leaders need to be cautioned against counting too quickly.
2. The source of this question comes from many conversations with my friend David Fitch.
3. Daniel H. Kim, *Systems Archetypes 1: Diagnosing Systemic Issues and Designing High-Leverage Interventions* (Cambridge, Mass.: Pegasus Communications Inc., 1992), p. 13.
4. See Job 38:4—42:6. Christ alone knows truth completely, that is, perfectly.
5. David Hansen, *The Art of Pastoring: Ministry Without All the Answers* (Downers Grove, Ill.: InterVarsity Press, 1994).
6. See Galatians 6:1-5.
7. This model grows out of ideas expressed by Peter Senge, applying systems thinking to corporate learning. His book, *The Fifth Discipline*, published by Doubleday, is highly recommended.
8. Kim, *Systems Archetypes 1*, p. 21.
9. Peter M. Senge, *The Fifth Discipline* (New York: Doubleday, 1990), p. 109.

THIRTEEN

CREATING THE
RIGHT LEADERSHIP
CULTURE

HANS FINZEL

Architects tell me that one of the greatest challenges of making buildings pleasant places in which to work is designing the climate systems so that people have the right atmosphere for producing work. One of the newest and most beautiful buildings in all of Dupage County, Illinois, where I live, is among those that have the highest employee illness rates.

The newly constructed multimillion-dollar county courthouse was closed for weeks because of rampant illness among its workers. How can a new office building be responsible for employee illnesses? It is a HVAC-related (heating, ventilation and air conditioning) problem. It seems that the architects and builders misfired on the design of the heating, ventilation and air conditioning. So many county workers became ill after they had moved into the new building that they brought a lawsuit against management—who, in turn, sued the builders to completely redo the HVAC. A multimillion dollar leadership mistake in the climate systems!

Whether you like it or not, if you are a leader, you are the keeper of the organizational climate in your organization. Much like the physical HVAC, the unseen organizational climate systems can make or break your working environment. This invisible corporate climate creates a culture in which people flourish or perish as they work under your direction.

Leaders are the prime creators, keepers and cultivators of corporate culture. The founders and/or leaders of an organization create the cultural values that are the trademarks of the group. Whether it is a church, business or local Boy Scout chapter, the leaders determine the values and rules of the working environment. The power to determine how the group will work together and what kind of atmosphere will be maintained lies in the hands of those at the top.

As keepers of the culture, one of the primary responsibilities of leadership is to understand the organizational values and climate of the group. Corporate cultures can sabotage a new leader's dreams or create a culture that will foster the climate for successful work. Like feeding nutrients to the soil of a flower bed, the corporate culture must be carefully cultivated by leadership to build the positive context for fruitfulness. Keeping the culture healthy and productive requires as much diligence as maintaining a beautiful garden surrounding your home.

A FEW CLUES ABOUT WORK CULTURES

I have worked in many settings during my years of college, graduate school and professional life. Some bosses have helped me grow as a person and others have stifled my development. During several summers of my college years, I held a job driving a delivery truck in and around my hometown of Huntsville, Alabama. Don, my supervisor, did everything he could to slow me down. He was basically of that "get by" culture where everyone did as little as possible unless the corporate big shots came to town. If I had idle time, I was busy reorganizing the warehouse or cleaning the stockroom shelves. Don did not appreciate my industrious approach to my work, and was happy for the day when I finally finished college and moved on to other things. Although Don liked me personally, he thought I never "fit" into the culture he was responsible for maintaining. I appreciated that summer job; it enabled me to see how bosses affect the working values of all the workers.

Leaders determine the effectiveness of followers. A leader will hopefully seek to develop an atmosphere in which people are able to flourish as they are empowered to do their very best with the highest levels of motivation.

I constantly meet people who tell me horror stories of supervisors who seem to have a gift for stifling any good the followers might attempt to do. Even in the local church, a deeply spiritual pastor can create a defeating climate in which the followers cannot bear the fruit of effective and productive work. Some spiritual giants are miserable failures when it comes to organizational leadership.

I have a file folder full of unsolicited employment applications from folks who want to change jobs because they are defeated in the stifling cultures where they now work. As you dig deeper into their frustrations, you find that it is rarely an issue of pay, but of finding a place that allows the freedom to succeed. People are looking for work places in which the right atmosphere exists to follow a fulfilling and empowering career.

A young man who recently applied to work with us said to me during the interview, "I want a place where I can grow as a person in a team environment." I don't think that is too much to ask, and it is up to me as the leader to create that world for him.

Just as attitudes shape performance, so the environment a leader creates shapes the effectiveness of the followers. What can a leader do to build a positive, empowering, enabling setting that will foster the very best in people? A few key principles about creating the right culture for leadership to be effective are foundational to understanding the power of corporate culture and personal effectiveness.

> **Principle 1: Never underestimate the power of corporate culture.** The climate created by leadership has everything to do with the effectiveness and success of the followers. The same person doing the same work can flourish in one leader's climate and totally fail in another's. Like the jet stream's powerful effect on the travel of airplanes, corporate culture can work for or against your success.
>
> **Principle 2: Leadership must give attention to cultivating the culture.** It is the responsibility of leaders to understand corporate values and culture and to foster an atmosphere in which followers can grow. Like the diligent farmer who toils in his fields from sunrise to sunset, one of the few fundamental responsibilities leaders must never neglect is creating the right setting for workers and followers to succeed.

Principle 3: Only leadership can change culture. Many people in an organization may want to "change the way we do things around here," but only the ones in control of the organization have the power to do so. If you are not at the top, you must convince those who are, of your program for change. The environment of every human institution, be it a church, business or family, is set by the leadership, and only those at the top can bring about significant change.

Principle 4: Many a fine person has perished in the wrong culture. At times, leaders are matched to the wrong situation, and the best thing they can do for themselves and their followers is to leave. In such cases, the leader's values are too far different from those of the new corporate culture he has attempted to enter. Sometimes it is the fault of the search committee that recruited the new leader without adequately doing its homework: Matching the values of the group to the values of the recruit is a vital part of the process. At times it is the follower who does not fit. In this case, a new worker, volunteer or member joins an organization only to find out quickly that they have major problems with the values of their newly adopted group. Perish or parachute, the choice is yours! For the low person on the totem pole, change will be very difficult indeed.

Principle 5: Leaders that excel today know their cultures and shape them for optimal success. An effective leader must get a handle on the culture of his organization and shape it in such a way as to build a positive, empowering, enabling setting that will foster the very best in people. One of the few core essentials today's leaders must master is a deep understanding of the core values that drive the group. Those core values create the corporate culture.

STRONG CULTURES CREATE SUCCESSFUL ENTERPRISES

A great deal is being said today in secular management and leadership studies about corporate culture. Successful companies such as Avis and Motorola usually appear as examples of companies that are successful because they devote much of their energies on a corporate leadership level to promoting and cultivating corporate culture. They put much of their energy into managing employees' behavior through creating a strong culture.

In 1982, Tom Peters and Robert Waterman wrote an immensely popular book, *In Search of Excellence: Lessons from America's Best-Run Companies*, in which they showed the benefits and characteristics of the strong corporate cultures of America's best business organizations. Though the passage of time and corporate changes have undermined some of their analysis of corporate America, their work has taught us a great deal. They brought to focus the realization that strong cultures contribute significantly to the organizational success of companies when the culture supports the mission, goals and strategy of the organization.

The pursuit of excellence is certainly something anyone involved in the leadership of a Christian organization ought to be about. The Scriptures exhort the Church in many places to do whatever it does to the glory of God, "So whether you eat or drink or whatever you do, do it all for the glory of God" (1 Cor. 10:31, *NIV*). We are also implored to perform our duties to the best of our abilities, as when Paul states, "Whatever you do, work at it with all your heart, as working for the Lord, not for men, since you know that you will receive an inheritance from the Lord as a reward. It is the Lord Christ you are serving" (Col. 3:23,24, *NIV*).

If you desire to be successful as a leader you desire a good thing. To create the culture that enables your followers to succeed may make all the difference in how you will be remembered as a leader. To this pursuit we will now give our attention.

CORPORATE CULTURE: THE WAY WE DO THINGS AROUND HERE

Before we move to the concrete steps necessary for building a successful culture for followers to flourish, it is necessary to get a handle on the nature of this powerful yet unseen world we label "corporate culture."

The word "culture" can be as vague as the word "love"—it means different things to different people. To my wife, Donna, it may mean an evening concert in downtown Chicago. To a biochemist, it refers to something grown in a petri dish. To anthropologists, culture is that formidable barrier that must be penetrated to understand a foreign audience. To leaders, organizational culture is the unseen set of rules and expected behaviors that embody the values of the group. The corporate culture is the environment created by the leaders of an organization in which everyone must work. As we have already stated, that environment can either foster or hamper productivity and corporate success.

The term "culture" was for many years reserved as part of the descriptive domain of anthropologists and sociologists. Today, however, it has become a buzz word in leadership and management circles. Anyone who has an interest in leadership or management will run into the concept of "corporate culture" regularly. It is discussed widely and is increasingly recognized as one of the fundamental building blocks of organizational life.

Traditionally, culture has been defined as simply the unique customs, values and artifacts of a people. Today, a growing consensus prevails in the business community that organizations have distinct cultures as well, the same distinct customs, values and artifacts we usually think of societies as possessing. It is also a growing conviction in management circles that those cultures need to be understood, nurtured and managed. For those who work in churches and Christian organizations, the principles are equally valid.

I define corporate culture with this simple phrase: "It's the way we do things around here." Or, if you prefer a definition with a bit more meat: "Corporate culture is the way insiders behave based on the values and group traditions they hold."

Ralph Kilmann writes this about the power of corporate culture: "The organization itself has an invisible quality—a certain style, a character, a way of doing things—that may be more powerful than the dictates of any one person or any formally documented system. To understand the essence or soul of the organization requires that we travel below the charts, rule books, machines, and buildings into the underground world of corporate cultures."[1]

In my first few years at the helm of our global mission organization, I have probably given more attention to cultivating issues of our organization's culture than to anything else. If I do not create the right culture for others to succeed, I can never hope to realize my bold dreams for us as an effective ministry.

I have come to see the great value of creating and sustaining the right leadership culture because organizational culture is like glue in plywood: you don't see it and are not fully aware of it until you try to take it apart. It is in fact one of the most powerful forces that determines what can and cannot be accomplished by the group. The success or failure of the leader depends on it. The fulfillment of all followers is cultivated within it. The leader who fails to understand the culture of his organization can never hope to harness it for visionary purposes.

Organizational culture is like a unique corporate fingerprint, unique face and unique personality that is part of your organization. Considering the billions of people on earth, God in His infinite creativity has designed every one of us with a different face, voice print, fingerprint and personality. Organizations are the same way. Each one has a totally unique and distinct composition we call its corporate culture. That culture is built upon the values and belief systems that percolate up from the core of its leadership like molten lava bubbling out of a volcano. We may think one church is like the next, but in reality each has its very distinct culture, built on the heritage of its leaders. To understand the culture is to learn what makes this group unique in its contribution to the world. These values form the bedrock for developing mission statements, vision and momentum.

KEY STRATEGIES FOR CREATING CULTURES WHERE FOLLOWERS SUCCEED

Now let's get to the bottom lines. How does the leader create the culture that can foster energy, forward momentum and success? It is accomplished by implementing seven key strategies, which might be recalled by using the word CULTURE as an acrostic. The letters stand for the following strategies:

C reate and sustain a compelling vision.
U nderstand the culture you are leading.
L isten to your followers and foster a learning atmosphere.
T rust others with a piece of the action.
U nderstand your special role as a servant-leader.
R espect every person on the team.
E mphasize your corporate values every chance you get.

Once a leader recognizes that his organizational climate has everything to do with his success as a leader, then he is more likely to be ready to get to work on creating that culture.

CREATE AND SUSTAIN A
COMPELLING VISION

Leadership is about the future. "Leader" implies that someone is taking others to a destination beyond the here and now. If I don't know where we are going, can I really expect others to find fulfillment in following me? That would be like the time I got hopelessly lost jogging in the backwoods of Prescott Pines, Arizona, and tried to convince the runner who was with me that I knew where I was going. It soon became obvious and as soon as it did, he quit following me!

Every group, organization, church, club or government agency needs a compelling vision people can believe in. This is especially true for the younger generations today. The busters and generation Xers are looking for a cause to believe in, something to which they can become committed. Vision is that which galvanizes the group, the compass that is constantly pointing out to everyone the group's agreed-upon destination.

A leader who has articulated vision carefully and continually will build up a large measure of trust among his followers. In the words of Warren Bennis and Burt Nanus:

> In order for followers to trust their leaders they expect the leadership to create and sustain a compelling vision. The leader's vision for the organization must be clear, attractive and attainable. We tend to trust leaders who create these visions, since vision represents the context for shared beliefs in a common organizational purpose.[2]

The people who follow you must have a sense that you are taking them somewhere—a sense of momentum and forward movement. The more you can communicate that direction—what we are calling "vision" these days—the more the workers/members have a good sense of motivation about the future.

Have you specified your corporate vision and mission? Do the troops know it? Have they memorized it? Job number one of leadership is to determine, carefully craft and preach the vision inside and outside the organization. Based on your group's values, develop a distinct expression of where you are going as a group. Learn how to state that direction in a mission and vision statement.

As a leader, spend some time alone and sort out your own values for the organization. Then work it through with your leadership team and decide on a set of beliefs the whole team stands for in relation to what your work is about and how you plan to accomplish it. From those core values and beliefs arise mission and vision statements that become the rallying cry of your group.

MISSION AND VISION STATEMENTS ARE LIKE: GLUE—THEY HELP LEADERS HOLD AN ORGANIZATION TOGETHER. A MAGNET—THEY ATTRACT NEWCOMERS AS MEMBERS, EMPLOYEES, CUSTOMERS OR DONORS. A RULER—THE TOOL BY WHICH A LEADER CAN MEASURE HOW HIS GROUP IS DOING.

During my first year as CEO of our mission, I carefully took our leadership team through the exercise of developing a fresh mission and vision statement. Out of those two statements flow our nine strategic priorities as an organization. The mission statement more than anything else embodies what we as a group hope to accomplish. It has galvanized us together in one spirit and we are working toward the common goal with a renewed passion. Our mission statement looks like this:

THE MISSION OF CB INTERNATIONAL
In vital partnership with churches at home and abroad, the mission of CB International is to be a pioneering force in fulfilling Christ's Commission to the final frontiers of the harvest.

This mission statement has caught on well and defines our essence. At strategic decision-making points, as we grapple with issues and draw conclusions, we test those conclusions against the mission statement: it is our standard. We constantly ask ourselves this question: Will this help us reach our mission or are we merely prolonging traditions that should be allowed to die a natural death?

I have challenged everyone in my organization to memorize our mission statement. They know they can make points with me if they recite it by heart. I preach it from the housetops and print it on every brochure, flyer and piece of literature we produce. You will even find it on our official CBI coffee mugs!

As Leroy Eims has said, "A leader is one who sees more than others see, who sees farther than others see, and who sees before others do."[3] The future is our business as leaders. That future must be packaged in a vision that can clearly communicate your leadership ideals.

UNDERSTAND THE CULTURE YOU ARE LEADING

The organizational culture of a group is the way insiders behave based on the values and group traditions they hold. If you are a new leader, your number one job is to study the values and group traditions that make people behave as they do. It will help you lead effectively and it will help enormously in the process of enfolding new members into the group.

Even if you have been around your organization a long time, you have perhaps never stopped to think about the culture of your organization. The time is now and you need help, because those closest and most familiar with the culture have the hardest time seeing it for what it really is. You cannot truly appreciate the uniqueness of your own culture until you get outside of your context and experience other cultures. If you are too familiar with your organization, gather others around you who can interpret your culture for you from an outsider's perspective.

Each time we gain two or three new employees at our home office, or each time we recruit a new group of missionaries for service overseas, I spend an hour with them describing our corporate culture and values. They will have already learned a great deal as outsiders who are entering with the fresh perspective of outsiders. As new insiders, however, they need to hear from me exactly what are our values and group traditions.

It is amazing just how different two organizations can be. A leader must understand those differences. In the past decade I have worked in two entirely different kinds of corporate cultures, which I will label in the following diagram as organization 1 and organization 2. Making the leadership jump from one to the other caused greater culture shock than any experience I have ever had—including my experiences as a missionary on foreign soil.

Here is a comparison of the two organizations as I experienced them:

Organization 1	Organization 2
Paper culture	Oral culture
Policy driven	Idea driven

Reserved	Cutting edge
Historically driven	Future driven
Traditional	Avant-garde
Little change	Constant change
Coats and ties	Jeans and T-shirts
Quiet	Noisy
Low tech	High tech
Slow pace	Kinetic pace
Male dominated	Dual gender leadership
Created by WWIIers	Created by boomers

Of course, no two organizations are the same. And some are at opposite ends of the culture continuum. Imagine the shock of moving from one of these organizations to the other. As a member. As a follower. As the leader! You could go schizophrenic if you did not take the time to understand how different values and different principles have caused their cultures to emerge the way they have.

How can you get a handle on corporate culture? Take time out with your leaders and study your culture and find out what your values really are. Two excellent resources are *The Power of Vision* by George Barna and *Visionary Leadership* by Burt Nanus.[4]

LISTEN TO YOUR FOLLOWERS, FOSTER A LEARNING ATMOSPHERE

Two of the most important words in any leader's vocabulary should be these: "listen" and "learn." Listening means you truly respect your followers. Learning means changing—demonstrating to your followers that you are a change agent and not merely a protector of the institution and the status quo.

"IN TIMES OF CHANGE, LEARNERS INHERIT THE EARTH, WHILE THE LEARNED FIND THEMSELVES BEAUTIFULLY EQUIPPED TO DEAL WITH A WORLD THAT NO LONGER EXISTS."

Listening and learning are the two keys leaders must use to combat institutionalization and stagnation—constant threats that will calcify us unless intentionally rejected. Organizations get into deep trouble when they shift from a primary focus on their *purpose* to primary focus on *preservation*. Leaders trying to preserve the status quo close themselves off to reality and new possibilities and listen to only those voices that agree with them. In contrast, learning leaders listen.

The more people you lead, the more you must listen. That is why God gave us two ears but only one mouth. Effective leadership has more to do with listening than with talking. Some days I get literally worn out listening to the problems and ideas my staff bring me. I do not want to listen to one more person, but I realize that leadership demands it and they deserve it from me.

Leaders by their very nature tend to be removed from the front lines of battle in the organization. Therefore they must listen to those in the trenches, and rely on the information they provide to make wise decisions. I am thoroughly convinced that the greatest innovations and strides forward we will make will arise from ideas generated at the fringes of our organization. I certainly do not have all the answers; I do not even know some of the key questions that will unlock our future. The answers come from those doing the work. How will we ever harvest those profound ideas if we do not listen long, listen hard and listen often?

Trust Others with a Piece of the Action

Blessed are the control freaks, for they shall inhibit the earth.

Of all the leadership sins I have ever observed, nothing destroys morale more than the control freak. Leaders who major in control have the following traits:

Think they, alone, have all the answers;
Think they know best because they were there first;
Have "founderitis"—they are unable to let go of their baby;
Delegate responsibilities without the authority to act;
Reverse decisions others were asked to make;
Keep colleagues in the dark about important decisions that
    affect them;
Won't give others room to make their mark in the organization.

The great problem that caused the collapse of the Soviet Union was not political, but economic—communism did not believe in private ownership. Everyone had a job but no one worked because they had no pride of ownership or the incentive of personal profitability. Ownership, of an idea, a purpose, a process or an outcome, is the key to human motivation. Because the Russian government controlled everything, no one was given a piece of the action to be responsible to build a productive society of responsible citizens.

To use another analogy, giving a worker a serious piece of the action with ownership authority is like moving from renting an apartment to owning your own home. All of a sudden the pride of ownership kicks in, and personal motivation shoots skyward. The worker is no longer just passing through and punching a clock, but realizes he will be evaluated as a person based on the quality of the job he is doing. He begins to see that his piece of the organization can make a real difference in the outcome of the whole group. When the ownership stakes are raised, the followers' level of commitment soars proportionately.

In creating a culture in which workers flourish, leaders must give followers a real stake in the organization. Every member of the group must be allowed to have authority and ownership over some part of the work. A leader must quit looking over everyone's shoulders and give people freedom to work their plans on their own. That includes giving people room to fail, for failure is part of learning and part of developing successful team players.

UNDERSTAND YOUR SPECIAL ROLE AS A SERVANT-LEADER

Top down leadership is dead. Today's workers, employees and volunteers expect to be a part of the decision-making process in their organizations. Effective leaders today have closed the distance between leader and follower, coming out of closed off mahogany executive suites and into the open-office world of the workers. Leadership accessibility and teamwork are the buzzwords of the 1990s.

I probably spend an average of half of each office work day at my desk, and the other half wandering around the organization touching base with employees. I want them to know I am accessible, and that I will be glad to step in and help them be successful in their work. I know that when they are successful, I am doing my job and will get good reviews from my board of directors.

A servant-leader sees his role differently than does a traditional, top down, dictatorial leader. The servant is present to make the worker successful, not vice versa. My workers/employees are not hired to serve me, but to serve the mission of the organization. My role as their leader is to facilitate their effectiveness in any way I can, much like a coach tries to get optimum performance out of the team players.

For those of us who claim to be Bible-adhering Christians, servant leadership should be a no-brainer. Our Lord modeled and taught this style of leadership right up to the night He was betrayed, even washing the feet of His disciples to demonstrate servanthood: "Now that I, your Lord and Teacher, have washed your feet, you also should wash one another's feet. I have set you an example that you should do as I have done for you" (John 13:14,15, *NIV*). Then in Mark 9:35 *(NIV)*, we read, "Sitting down, Jesus called the Twelve and said, 'If anyone wants to be first, he must be the very last, and the servant of all.'"

Because the leader is the keeper of the culture, it falls on his shoulders to cultivate a culture that is distinctly Christian. Usually, whatever the values and beliefs of the leader may be, those same values and beliefs become the operative assumptions of the followers. That puts a great deal of responsibility on the shoulder of the leader. Christian leaders should strive for model servant leadership, leading in ways that are clearly distinct from the hierarchical secular model.

Here is the bottom line on servant leadership: The focus of a servant-leader is creating the best climate and investing in human cultivation, not majoring in control.

RESPECT EVERY MEMBER OF YOUR TEAM

The smaller the ego, the bigger the leader. About a year ago I called my staff together and informed them that I expected the greatest ideas and most important advances in CB International to come from them—the troops, not us, the leaders. Our role, as leaders, is to make them successful. To back up that leadership philosophy we drafted and circulated a set of core values we believe about our workers.

When you not only invest the resources to develop such a statement of beliefs about the importance of each person who comprises your team, but also share those perspectives with them in a way that says "you really count," your colleagues will have a tangible understanding of how much you respect them as partners in ministry. If you treat them like cogs in a machine, mere "worker ants," their loyalty and productivity will reflect that culture. Give them respect and the dignity they deserve, and soon they will be ready to do anything for you. Be careful, though: respect must be genuine; it cannot be faked.

CB International's Core Values

Values create, shape and perpetuate the ethos of an organization. In pursuit of CBI's objectives, the following underlying values characterize every aspect of CBI's endeavor as it relates to the members of our organization:

1. *Individual Dignity*

We diligently maintain and promote the dignity and worth of each individual within CBI's ministries worldwide. People with a proper sense of spiritual and emotional well-being are freed for productive ministry that is committed to goal-oriented planning and team accountability.

2. *Corporate Creativity*

We encourage creative and innovative strategies directed by the Spirit of God and implemented through policies and structures which are characterized by mutual trust and cooperation.

3. *Uncompromising Integrity*

We adhere uncompromisingly to honesty and integrity in all matters pertaining to the missions enterprise whatever the consequences. This will always be manifested by biblical standards of ethics, morality and financial accountability wherever CB International's personnel are involved.

4. *Personal Development*

We are committed at all levels of leadership to creating an organizational climate conducive to continuing personal growth and development in missionary service. Management is implemented as a ministry of enablement and encouragement.

Emphasize Values Every Chance You Get

Corporate culture is the lifeblood of an organization. A fundamental task of a leader is to convey that culture at all times, to all who will listen.

> A corporation's values are its life's blood. Without effective communication, actively practiced, without the art of scrutiny, those values will disappear in a sea of trivial memos and impertinent reports.[5]

If the leader cannot and does not articulate the values that should be emphasized, organizational drift occurs. On the other hand, leaders who understand values and can articulate them well to the organization have a proven track record of superior performance. These leaders have harnessed the culture for the good of the group, and have created a truly effective organization of fulfilled followers.

James Kouzes and Barry Posner found six significant payoffs for both managers and their organizations when the leaders were well versed in articulating a unified and distinct organizational culture. They wrote the following about such a culture:

1. Fosters strong feelings of personal effectiveness.
2. Promotes high levels of company loyalty.
3. Facilitates consensus about key organizational goals and stake holders.
4. Encourages ethical behavior.
5. Reduces levels of job stress and tension.
6. Promotes strong norms about working hard and caring.[6]

So how do you articulate the values of your group? Two examples will show how two very different organizations have summarized the basics in a document about their values. The first is Church Resource Ministries, a cutting-edge, West Coast ministry designed to foster the healthy development of church leadership. Each new member of CRM's team is given a copy of the following document. The content identifies a set of foundational values that will form the basis of leader-follower relationships at CRM.

The second example is from my own experience leading CB International. After two years into the CEO role, one of my key leaders asked me to put in writing what I valued most from our followers. I appreciated her request and the following is the result, now handed out widely throughout our organization.

THE EXPECTATIONS AND PRIVILEGES OF CRM STAFF

As a staff person with CRM, it is fair for me to expect the following from those whom I follow throughout the organization. I can expect:

* To know those who lead me and what they believe.
  If I follow you, will I know who you are? What are you like? Are you authentic? Are you honest? Will you deal with me with integrity?

* To have leaders who will explain to me their vision.
  What do you see for me? What's the future and how do I fit? Do you care about my future? Will you have a place for me or will you simply use me?

* To never be left in isolation.
  Are you there for me? Do you love me? Will you love me? Do you care about my cares? My concerns? My needs?

* To be heard.
  To whom will you listen? Will I be heard? Taken seriously? Appreciated?

* To be trusted.
  Can I take initiative without fear? Will my creativity be rewarded and encouraged? Will I be respected?

* To be provided a context for growth.
  Will I be encouraged to be a lifelong learner? Will my gifts be increasingly identified and expressed? Can I live in a context where God's power can be freely manifested in my life? Will I be developed?

* To be held accountable.
  Will I be held accountable for personal godliness and holiness in all aspects of life and ministry? Will I be fairly evaluated for the performance of my responsibilities? Will I be lovingly held to God's best for my life?

* To be the object of grace.
  Will I be forgiven, even in the face of shortcomings, inadequacies and failure? Will I have the freedom to be whom God has made me? Will I be led with kindness?

WAYS TO SCORE AT CB INTERNATIONAL

Success in any organization comes from following this simple rule: "Find out how they keep score, and score!"—Hans Finzel

Demonstrate Belief in CBI's Mission, Vision and Values:
Believe in CBI's mission and vision—memorize our mission statement
Have a passion for growth—it's a sign of abundant life
Think of new ways for CBI to fulfill its mission and to do it more effectively.

Be a CBI Pioneer:
Take risks to accomplish greater things
Develop a pioneer mentality for problem solving
Display creativity and innovation in your work area—new ways to approach old problems
Generate new ideas that work to make things better
Strive daily for continuous improvement—"kaizen"
Push the technology envelope—work smarter.

Practice Excellence:
Care about a high standard of excellence
Set the standards—don't just follow what others do
Develop a disdain for mediocrity
Promote the use of state of the art graphics and publications
Strive for customer satisfaction: our donors, pastors, missionaries and nationals.

KISS—Keep It Simple:
Reduce paperwork and increase efficiency
Simplify the bureaucracy and fight institutionalism
Flat organizations work better—reduce layers of decision-makers
Practice the ODD approach: outsource, downsize and deconstruct layers of inefficiency
Ask for the authority to make more decisions that affect you.

Promote a Team Mentality—"We" Is Better Than "Me":
Develop ways to work in teams
If you lead—delegate!

Whether you lead or follow—communicate!
If you lead—empower others
If you lead—push responsible decision-making downstream
Recognize that teams come up with the greatest ideas.

Display a Kingdom Mentality:
Don't be concerned with who gets the credit
Share the blessing with others—don't worry about "turf"
Have a kingdom mentality, don't beat the denomination drum
Give outsiders what they request
Network, network and network.

Help Create a Fun Place to Work:
Believe that work is fun
Avoid whining at all costs
Show grace with everyone inside and out
Be positive and encourage a job well done.

GET TO THE POINT

I am a bottom-line kind of person. If I had to point to two or three keys that will create the kind of culture in which followers will reach peak performance, I would settle on these:

- *Propel your group forward with a clearly articulated vision.* Forward momentum is an essential building block for any healthy group, and it is up to the group's leaders to provide it. Without it, followers degenerate into nothing more than lukewarm clock punchers or frustrated dreamers. Rally the troops and instill enthusiasm for a bright future by developing a compelling vision for tomorrow.
- *Create a learning spirit among your leaders.* Humility is the key to learning, and leaders who are servants humbly admit that they do not even know half of the answers. You can provide strong leadership and direction for an organization but still cultivate a learning spirit in all the members. If you believe your followers are your greatest resource, you will listen to them and teach them to listen to others.
- *Demonstrate a commitment to grace in relationships.* Too

many people are too hard on each other, and this seems particularly true in the Church. Why would the very community founded on the greatest display of grace be so harsh with one another? Leaders should approach their followers in a spirit of gentle grace and allow room for failure. This is not to excuse habitual irresponsibility or chronic incompetence, but to give people who want to grow a chance to rise to their full potential.

Servant leadership will go a long way to create this kind of climate in your organization, by having those in charge display a better way to be out front:

Also a dispute arose among them as to which of them was considered to be greatest. Jesus said to them, "The kings of the Gentiles lord it over them; and those who exercise authority over them call themselves Benefactors. But you are not to be like that. Instead, the greatest among you should be like the youngest, and the one who rules like the one who serves" (Luke 22:24-26, *NIV*).

Notes
1. Ralph Kilmann, *Beyond the Quick Fix* (San Francisco: Jossey-Bass, 1984), p. 92.
2. Warren Bennis and Burt Nanus, *Leaders* (San Francisco: Harper & Row, 1985), p. 154.
3. Leroy Eims, *Be the Leader You Are Meant To Be* (Wheaton, Ill.: Victor Books, 1975), p. 55.
4. The full citations for these excellent resources are George Barna, *The Power of Vision* (Ventura, Calif.: Regal Books, 1992); and Burt Nanus, *Visionary Leadership* (San Francisco: Jossey-Bass Publishers, 1992).
5. Max DePree, *Leadership Is an Art* (New York: Dell Books, 1989), p. 108.
6. James Kouzes and Barry Posner, *The Leadership Challenge* (San Francisco: Jossey-Bass Publications, 1987), p. 193.

FOURTEEN

THE IMPORTANCE
OF PRAYER IN
LEADING PEOPLE

C. PETER WAGNER

Christian leaders can lead with or without prayer. This, I realize, is axiomatic. Christian parents can raise a family with or without prayer. Christian students can study with or without prayer. This chapter, however, is based on a fundamental premise: Whatever Christian people do, things will go better with prayer. This, of course, includes Christian leadership, whether it be a pastor leading a church, a coach leading an athletic team, a construction supervisor leading a work crew, an office manager leading a staff or you name it.

My remarks in this chapter are directed a bit more specifically toward pastoral leadership than toward other kinds of leadership. My professional role is that of a trainer of pastors, and consequently most of my thinking has revolved around the church leadership context. If your context for leading is not the pastorate, however, take heart: You will not find it difficult to adapt these principles for powerful prayer to your own situation, whatever it may be.

I imagine that many who turn to this chapter will expect it to suggest they should pray more. Although I firmly believe that most of us, including me, should pray more, I am not going to focus on the quantity of prayer as much as on its quality. Christian bookstores are well stocked with books that give excellent reasons why we should pray more and how to do so. Few of them, however, elaborate on the premise that not all prayer is equal. That is what I hope to do in the next few pages.

ALL PRAYER IS NOT THE SAME

If it is true that prayer will make leadership more effective, it follows that the higher the quality of prayer, the higher might be the quality of leadership. The rather common, but naive, notion that all prayer is of the same quality can greatly dilute the effectiveness of prayer. James says: "The effective, fervent prayer of a righteous man [person] avails much" (Jas. 5:16). As if anticipating the question, "But how can we know the difference?" James immediately goes on to use Elijah as his example of one who engaged in effective prayer. It is very simple: Elijah prayed that it wouldn't rain and it didn't; he prayed that it would rain and it did!

Is that kind of prayer possible today? James seems to think it is because he immediately adds, "Elijah was a man with a nature like ours" (v. 17). I realize that most of us may not have experienced prayer quite that powerful regularly, but if not, I am going to suggest in this chapter at least three things leaders like us can do about it.

First, we can individually move to improve the quality of our prayer life.

Second, we can move the people we lead in that direction as well.

Third, we can recruit intercessors whose prayer lives may already be much nearer to Elijah's example to pray specifically for us.

PRAYER AND CHURCH GROWTH

My title at Fuller Seminary is Professor of Church Growth. I have spent the better part of three decades studying and analyzing why it is that some churches grow while others do not. Many principles of church growth have been discovered and thoroughly field tested in recent years. Although much more is yet to be learned, we nevertheless have accumulated quite a good bit of knowledge concerning the dynamics of church growth. Curiously, however, relatively little has been discovered about how prayer can exert a cause-and-effect relationship to church growth.

This surprised me when I first began to research, write and teach about prayer back in 1987. I had previously heard so much about the importance of prayer that I expected to find many available resources about prayer and church growth when I began to build my library on the subject. But, no. In 1987 I could not find a single work on how prayer might or might not affect the growth of churches. Many sermons were on record declaring the importance of prayer, but very little confirming research. I say "very little" because there was one exception to the rule: the remarkable church growth in Korea, which, in almost every analysis, was attributed largely to prayer.

Since 1987, a bit more research has been done. The first work on the subject I am aware of was Terry Teykl's booklet *Pray and Grow*, which was published in 1988. Kirk Hadaway included a section about prayer in his book *Church Growth Principles*, reporting that there seemed to be somewhat more of an emphasis on prayer in the Southern Baptist churches, which broke out of a growth plateau as compared to churches that remained on the plateau. Marlin Mull conducted a study of Wesleyan Churches and found that the growing churches registered a higher degree of participation in their annual "Forty Days of Prayer and Fasting" program than did the nongrowing churches.

At the same time, John Vaughan, regarded as the national expert on large churches, wrote a book entitled *Megachurches and America's Cities*. In it, he analyzes the characteristics of churches that draw two thousand or more in weekly worship attendance. One of Vaughan's most interesting chapters is "Predictable Changes in Growing Churches," in which he lists twenty of the differences he sees as most significant in the growth of large churches as compared to smaller ones. Not one of the changes mentioned talks about prayer! This does not mean that John Vaughan belittles prayer. As a personal friend, I can attest that he holds prayer in high esteem. It does mean, however, that after extensive research, it did not occur to him to list prayer among the twenty most important growth characteristics.

A similar study was published by the Evangelistic Association of New England in 1995. They attempted something that many of us had been hoping would be done for quite some time. They undertook the task of developing a measuring instrument to measure the quality of a given church. Overall, it is an excellent piece of work. Ten salient characteristics of church quality appear on their scale. Again, though, not one of the ten is prayer! The word "prayer" is mentioned only once in the document, "Ten Characteristics of a Healthy Church"—and that almost in passing.

THE PRAYER CREDIBILITY GAP

Prayer is so prominent in the Bible and so dear to the hearts of Christian people everywhere that it would be virtually unthinkable for a pastor to entertain the thought that there might not be a direct cause-and-effect relationship between prayer and church growth. Because of that, a standard rhetoric has emerged. Locate the pastors of one hundred growing churches and ask each of them what role prayer plays in the growth of their churches. Without exception, all one hundred pastors would respond with words to the effect: "Prayer plays a key role. Without prayer our church definitely would not be growing."

Suppose, however, we examined and analyzed the prayer life and ministry of these one hundred growing churches? I would be surprised if more than five of the one hundred churches would have a prayer ministry any more active and more dynamic than that of the many other churches in their community that were not growing. In other words, probably ninety-five of them would have a mediocre prayer ministry. Why, then, are they growing? It is quite simple. They are employing sound church growth principles backed by a little bit of prayer. They talk about prayer, but much of it is rhetoric, not action.

I would think that the ninety-five could be compared to an 8-cylinder automobile running on 5 or 6 cylinders. It may be able to move forward, but it is certainly not all it was intended to be. If our hypothetical churches could change their rhetoric prayer into action prayer, I believe they would better fulfill God's true potential for them. Prayer, as most pastors affirm, really is important. It is a recognized divine principle that spiritual power will tend to increase as effective prayer increases in congregations.

MAKING PRAYER MORE EFFECTIVE

I personally know a good deal about prayer as rhetoric. For about the first twenty-five years of my professional career, I could have been described as an ordained minister of rhetoric prayer. I have now changed, and enough time has elapsed for me to analyze the specific areas in my own life that needed new attitudes and new thinking. If leaders desire to pray more effectively, and to help those whom they lead draw on God's supernatural power through prayer, they would do well to consider the following principles:

• *Prayer is a two-way street.*

At its very core, prayer should be seen as a relationship between two persons. Prayer leaders are virtually unanimous in asserting that the most important quality of prayer needs to be establishing an intimacy with the Father. My research on prayer and prayer movements has made it clear that certain people are capable of attaining more intimacy with God through prayer than are others.

Interacting with them can easily foster an unnecessary and frequently counterproductive guilt trip. I was somewhat susceptible to that myself, and it took me awhile to learn to live with the fact that on good days I might rank at only about a 7 on an intimacy scale of 1 to 10. But 7 is better than 5—or zero! My advice is that you set a goal to move as high on the scale as you can, but not to be overly disappointed if you fall short of perfection. Meanwhile, we must realize that intimacy at any level, if it is between two persons, requires a give and take.

A common assumption about prayer is that it is a monologue. In our church services, many of us have never seen or heard prayers that are anything but a one-way street. The pastor, other people, or the whole congregation together talk to God, expecting Him to listen. Even in times of silent prayer, each of us as individuals are expected to do the same thing. Period.

I now see prayer as not only talking to God, but also listening for, and actually hearing His voice. If God is our Father, it stands to reason that we should do this. When my own father was alive, I called him on the phone every Sunday. It would not have entered our minds for me to talk and him to listen and say nothing.

Many of us, particularly those who come from the more traditional streams of Christianity, have shied away from trying to hear the voice of God because of an exaggerated application of a good theological principle. The principle, a very important one, is the inspiration and authority of the Scriptures. We have been taught to regard the Bible not only as the *Word* of God, but as *the* Word of God. A corollary for many of us has been that all that God has desired to reveal to the human race is contained in the sixty-six books of the Bible. Expecting to hear God's authentic voice outside the Scriptures is then seen as wrong. God, we have been told, does not engage in "extrabiblical revelation."

What I have just said sounds strange to growing numbers of Christian people today. Believers in Pentecostal and "new apostolic" (sometimes referred to as "postdenominational") churches in the Western world, and in most all churches in the Third World, believe they hear the voice of God apart from what is written in the Bible (although not contradicting what is in the Bible) regularly, even in their church services. Frequently what God is saying will be announced publicly through prophecy. Many are bold enough to declare "Thus saith the Lord," followed by the prophetic message.

I realize that some leaders may not be open to this because they have been taught what is known as the doctrine of "cessationism." The premise is that the so-called "sign gifts" (e.g., tongues, miracles, healing) ceased with the end of the apostolic age. After the New Testament had been written and compiled, such sign gifts as prophecy were no longer needed. It goes without saying that cessationist theology, which has been very popular for several generations, has been a chief contributing factor to the assumption that prayer is only a one-way street. Fortunately, cessationism is quite rapidly going out of style.

• *Prayer works.*

The second important change that many of us need to make is to realize that prayer really works. Without this, we will never get far beyond rhetoric prayer. By this I mean that if we pray, things will happen that would not have happened if we had not prayed.

Not all Christian leaders believe this. This weakness is again because of an exaggerated application of a good theological point: this time, the sovereignty of God. If God is not sovereign, He is not God. He is the creator and sustainer of the whole universe. So far, so good. Does the fact that the sovereign God knows everything in the past, present and future, also mean that He has predetermined everything that will ever happen in history? If so, forget about action prayer. The best that prayer could possibly do under such circumstances would be to benefit those who pray so that they can more cheerfully conform to what God has determined to do anyway, whether they pray or not.

One of the best statements of what I consider a more correct and more helpful theology of prayer comes from a chapter title in Jack Hayford's book *Prayer Is Invading the Impossible.* Hayford says, "If we don't, He won't." Neither Hayford nor anyone else would say, "If we don't, He can't." This would deny that God is sovereign. Fortunately, we can have it both ways. How?

• *Plan A or Plan B?*

A sovereign God would create the universe exactly the way He wanted it. For reasons of His own, God designed human history with what we might call in current language "Plan A" and "Plan B." The difference about whether, in a particular situation, we end up with Plan A, the best, or Plan B, the second best, can frequently depend on the choices we make, as human beings created in the image of God. For a starter, look at Adam and Eve. If, in the Garden of Eden, they had obeyed God rather than the devil, human history would undoubtedly have been a lot different. The same thing can be applied to our understanding of prayer. I like the way Richard Foster puts it in *The Celebration of Discipline*: "We are working with God to determine the future. Certain things will happen in history if we pray rightly."

As an example, I need only to repeat the illustration of effective prayer seen in the book of James. Elijah prayed that it would not rain, and it didn't; then he prayed that it would rain, and it did. James's presumption is that history would have been different if Elijah had not prayed.

Or let me cite one of the more dramatic examples in my own life, told in detail in my book *Prayer Shield*. A few years ago, I fell from a ladder, landing on the back of my head and neck on a cement floor. At exactly the same moment, an intercessor, several miles away, heard the voice of God, prayed intensely and effectively, and not only was my life saved, but I also received no major injury from the fall. Both my wife and I are convinced that history would have been different were it not for her specific prayer. Doris most likely would have been a widow!

Without entering into two-way prayer, hearing the voice of God, and realizing that prayer really works, effective prayer for a leader and for those being led will continue to be elusive.

MOBILIZING YOUR PEOPLE FOR PRAYER

The task of leading people in prayer involves bringing the whole group to the place where prayer is a significant part of their daily lives and where positive changes can reasonably be attributed to God's answers to prayer. In the case of a pastor, the congregation should be recognized by themselves and by others as a praying congregation and the growth and health of the church will presumably rise to levels not previously seen. How can this be done?

I recommend that pastors who wish to lead their congregations to a superior lifestyle of prayer allocate adequate amounts of time and energy to three primary tasks: (1) teaching the people the rules of prayer, (2) visibly modeling a lifestyle of prayer and (3) organizing and programming for prayer.

1. Teach the rules of prayer.

The field of prayer is so vast that it would be difficult to catalog all the varieties of prayer, the rules of prayer and the methods of prayer known to Christian people. The nearest I have seen is Richard Foster's book *Prayer*, which some have referred to as our "cookbook of prayer." I mention that because in this section on the rules of prayer, I have chosen the four I feel are the most important rules for a leader to communicate to others, knowing full well that these four do not comprise an exhaustive list and that other authors might have chosen a different set of four.

Nevertheless, I would not expect many congregations to reach significantly higher levels of prayer without thoroughly absorbing these four rules into their daily thinking and acting.

Praying with Faith

The first rule is praying with faith. "Jesus answered and said to them, 'Have faith in God. For assuredly, I say to you, whoever says to this mountain, "Be removed and be cast into the sea," and does not doubt in his heart, but believes that those things he says will be done, he will have whatever he says'" (Mark 11:22,23). The stress here is on faith that means not to doubt, but to believe. Faith is the "substance of things hoped for" (Heb. 11:1), or facing the future with the confidence of God's blessing.

The more certain we are that what we are praying for is God's will, the more faith we can have. When we become accustomed to two-way prayer, we often hear the voice of God telling us what He desires for those of us who lead, as well as for our followers. If and when this happens, our faith level rises enormously because, "This is the confidence that we have in Him, that if we ask anything according to His will, He hears us" (1 John 5:14).

A Pure Heart

The second rule of prayer we need to teach our people is praying with a pure heart. We must constantly be on guard that the motives behind our prayers are the right motives. The higher we find ourselves on the holiness scale, the more powerful will be our prayers. On the other hand, unforgiveness, unconfessed sin and a worldly lifestyle are some of the best known inhibitors of effectiveness in prayer. If such things are not cared for, as they can be with the spiritual resources God gives to every believer, more than likely, our motives in praying will not always be the best. "You ask and do not receive, because you ask amiss, that you may spend it on your pleasures" (Jas. 4:3).

Prayer and Power

Praying with power is the third rule of prayer. The key variable here is being filled with the Holy Spirit. All spiritual power we ever have comes through the Holy Spirit, so it stands to reason that the more filled we are with the Holy Spirit, the better. Is it really possible to be filled with the Holy Spirit? Of course. The reason I mention this is that, in my opinion, some Christian leaders have overcomplicated the explanations of how this normally happens. We sometimes get the idea that to be filled with the Holy Spirit we have to go to a certain kind of meeting, come forward in response to an invitation, have people pray for us and expect some kind of visible, tangible sign to confirm that we have really been filled.

Some may think I oversimplify it, but it seems to me that all we have to do is to ask God to fill us with the Holy Spirit, and then take Him at His word that He will do it. Jesus said, "If a son asks for bread from any father among you, will he give him a stone?" and then He immediately adds: "If you then, being evil, know how to give good gifts to your children, how much more will your heavenly Father give the Holy Spirit to those who ask Him!" (Luke 11:11,13).

Nowhere does the Bible tell us just how long each filling of the Holy Spirit lasts. To be on the safe side, I ask God to fill me each and every day. Furthermore, I believe that He keeps His word and does it. Consequently, as a general rule, I live my life from day to day filled with the Holy Spirit, and I can pray with a good bit of confidence. By this I do not mean I am immune from spiritual ups and downs. No, I am very susceptible. The more mature I become, however, the more the spiritual downs become exceptions rather than the rule.

Practicing Persistence

The fourth rule of prayer is praying with persistence. Almost everyone who has read what the Bible teaches about prayer knows that in most cases praying about something just one time is not enough; we must pray for it again and again before we see the answer we are expecting. How long do we keep praying? We pray persistently and fervently until one of three things happens. First, we pray until we see the answer. For example, I prayed for decades (sometimes not as persistently as I should have) for my father to be saved. When he accepted Christ, I no longer prayed for his salvation.

Second, we pray until God releases us. As we listen to God's voice, frequently He will say words to this effect: "O.K., you've prayed enough about that. I'm releasing you from the burden." We may not have seen the answer, but we obey Him and quit praying about it.

Third, we pray until God says no. An excellent biblical case of this is when Paul prayed that God would remove his "thorn in the flesh," but God told him He felt Paul would be better off with it. This is especially interesting when we realize that the "thorn" was not from God, but a "messenger of Satan." Nevertheless, this was God's answer and Paul was obedient enough not to talk about it to God anymore (see 2 Cor. 12:7-9).

2. Modeling a lifestyle of prayer.

If prayer in leading people is going to be most effective, not only do leaders need to teach the rules of prayer, but they also need to model those rules through their lifestyles. This particularly applies to pastoral leadership. As I began researching the prayer life of local congregations seriously, I found myself coming to what was for me a reluctant conclusion. Let me explain.

As readers of my books such as *Leading Your Church to Growth* will know, a prominent part of my theory of church leadership is that the senior pastors must learn to delegate the ministry to the congregation. The more the pastor leads and the people minister, the greater the church's growth potential. I strongly teach that pastors should help people discover their spiritual gifts, train them in their use, then delegate, delegate, delegate. My assumption was that the senior pastor could delegate the prayer ministry of the church.

On this I was wrong. My reluctant conclusion now is: The prayer life of a local church will rise or fall on the visible modeling of the priority of prayer in the life and ministry of the senior pastor. This is not the only factor in developing a praying church, but it is a prerequisite. I hasten to say that this does not mean the senior pastor needs to be a prayer giant or have the spiritual gift of intercession. Very few pastors have this gift.

It does mean, however, that the pastor or any leader who desires to create a powerful atmosphere of prayer should talk about prayer publicly and privately, should prioritize prayer in the church or organization's program, should provide a budget for prayer and the prayer ministry and should feed the congregation a rich diet of testimonies to answered prayer. Above all, the followers must know that their leader prays for them faithfully and systematically. Several leaders I know announce to their people that they are going to take a whole day, or two days or more, to lock themselves into a hotel room or a retreat center, just to pray for each member of their congregation or for their employees. Before they go, they ask for written requests, assuring the people that once prayed for, the correspondence will be shredded and destroyed, never to be mentioned again in the future.

3. Organization: adding the nuts and bolts.

Once leaders and their people agree about the rules of prayer, and when the leaders are perceived by their followers as individuals for whom prayer is a vital part of their everyday lives, the groundwork has been laid for implementation. Except in cases of extraordinary revival, prayer does not usually happen by itself. It requires intentional structuring and programming. Wise leaders will make sure this happens.

This brings us back to delegation. At the nuts-and-bolts level of structuring a program for prayer, the leader can, and in most cases should, delegate a middle-management person to oversee it, administer it and monitor it. This will work well, providing the leader is continually perceived as a person giving high priority to prayer in every aspect of life. The prayer leader, minister of prayer, prayer coordinator or director of prayer should be a person for whom prayer is a vital part of life, both in conviction and in practice. The ideal person is one who has both the gift of intercession and the gift of administration, but such are few and far between. Intercession is a right-brained activity, while administration is left-brained, and not many people have the ability to operate well in both. The larger the church or organization, the more weight should be given to the administrative side of the equation.

As the prayer movement continues to mature, it is becoming more evident that these persons assigned the day-by-day responsibility of keeping the prayer ministry a vital and active part of the organization are crucial to sustaining prayer past an initial burst of enthusiasm. I can hardly overstress the value of the visible, ongoing investment of time, energy and money in making this happen. I am happy to report that it can now be considered a trend for local churches to open full-time or part-time staff positions for ministers or pastors of prayer. Some of these positions are staffed by volunteers, which is satisfactory providing that the minister of prayer is awarded full staff status in the church.

In the business world, this is not yet a discernible trend, but substantial beginnings have been made. Conversations I have had during the past few months indicate that the Holy Spirit has been speaking to prominent Christian business people about organizing overt prayer ministries in their businesses, starting by adding a prayer manager (or whatever other title) to the payroll. I regard this as one of the most significant new developments in the kingdom of God.

Having said this, it becomes obvious that prayer ministries in secular businesses will have to operate under different sets of rules than will the prayer ministries in local churches. The rule books for this have not been written, but look for them in the near future. If this is something the Holy Spirit is truly saying to the churches, as I believe it is, God will show us the ways and means of moving forward.

Spiritual Protection for the Leader

If the aforementioned is in place and operative, it is not enough. I want to end this chapter with what, in many cases, might turn out to be the most important advice for leaders. Christian leaders need the spiritual protection that comes through specific, intentional prayer for them as individuals.

Nothing threatens the devil more than effective prayer. Keep in mind that he is not greatly disturbed by much of the pabulum, rhetoric praying that characterizes many Christians and many churches. As soon as aggressive Christian leaders move into action prayer, however, teaching and modeling the rules of prayer and installing intense, systematic prayer ministries in their churches and other organizations, the world of darkness takes serious note. Satanic attacks of all kinds that may not have been noticed at all in the past may begin in earnest. Demonic forces may issue what amounts to a declaration of war!

How do Christian leaders rise to meet such a formidable challenge?

Some might think it is up to the leader to pray longer, harder and more powerfully to avoid Satan's attacks. This is not a bad idea, and I strongly recommend that Christian leaders improve their personal prayer lives. Experience, however, has shown that if we leave it at that, the chances of success are not as high as we might hope. Few pastors or other Christian leaders are able personally to provide all the prayer that they, their churches, their ministries or their organizations need to survive high-level satanic attacks.

Furthermore, this does not seem to be God's design. All Christians, including Christian leaders, are members of the Body of Christ. The Scriptures teach that the Church functions like a human body; many different parts carry out their specialty for the benefit of all the other body parts. The function or specialty of each believer is determined by the spiritual gifts received from the Holy Spirit. Of all the spiritual gifts (my list includes twenty-seven of them), the one most valuable for providing spiritual protection for Christian leaders is the gift of intercession.

The Prayers of Intercessors

Intercessors, by definition, stand in the gap between God and the human being for whom they are praying. The prayers of intercessors never substitute for the personal prayer life of Christian leaders, but they very definitely supplement them, in many cases to a surprisingly large extent.

A graphic biblical example of this is the story in Exodus 17 of Joshua fighting and winning the battle of Rephidim, defeating the forces of Amalek. While Joshua was fighting, Moses was on the mountain overlooking the battlefield and interceding before God with the help of Aaron and Hur. When Moses' arms were up, Joshua was winning; when they were down, Joshua was losing. The whole point of the story is that this physical battle was really won by intercessory prayer in the invisible world. Was it the prayer of Joshua, who eventually got credit for the victory? In all probability, Joshua was not doing much praying at all. No, it was the prayer of Moses, the intercessor, that brought down the power of God into the visible world.

Joshua reminds me of many pastors and other Christian leaders today. They are out on the front lines fulfilling whatever assignments they may have received from God. Their ministries are often every bit as strenuous as Joshua's battle must have been, and they realize they need prayer. Most Christian leaders I know will admit, in their honest moments, though, that their personal prayer lives are probably not enough in themselves to carry them to victory. They need help, and that help has been made available by God.

A Team of Prayer Partners

The best advice I can give to Christian leaders is that they do whatever is necessary to build a team of personal prayer partners, the more powerful the better. These are individuals, some with the spiritual gift of intercession and others just good, committed Christian pray-ers, who have sensed a special assignment from God to dedicate a significant part of their regular prayer time to a certain leader. The full details of how such intercessors can be recognized, recruited and nurtured are provided in my book *Prayer Shield*. I have said many times that of the dozens of books I have written for pastors, *Prayer Shield* is undoubtedly the most important.

How important can personal intercessors be? I mentioned earlier how one saved my physical life through prayer. I believe the same thing was true of the apostle Peter when King Herod put him on his hit list and tried to execute him (see Acts 12). Herod actually succeeded in executing James, but Peter seemed to have special protection. From where did that protection come? Acts 12:5 says, "Peter was therefore kept in prison, but constant prayer was offered to God for him by the church." The prayer took place in the home of Mary, the mother of Mark, whom, I would surmise, was Peter's personal intercessor.

The apostle Paul also had personal intercessors, named Euodia and Syntyche, members of the church in Philippi. He fondly refers to them by name in his letter to the Philippians, mentioning that they "labored with me in the gospel" (Phil. 4:3). A more probable translation of the original Greek would be that they "did spiritual warfare on my behalf," just what faithful personal intercessors constantly do for the leaders they are called to pray for today.

My wife, Doris, and I have about two hundred prayer partners who intercede for us regularly. Twenty-two of them are in a separate category, not because they are more spiritual or more holy than the others, but because we have mutually recognized that God has given them a very special anointing for high-level prayer on behalf of us and our ministry. We keep in touch with all of them through a regular prayer partners letter, but the twenty-two have more access to us, they are better informed and they are privy to a considerable amount of confidential material we believe needs extraordinary prayer. We feel well protected, although we have clear evidence that Satan has elevated us higher on his hit list than most. Needless to say, these intercessors are among the most important people in our lives.

GREAT LEADERS PRAY!

You can be a leader who draws on the power of God through prayer. Whether you lead a church, a parachurch ministry or a secular organization, you can begin to see the power of God blessing your people as never before. If you are serious about it, you will work on your own prayer life, you will stimulate effective prayer in the lives of your followers, you will generate serious prayer for your organization and you will recruit a team of personal prayer partners who will serve as your "prayer shield."

References

Evangelistic Association of New England, "Ten Characteristics of a Healthy Church," (Lexington, Mass., 1995).

Richard Foster, *Celebration of Discipline* (San Francisco: HarperSanFrancisco, 1988).
———— *Prayer* (San Francisco: HarperSanFrancisco, 1991).

Kirk Hadaway, *Church Growth Principles* (Nashville: Broadman Press, 1988).

Jack Hayford, *Prayer Is Invading the Impossible* (New York: Ballantine Books, 1983).

Terry Teykl, *Pray and Grow* (Nashville: Discipleship Resources, United Methodist Church, 1988).

John Vaughan, *Megachurches and America's Cities* (Grand Rapids: Baker Books, 1988).

C. Peter Wagner, *Prayer Shield* (Ventura, Calif.: Regal Books, 1990).
———— *Leading Your Church to Growth* (Ventura, Calif.: Regal Books, 1986).

FIFTEEN

TRANSITION IN
LEADERSHIP

WALLACE ERICKSON

Early in my youth, I began forming important concepts about responsible leadership. My boyhood days were totally absorbed by the Boy Scout movement. I spent every summer in camp and outdoor activities from age eight through my early twenties. From the time I was thirteen years old, I served in staff positions in the woods or on the waterfront. Not only did I progress through the ranks to the highest position possible in Scouting, but for several years I also served on national camp staffs, leading and training other boys.

My early adult training and ministry were directed toward the pastorate, where I served four congregations in three states during a fifteen-year period. Feeling called to minister full-time to youth, I then joined Compassion International. I lived overseas and traveled the world, serving that ministry for twenty-six years. During the last eighteen years, I fulfilled the role of president and CEO.

At every age, each time my life changed direction, I felt either the joys of accepting the gavel or the emptiness of passing it to another. In each transition, I experienced the challenge of a new adventure or the loss of a goal.

THE IMPORTANCE OF SUCCESSION

Have you ever witnessed the changing of the guard at Buckingham Palace or the passing of the baton during the Olympic relays? If so, then you have seen succession in action. You have also realized that the skill and timing involved in passing on that baton can make the difference between winning or losing the race.

The events of history and observations in my lifetime reveal that transition in leadership can easily be the most traumatic event in any organization's history. Succession in leadership makes a tremendous impact on any ministry. It dramatically affects the leader, his executive team, staff and board; the constituency, donors and outside publics.

In every succession, the organization's credibility, momentum, vision and values are at risk. A poor transition can drain corporate energy and resources for years to come. Every ministry, regardless of its size or purpose, must carefully plan and execute the transition of leadership. Without a smooth succession, lasting success cannot be achieved.

Some of the world's leaders experienced great success, but because they failed miserably at succession, their life accomplishments collapsed shortly after their departure. It is true that "succession" follows "success" in the dictionary; however, it rarely follows in real life. Hundreds of books have been written about the subject of success; almost none about succession.

At a convention of the National Association of Evangelicals, Ted Engstrom told an assembly of pastors and CEOs that "one of the most important legacies a leader can give or leave the institution is a smooth transition in leadership where the organizational alliance can be quickly and readily given to the new leader."[1]

THREE MAJOR PLAYERS IN SUCCESSION

In this chapter I hope to help you, as a leader, to identify, prepare and install your successor. Whether you are involved in a nonprofit organization, a parachurch ministry, a denomination or local church, you can have some input into this important event. I realize that, according to the church polity of some denominations, restrictions may prevent input by the incumbent pastor or executive. Procedures that are chiseled in stone are out of his control. Whether he has little or great opportunity, he must be a participant. No other activity guarantees the perpetuation of the ministry after the incumbent is gone as much as a well-planned and carefully executed transition.

In any kind of leadership transition, the three key players are: the incumbent, the board and the successor. For the transition to be smooth, efficient and successful, each player has a major role to play. In each of these areas there is a mind-set to develop, decisions to make, tasks to perform and hindrances to overcome. If each of the three players is successful, they can celebrate.

THE ROLE OF THE INCUMBENT

The transition from leader to former leader is not a passive event for the incumbent. In most cases, the incumbent has an opportunity to demonstrate his leadership abilities by playing a major role in the development process. The nature of that role will vary from organization to organization, but in a healthy situation the incumbent helps to map out the transition.

Attitude

In his book *Passing the Baton,* Richard Vansal of the Harvard Business School said, "The process of managing the succession to the corner office, of handing over the baton of power, is one that begins soon after the CEO is named."[2]

I agree that preparation should begin the day the CEO steps into his office. One of his top priorities is to begin thinking about succession. However, that is a message new leaders do not want to hear. They respond, "I've just arrived. I've spent years preparing for this promotion. Why should I think about leaving?" The best reason is that "any leadership position is transitory and likely to be short-lived."[3]

Mentally, each executive must prepare himself for this event. It is not necessary to become preoccupied with the subject. The leader can let it simmer on the back burner, stirring it periodically during his term of service. The human tendency is to procrastinate, putting off those things that seem a long way off. Often we do not approach an issue because we believe we have plenty of time. Time, however, does not wait for us to accomplish our goals. The reality is that time is as relentless as the ocean tide. It just keeps moving on. Tomorrow comes sooner than we expected, and along with tomorrow comes change.

Change is inevitable. Too often I have watched change catch leaders by surprise and they are totally unprepared. Everyone has a choice: Plan today and help direct change, or procrastinate and become its victim. The title of a recent management book offers good advice for the CEO: *Control Your Destiny or Someone Else Will*.[4]

When it comes to transition, some leaders face change, embrace it and make it their own. Others fight the process, and as a result are forced out, usually destroying relationships and tarnishing the ministry's good name.

I went through a transition once that left me with a sense of failure. It was such a devastating experience I made up my mind that my calling was from God, not from man. Therefore, I would always allow Him to interpret ministry for me; I would seek His approval rather than the approval of people. I determined that I would survey my gifts and identify possible avenues of option for ministry so that any time I faced difficult problems or the feeling of being trapped, I could say to myself, "I don't have to do this. I have the gifts to do many things well."

This mental exercise was a reassuring experience, relieving me of that trapped feeling. I did have other options. Then I could face the current problem with confidence, and I never had to feel that my self-worth was tied to the job. Someday that job would end, but I knew I could always do something else and do it well. I believe that kind of mind-set is important as leaders plan for and face the future.

Spiritual Commitment

God has a time line drawn out for each one of His children. Not only does God have a purpose and plan for each of us, but He also has one for the ministry where each serves. If a CEO can acknowledge that "this ministry is His, not mine; it belongs to God, not me," he will be able to surrender to God's timing and plan.

One reason David was such an effective general and king was that he was aware of God's leading. He constantly asked God for direction and then obeyed. Later in his reign when God told him he would not build the Temple, David surrendered to God's plan and turned over the project to his successor.

Like David, we, too, are mortal. We do not know how much time we have left to serve in our present positions. God is sovereign and His timing is always at play. We have all watched the career path of a friend change direction. We have seen the health of others deteriorate or their lives cut short.

When we make our plans for tomorrow, we must remember the admonition in James 4:15 (NIV). "You ought to say, 'If it is the Lord's will, we will live and do this or that.'" We have no guarantee that we will have many tomorrows, so we need to surrender to God's will, trusting in His wisdom and following His direction.

Financial Preparation

Everybody needs to have a personal financial plan and make steady progress for the day when it becomes necessary to move on. Ideally, it would be great if a person had plenty of lead time. I have seen too many pastors who reached retirement age having accumulated very little financial stability. Too often I have heard executives say, "I can't retire. I can't afford it."

A wise person will start early to lay aside resources so when change comes, he will be prepared. An oak tree was once an acorn, but with time it grew into a tall impressive tree. Money is like that oak tree: with time, little can become much. A mind-set of long-term preparation is critical to successful financial planning.

Procrastination can be destructive in this area of our lives. An old Chinese proverb says: If we don't change direction soon, we will likely end up where we are headed.

Knowing When to Step Down

"Executive successions are rarely easy, especially today when so many of our leaders have become heroes, often unwilling to surrender control of a firm to which they have dedicated their lives."[5] This is particularly true when the succession leads to retirement. Retirement is ranked tenth in the list of the most stressful events in life—close behind being fired, which is eighth.[6]

Knowing these statistics makes it easy to understand the polls by Louis Harris and Associates indicating that 50 percent would happily work beyond age 65, and 46 percent of retired CEOs wish they were still working full- or part-time.[7]

Otto Rank described the fears that beset many high corporate officers as "leaving office means a loss of heroic stature, a plunge into the abyss of insignificance, a kind of mortality."[8]

During the eighteen years I served as president of Compassion International, I became aware of many founding directors or aging CEOs who stayed too long in their positions, making it mandatory for them to be forcibly extracted. These leaders may have had good intentions, but they did not recognize when it was time to leave.

Some CEOs labor with the mind-set that their work is not yet done. They measure their success in life by their own career accomplishments. History has shown us, however, that many outstanding accomplishments were started by a talented individual whose life or career ended before all his goals and visions became reality. That person's successor then accepted the responsibility to fulfill that vision and complete the unfinished task. One of the best tests of leadership is the willingness to pass the baton to a successor and let him carry it across the finish line.

How can a leader know when to pass the baton? I do not believe any single condition or activity should prompt this. The answer lies in a combination of understanding God's plan for his life and the ministry he is now serving, of accurately assessing his own gifts against the current realistic needs of this ministry and of evaluating the level of satisfaction and support he is receiving from the board and staff.

Before the privilege of leading slips away, it is critical for the board of directors to give realistic, candid feedback to the CEO. An annual assessment needs to be made against well-defined performance criteria that the board and CEO have previously agreed upon. There should be no surprises to the CEO or the directors if they have been adequately communicating and working as a team.

Several signals should trigger a need for an honest and extensive self-evaluation. Periodically, a CEO should ask himself the following questions:

1. Is there a concern that the blessing of God no longer rests upon your work or on the ministry?
2. Are you losing the approval and appreciation of the board of directors?
3. Are you losing the support and cooperation of your staff?
4. Do you feel that the organization has grown beyond your unique abilities or experiences? Do you feel like a misfit—no longer the right person for the job?
5. Have you run out of enthusiasm and energy? Are the daily demands draining you physically and emotionally?
6. In your own heart, do you feel that God is closing the door on this chapter of your life?

If the leader recognizes that his position exists
for the ministry's benefit, not his,
If he can express thanks to others and give glory
to God for all achievements,
If he can communicate openly and effectively
with his board and staff,
If he can honestly evaluate his own strengths
and weaknesses,
If he willingly chooses his own departure date,
then he can preserve his heroic image
and his leaving will be a day of celebration,
not a day of tragic loss.

Attracting Quality Staff

One of the greatest challenges facing leaders is to replace themselves, and train others to become leaders. "An organization that is not capable of perpetuating itself has failed. An organization, therefore, has to provide today the men who can run it tomorrow."[9]

The success of an organization depends on its ability to attract and hold the right kind of people. Drucker advises the CEO to ask himself four questions:

1. Are we attracting people we are willing to entrust this organization to?
2. Are we developing them so that they are going to be better than we are?
3. Are we holding them, inspiring them, and recognizing them?
4. Are we building for tomorrow as we make our people decisions today?[10]

In my search for quality people, I had a standing order with Human Resources during my last fifteen years as CEO of Compassion International: Always fill each vacancy with people better qualified (experience, academic training, spiritual maturity) than those we had before. Each vacancy gave us the opportunity of stepping up in quality. To maintain momentum and experience growth, an organization must steadily upgrade its human resources.

The natural tendency is to shy away from hiring people who are better equipped than oneself. Yes, able people are aggressive and ambitious. The wise leader, however, will recognize that it is better to have strong, effective, challenging people around him than to risk being served by mediocrity.

"There is no prouder boast, but also no better prescription, for executive effectiveness than the words Andrew Carnegie, the father of the US Steel Industry, chose for his own tombstone: 'Here lies a man who knew how to bring into his service men better than he was himself.'"[11]

Developing Potential Leaders

A good CEO gathers a complement of men and women around him—people who have different sets of gifts. This is critical in developing future leaders.

As a young man I was a director of Boy Scout camps and church camps, and I learned then that former campers make the best camp staff. From an early adult age, I believed in growing my own staff. If and when a leader finds good people who have unusual natural gifts and are receptive and excited about the vision of the ministry, he should invest time, energy and money to develop them in every conceivable way he can.

When "leaders enable followers to develop their own initiative, they are creating something that can survive their own departure. Some individuals who have dazzling powers of personal leadership not only fail to build institutional strength, but create dependency in those below them. However spectacular their personal performance, they leave behind a weakened organization staffed by weakened people. In contrast, leaders who strengthen their people and have a gift for institution building may create a legacy that will last for a long time."[12]

The CEO who gives of his time and self to develop people will receive a double blessing: (1) growth and effectiveness in the organization as a whole and, (2) a larger pool of quality managers and executives from which to select his future leaders and a possible successor.

Orientation of the Successor

Let's assume for a moment that the choice of the successor has been made and the incumbent is still in office. Now, the incumbent has responsibility for the orientation and possible training of the future CEO. This period of time could last for weeks, months, or even several years, depending on the specific plan of transition the board and the incumbent have agreed upon.

I am aware of some plans that amounted to no more than an introduction to the staff and a tour through the office. That style assumes the transfer of leadership is an easy task. In other cases, the board thought it was wise to have trial periods of leadership and extended orientation.

In the transition I recently completed, the board chose a three-year time frame, transferring heavier responsibility each year to the appointed successor—Dr. Wess Stafford—who had already been with Compassion for fourteen years. Early in our association, Dr. Stafford was involved in a doctoral program for three years. He had served with Compassion for four years in Haiti, two years in the program division, two years as assistant to the president, and the last five years as the director of development.

Three years prior to my intended retirement, the board made our plan public, announcing that Dr. Stafford was the current candidate. He was promoted to the position of vice president. In addition to leading his own division, he was given a second division to lead and manage. During the second year, a third division was added to his responsibility. In the third and final year of the transition, he was promoted to executive vice president and chief operating officer. At that time, he acquired all five divisions for his oversight and responsibility.

Post-Transition Involvement

I think it is important for the incumbent to disconnect from the ministry he is leaving as soon as possible. The board needs to build a relationship with the new CEO. The successor needs time to adjust to his new responsibilities. The staff and friends of the ministry need time to transfer their loyalties and confidence to their new leader. Disengagement from the past is also important for the incumbent because it is difficult to start a new phase in life if he is constantly being drawn into issues of personnel and operations or asked questions about problems and solutions.

In my seminary training, it was espoused that when a pastor moved on to a new assignment, he should be cautious about maintaining close personal friendships in the former church. Members of a congregation have difficulty establishing a new relationship if the former pastor is still vying for people's attention and time.

When a pastor moves to a different church or an executive to a new organization, he usually moves to a new community, sometimes to another state. That helps tremendously in the transition. When I retired from Compassion, I actually moved to a different state for some of the same reasons previously outlined. I now wait for my counsel or advice to be sought.

Any time in our lives, at every age, when we lose a goal or lay down a responsibility, we create a void. We must not leave that vacancy open. It must be filled with something else. This is the only way we stay connected to life and find our purpose (His purpose) for living.

Throughout my life, I have been blessed with an array of diversified interests and hobbies. I say "blessed" because there is always a new challenge waiting. I am often frustrated because there is never enough time to pursue them all. A happy transition requires that we have somewhere else to go, something new to do, or something old but neglected to challenge and excite us afresh.

On my retirement, the board elected me to a three-year term. Now I am learning a new role in relationships. I am an encourager and supporter of the new CEO and his staff.

I believe my action supports the research of Sonnenfeld. In a survey, he found that the more an executive thought and talked about retirement as an opportunity to build an identity independent of his previous leadership role, the healthier the adjustment. The respondents felt that retirement was an opportunity to enjoy time for themselves, a chance to spend quality time with family members, a long-desired escape from public exposure of their private lives, and a chance to become involved in community, recreational, academic, business, or other activities with enthusiasm and anticipation.[13]

THE ROLE OF THE BOARD

In every nonprofit entity, the governing board's first and foremost task should be to select and appoint the senior executive. One important prerequisite is developing a comprehensive transition plan.

"In most large, publicly-held companies this is a normal procedure; however nonprofits are much less likely to think systematically about this important issue."[14] It is far too prevalent today for a nonprofit board or some other authority to remove the CEO before well-defined plans are in place for the succession. When this happens, the change in leadership can be awkward and sometimes even divisive.

UNDERSTANDING THE INCUMBENT'S ATTITUDE

In a study designed to help boards understand how CEOs exit their positions, Jeffrey Sonnenfeld surveyed two hundred and fifty chief executives, officers and recently retired CEOs. From those interviews he discovered four distinct styles of exiting behavior: monarchs, generals, ambassadors and governors. (These terms do not refer to their management styles.)[15]

I have gleaned information from Sonnenfeld's book about these four styles and have prepared the following chart (see next page). Having this information, the board can identify its incumbent and make better plans for its role in the succession process. For a deeper understanding of these personalities, you may want to read Sonnenfeld's book *The Hero's Farewell*.[16]

ESTABLISHING CRITERIA

Choosing the successor is the single most important decision the board will ever have to make. Drucker states: "The most critical people decision, and the one that is hardest to undo, is the succession to the top. It is the most difficult because every such decision is a real gamble."[17] Therefore, it deserves thoughtful attention, wisdom and prayer.

The board should not start a search, though, until it has reviewed its mission and the reason for the existence of the nonprofit organization. In his book *First Things First*, Stephen Covey suggests an unusual exercise. We should ask ourselves, "Do you know what 'true north' is for this organization?"[18]

The board will also want to answer the following questions: What challenges are we going to face during the next few years? Where do we want the organization to go? What kind of leader do we need?

From the answers to these questions, the board now formulates a job description and profile for the CEO. The profile list will contain two divisions. First, the "must-haves" or nonnegotiable qualities; these are characteristics the ministry cannot do without. Next are the ideal qualities, which are characteristics the board would like the new leader to have, but are qualities on which they would be willing to compromise. The must-have list can be fairly short, but the second list should be longer and needs to be prioritized.

How Heroes Exit the Organization

Monarchs 12% of those surveyed	Generals 21%	Ambassadors 38%	Governors 29%
Deeply attached to executive position	Love heroic stature of executive position	Identity not tied to executive position	Little attachment to executive position
Long term in role	Short term in role	Long term in role	Short term in role
Resist succession "I'm not done yet"	Reluctantly accept succession "I'm the best"	Enjoy succession process Content with accomplishments	Accept succession Move on to new challenges
Choose weak successors Undermine the successor	Choose strong successors "I'm even better"	Mentor strong successors Commit to their success	Unconcerned with successor "I'm out of here"
Leave bitter and hurt Feel he was forced out	Plot and fight to return to power Leaves the office in pain	Provide continuity and counsel Believe ministry can succeed without them	Break all ties Move on

Responsibilities of the Board

Press for realistic succession plan	Insist on leadership depth on team	Clearly define his responsibility and terms on the Board	Encourage to remain in contact for brief Board term
Oversee the time frame, candidates, development process	Keep Board and successor involved in succession plan	Break old patterns with former staff and successor	Support for successor comes from the Board

INVOLVING THE INCUMBENT

Ideally, the incumbent who has the ministry at heart should be brought into the process at this point. His consultation could be valuable and can help make a smooth transition. I said "ideally," because I realize a variety of circumstances and church polities may not make that possible. The current leader may have resigned, been relieved, developed a major health problem or even died. Or the current incumbent may not be willing to participate because of psychological or personality barriers. Another hindrance is that many churches having an Episcopal government do not allow for incumbent input.

An incumbent should always be concerned about succession and should work closely with the board in addressing that issue. Who knows better than the CEO the strengths and weaknesses of the organization, or the qualities and capabilities of those who worked directly under him? Wise directors will welcome and listen carefully to the opinions of the retiring CEO.

CREATING A MASTER PLAN

"Without a clear master plan, everyone has the feeling of being part of the same band, but playing different music...or running a race without a finish line."[19] The master plan outlines the progressive steps and targets the time frames. It will take thoughtful planning and discipline.

In the Old Testament, we find an example of a successful transition from Moses to Joshua.

1. **Pray**
   Moses said to the Lord, "May the Lord, the God of the spirits of all mankind, appoint a man over this community to go out and come in before them, one who will lead them out and bring them in, so the Lord's people will not be like sheep without a shepherd"(Num. 27:15-17, *NIV*).

2. **Select**
   So the Lord said to Moses, "Take Joshua son of Nun, a man in whom is the spirit, and lay your hand on him" (v. 18, *NIV*).

3.   **Develop**

Give him some of your authority so the whole Israelite community will obey him. He is to stand before Eleazar the priest, who will obtain decisions for him by inquiring of the Urim before the Lord. At his command he and the entire community of the Israelites will go out, and at his command they will come in (vv. 20,21, *NIV*).

4.   **Support**

But commission Joshua, and encourage and strengthen him, for he will lead this people across and will cause them to inherit the land that you will see (Deut. 3:28, *NIV*).

5.   **Commission**

Moses did as the Lord commanded him. He took Joshua and had him stand before Eleazar the priest and the whole assembly. Then he laid his hands on him and commissioned him, as the Lord instructed through Moses (Num. 27:22,23, *NIV*).

SELECTING THE SUCCESSOR

Some boards appoint a search committee and define definite guidelines and instructions. If the incumbent could serve on this committee, it might prove helpful. He could provide advice and counsel about in-house executives as well as be a part of the interview team for potential outside candidates.

In churches and denominations, a nominating committee plays an important role. Without quality work from an efficient nominating committee, the voting process turns out to be a popularity contest or a vote by acclamation, rather than judging the candidates on the basis of proven skills and effective leadership.

Although the committee may carry on the preliminary interviews, sort candidates and make recommendations, it is the responsibility of the entire board to make the final decision in choosing the new CEO.

In their book *Increasing Your Boardroom Confidence*, Bobb Biehl and Ted Engstrom have written a chapter entitled "Selecting the Right Senior Executive." They chart the activities and give detailed lists of the step-by-step process.[20]

The entire process can become quite involved, therefore the board must allow plenty of time for deep consideration and judgment. Be patient.

"People decisions are time consuming, for the simple reason that the Lord did not create people as resources for organizations. They do not come in the proper size and shape for the task. They cannot be machined down or recast for their tasks. People are always 'almost fits' at best."[21]

An old proverb says: One cannot hire a hand; the whole man always comes with it.

The spirit of any ministry is exemplified, nurtured and perpetuated by its leaders. Central to that position is the person appointed to be the senior executive, whose actions and attitudes affirm the beliefs and positions of an organization. I thought it might be helpful to list and discuss briefly the leadership attributes I consider to be of paramount importance.

- **Christlike.** Is the candidate committed to follow the will of His heavenly Father? Is he humble and compassionate? Is he a person of prayer, mature in his walk with God, biblical in his standards for living as well as his leading? Does he have a servant attitude? Is he more excited about the opportunity to serve others and the ministry and less enamored with the title and prestige of the office?
- **Character.** The stature of a man is measured by his character—his moral excellence. The first of the twelve Scout laws is: "A Scout is trustworthy." Can this man be trusted to live up to his word, to keep his promises? What about his integrity? His reputation?

WHEN WEALTH IS LOST, NOTHING IS LOST; WHEN HEALTH IS LOST, SOMETHING IS LOST; WHEN CHARACTER IS LOST, ALL IS LOST.
ANONYMOUS

- **Competence.** Is the candidate qualified? Does he have the skills, education, training, experience, wisdom, business acumen and maturity to handle the top position in this organization?

- **Charisma.** Does he have a personal magic of leadership that will arouse special loyalty or enthusiasm? Will he be able to build and lead an effective and cohesive human organization? Do his actions and appearance command respect?
- **Communication skills.** Can he express ideas effectively in both speaking and writing? Does he possess the ability to help others see and understand as well as to excite them to action?
- **Compatibility.** Is the candidate a good fit for the position, the unique culture of this ministry or congregation, the staff and local community?
- **Coachable.** Does this person have a desire to learn and grow? Is he teachable? Is he receptive to constructive criticism?
- **Commitment.** Will he give his loyalty to this organization? Could this ministry become his passion and calling? Will he ride out the stormy weather? Are his wife and children committed to support and encourage him?

Celebrating

A smooth succession includes a gracious exit for the incumbent and a wise takeover by the new leader. Too often we admire the rise and ignore the exit, but both are important.

The board will want to plan a time when the organization celebrates the passing of the old and the starting of the new. Take time to praise and honor the incumbent and to welcome and introduce the successor.

The celebration is the backward look of honor and the forward look of expectancy.

The Role of the Successor

Transition is a bridge that must be built by both the incumbent and the successor. That involves some things each needs to do separately and some things they do together.

Like Paul and Timothy, Dr. Stafford and I traveled, prayed and planned together, learning from each other during the three-year transition period. We shared openly and candidly the troubles and triumphs, the burdens and blessings of the executive office. We discussed what our relationship should be and agreed on seven important issues.

- **Prayer.** We would earnestly pray together, seeking God's leadership and blessing.
- **Honesty.** We would be totally honest in our communication with each other and yet compassionate in our relationship.
- **United front.** We would never confront each other about disagreements in public or in front of the executive staff. We would work those out in the privacy of the president's office
- **Decisions.** I would never reverse any of his decisions. I wanted him to build confidence in his own wisdom and ability. We would discuss and critique his decisions afterward, but I would always support them.
- **Timing.** If he wanted to make changes in personnel, structure, policy or procedures, we would do that on my watch. I would help guide those changes through before he took office.
- **Board relations.** He would regularly attend all board functions and report on his area of responsibility. This would give my successor intimate exposure to the board personalities and to its functions. It would also give the board exposure to his performance and spirit.
- **Authority.** He always understood that the board was his employer and that it was the board who would make the final decision if he should be elected president.

During our transition period, we tried to follow the example of John the Baptist when he said, "He must become greater; I must become less" (John 3:30, NIV). We allowed Dr. Stafford to increase in visibility, responsibility and authority.

The incumbent and the successor must work together to make the transition as comfortable as possible and see that loyalty is shifted. Be prepared, for a certain amount of tension seems to be unavoidable. Staff members have a concern; they want to know how this change is going to affect them. All the people involved need time to untangle their old loyalties and relationships with the era that is ending. To some, the transition is like a death; to others it may be a rebirth.

The staff need to see and feel unity and enthusiasm in the transition. Even the donors and the public need to sense that all is well within the walls of the organization. I do not believe a transition such as this can be successful unless the incumbent endorses the candidate and the process 110 percent. When he does, stepping out is right for the incumbent and stepping in is a win for the successor.

AFTER PASSING THE BATON

In the two years that have elapsed since my retirement, I have observed appropriate attitudes and conduct on the part of my successor that I would like to share, because I believe these elements contributed greatly to a harmonious transition.

- **Preserving the dignity of the predecessor** by speaking well of his record and accomplishments. Do not interpret past decisions in the light of today's needs and resources.
- **Being sensitive to the transition needs of the executive team.** Everyone feels vulnerable even under familiar leadership. When a new leader takes responsibility, their roles and responsibilities are uncertain. The staff need to know what is expected of them.
- **Building a relationship with the board.** Instead of depending on the predecessor for guidance, seek the counsel of the board.
- **Determining to keep the values and vision** that have historically built the ministry.
- **Committing to a learning process.** Spend the first year listening to and learning from the staff at every level.
- **Communicating face-to-face with the whole organization,** sharing his personal history, values, perspectives and vision.
- **Following up on the networked relationships** of the incumbent. Value these relationships, act quickly to build on them and make them his own.

These positive actions helped make the succession process a win for him, the board and the predecessor.

MAKING SUCCESSION
A WIN-WIN EXPERIENCE

This is a game in which every player has to win, but no one wins unless everyone is committed to helping the team win. Everyone benefits by a successful transition: the incumbent, the board, the successor, the ministry and the Kingdom.

Looking back on my personal experience with the succession process, I am glad I took adequate time to make plans—plans that affected my own personal life, and plans that affected the corporate life of Compassion International. I am happy with the role the board played in the plan. I am ecstatic that my successor was committed to the plan and always manifested an attitude of respect, cooperation and love toward me so that our succession process turned out to be textbook quality.

I am reminded of the Scripture that says, "Many are the plans in a man's heart, but it is the Lord's purpose that prevails" (Prov. 19:21, NIV). To God be the glory.

Notes
1. Ted Engstrom, *Succession, Challenges, and Concerns* (Tape from National Association Evangelical National Conference, 1988).
2. Richard Vansal, *Passing the Baton* (Quote from Lorne Sanny's tape "A Planned Transition," National Association of Evangelicals National Conference, 1988).
3. Peter F. Drucker, *Managing for Results* (London: Pan Books LTD, 1967), p. 20.
4. Noel M. Ticky and Stratford Sherman, *Control Your Destiny or Someone Else Will* (New York: Harper Business, 1994).
5. Jeffrey Sonnenfeld, *The Hero's Farewell, What happens When CEOs Retire* (New York: Oxford University Press, Inc., 1988), jacket.
6. Ibid., p. 11.
7. Ibid., p. 10.
8. Otto Rank, (Quote from Sonnenfeld's book, *The Hero's Farewell*), p. 3.
9. Peter F. Drucker, *The Effective Executive* (New York: HarperCollins, 1967), p. 32.
10. Peter F. Drucker, *Managing the Non-Profit Organization* (New York: Harper Business, 1992), p. 155.
11. Drucker, *The Effective Executive*, p. 73.
12. John Gardner, (Quoted by Ted Engstrom on his N.A.E. tape).
13. Sonnenfeld, *The Hero's Farewell*, p. 68.

14. William G. Bowen, *Inside the Boardroom* (New York: John Wiley & Sons, Inc., 1994), pp. 106-107.
15. Sonnenfeld, *The Hero's Farewell*, pp. 70-71.
16. Ibid., pp. 80-216.
17. Drucker, *Managing the Non-Profit Organization*, pp. 254-255.
18. Stephen Covey, and A. Roger and Rebecca R. Merrill, *First Things First* (New York: Simon & Schuster, 1996), p. 215.
19. Bobb Biehl and Ted Engstrom, *Increasing Your Boardroom Confidence* (Sisters, Oreg.: Questar Publishers, Inc., 1988), p. 179.
20. Ibid., pp. 172-177.
21. Drucker, *The Effective Executive*, p. 33.

RESOURCES FROM THE BARNA RESEARCH GROUP, LTD.

If you found this book to be useful, you may be interested in some of the other resources available from George Barna and the Barna Research Group, Ltd. A full-service marketing research company, their vision is to provide current, accurate and reliable information, in bite-sized pieces, at economical prices, to enable ministries to make strategic decisions that glorify God. Toward that end, the company conducts custom research projects for churches and parachurch ministries (as well as other organizations); conducts informational and training seminars for church leaders; and develops resources designed to inform and enable ministries to serve more strategically.

Among the resources currently available from Barna Research are the following.

Books (by George Barna):
The Index of Leading Spiritual Indicators (Word Publishing, 1996).
Turning Vision into Action (Regal Books, 1996).
Evangelism That Works (Regal Books, 1995).
Generation Next (Regal Books, 1995).
Turnaround Churches (Regal Books, 1993).
Today's Pastors (Regal Books, 1993).
The Power of Vision (Regal Books, 1992).
Baby Busters (Northfield Publishing, 1992).
A Step-by-Step Guide to Church Marketing (Regal Books, 1992).
User Friendly Churches (Regal Books, 1991).
The Frog in the Kettle (Regal Books, 1990).
Finding a Church You Can Call Home (Regal Books, 1989).

Newsletter:
The Barna Report, a bimonthly publication, published by Word Ministry Resources (1-800-933-9673 ext. 2037).

Video Seminars (featuring George Barna):
The Power of Vision (Gospel Light Videos, 1996).
Turning Vision into Action (Gospel Light Videos, 1996).
Raising Money for Your Church (Gospel Light Videos, 1996).
Understanding Today's Teens (Gospel Light Videos, 1996).
Trends That Are Changing Your Ministry World (Gospel Light Videos, 1996).
What Evangelistic Churches Do (Gospel Light Videos, 1996).
Ten Myths About Evangelism (Gospel Light Videos, 1996).
How to Turn Around Your Church (Gospel Light Videos, 1996).

Audio Presentations (by George Barna):
"Discovering God's Vision for Your Ministry"
"Pastoral Leadership Within the Church"
"Strategic Thinking for Your Ministry"
"Creating a User Friendly Church"
"Understanding Today's Teenagers"
"Effective Evangelism in a Gospel-Resistant Culture"
"How Churches Raise Money for Ministry"

Diagnostic Tools:
The User Friendly Inventory

For information about these resources, to acquire any of these materials, or to learn about other services available through the Barna Research Group, please call or contact them as follows:

Telephone: 805-658-8885
Fax: 805-658-7298
Mail: Barna Research Group, Ltd.
              5528 Everglades Street, Ventura, CA 93003

Resources for Cutting Edge Leaders

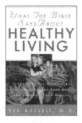

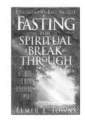

Setting Your Church Free

Neil T. Anderson and Charles Mylander

Spiritual battles can affect entire churches as well as individuals. *Setting Your Church Free* shows pastors and church leaders how they can apply the powerful principles from *Victory Over the Darkness* to lead their churches to freedom.

Hardcover • ISBN 08307.16556

What the Bible Says About Healthy Living

Rex Russell, M.D.

Learn three biblical principles that will help you improve your physical—and spiritual—health. This book gives you practical, workable steps to improve your health and overall quality of life.

Paperback • ISBN 08307.18583

The Healthy Church

C. Peter Wagner

When striving for health and growth of a church, we often overlook things that are killing us. If we can detect and counteract these diseases we can grow a healthy, Christ-directed church.

Hardcover • ISBN 08307.18346

Fasting for Spiritual Breakthrough

Elmer L. Towns

This book gives you the biblical reasons for fasting, and introduces you to nine biblical fasts—each designed for a specific physical and spiritual outcome.

Paperback • ISBN 08307.18397

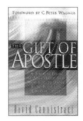

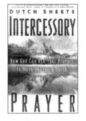

The Voice of God

Cindy Jacobs

Cut through confusion and see how prophecy can be used in any church. You'll get a clear picture of biblical prophecy and how an individual can exercise this spiritual gift to edify the church.

Paperback • ISBN 08307.17730

The Gift of Apostle

David Cannistraci

Find out why God has given the Church apostles—leaders with a clear mission to mobilize and unify the church—and see what the Bible says about the apostolic gift for today's church.

Hardcover • ISBN 08307.18451

Intercessory Prayer

Dutch Sheets

Find inspiration to reach new levels of prayer, the courage to pray for the "impossible" and the persistence to see your prayers through to completion.

"Of all the books on prayer I have read, none compares to Intercessory Prayer!" –C. Peter Wagner

Hardcover • ISBN 08307.18885

That None Should Perish

Ed Silvoso

Ed Silvoso shows that dramatic things happen when we pray for people. Learn the powerful principles of "prayer evangelism" and how to bring the gospel to your community, reaching your entire city for Christ.

Paperback • ISBN 08307.16904

Ask for these resources at your local Christian bookstore. **Regal**
A Division of Gospel Light

Continuing Education for Church Leaders

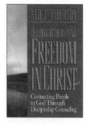

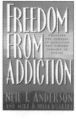

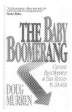

The Baby Boomerang

Doug Murren

The "Baby Boomers" are beginning to come back to the fold in large numbers. This book is a how-to resource for evangelical leaders who need solid, practical advice on reaching the boomers.

Paperback • ISBN 08307.13956

Generation Next

George Barna

George Barna provides thorough analysis and exploration into the minds of today's teens, examining their beliefs, habits and attitudes in terms of family relationships, the Church, the Bible and much more.

Hardcover • 08307.17870

Setting Your Church Free

Neil T. Anderson and Charles Mylander

Spiritual battles can affect entire churches as well as individuals. **Setting Your Church Free** shows pastors and church leaders how they can apply the powerful principles from **Victory over the Darkness** to lead their church to freedom.

Hardcover • ISBN 08307.16556

Crisis Counseling

H. Norman Wright

Crisis Counseling will give you the tools you need to provide honest, practical and biblically based assistance to anyone who is in crisis so that you won't be at a loss during the critical first 72 hours.

Hardcover • ISBN 08307.16114

Heart to Heart with Pastors' Wives

Compiled by Lynne Dugan

An excellent resource foe women married to men in Christian leadership. Here are the stories and wisdom of women who live day in and day out in public view. Readers will discover how they can support their husbands and find God's purpose for their own lives.

Hardcover • ISBN 08307.16483

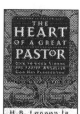

The Heart of a Great Pastor

H.B. London Jr. and Neil B. Wiseman

On these pages leaders will find inspiring wisdom and advice to help them "bloom where they are planted" and transform the ordinary circumstances of life into "holy ground".

Hardcover • ISBN 08307.16742

Bring George Barna to Your Church With the Leading Edge Video Series.

What Evangelistic Churches Do
Video • SPCN 85116.00973
Audio • SPCN 75116.00549

Trends That Are Changing Your Ministry
Video • SPCN 85116.00981
Audio • SPCN 75116.00557

With the **Leading Edge Series** you can conduct powerful video seminars, educating and mobilizing small groups, Sunday School classes and your entire congregation. Each video includes two 30–minute sessions with **reproducible** handouts, and an easy-to-follow format, making them great for retreats and weekend seminars.

10 Myths About Evangelism
Video • SPCN 85116.01007
Audio • SPCN 75116.00565

How To Turn Around Your Church
Video • SPCN 85116.01015
Audio • SPCN 75116.00530

Ask for these resources at your local Christian bookstore.

More Informative Resources from George Barna.

Church Marketing
A Step-by-Step Guide

For church leaders who want to implement the ideas from Barna's other books, here's a biblically based guide. Put successful marketing strategies into action, discover and apply God's unique vision for your ministry and maximize your effectiveness in your community.

Manual • 250p
ISBN 08307.14049

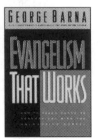

Evangelism that Works

A picture of the unsaved in the U.S. today and the methods that are reaching them. Provides leaders with practical real-life tools for the task.

Hardcover • 180p
ISBN 08307.17390

The Frog in the Kettle

If we share Christ's mission of reaching the world, we have to understand needs. This book gives a projection of the future and how we as Christians need to respond.

Trade • 235p
ISBN 08307.14278

User Friendly Churches

Discover the characteristics th today's healthiest churches h in common and learn how to develop biblical, user-friendly strategies for reaching people.

Trade • 191p
ISBN 08307.14731

Virtual America
The Barna Report
1994-95

Examines the direction our nation is heading in terms of people's beliefs, lifestyles and social habits. This all-new survey provides an insider's look into our rapidly changing society. It also helps readers understand those trends in the context of Scripture and God's plan for the world.

Hardcover • 300p
ISBN 08307.17153

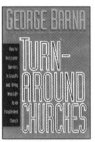

Turnaround Churches

Discover how dozens of churches have made the transition from stagnation to growth—from the pastors who took part in turning the churches around. A view of the techniques many churches are using to rekindle the flame of growth and renewal.

Paperback • 204p
ISBN 08307.16572

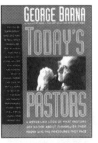

Today's Pastors

In the tradition of his best-selling book, *The Frog in the Kettle*, George Barna takes his analysis of the church one step further—this time by taking the pulse of the person at the top. Examines the way ministers feel about themselves, the work they do, their colleagues and the congregations they serve.

Hardcover • 180p
ISBN 08307.15916

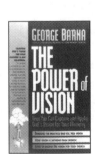

The Power of Vision

George Barna's message to thousands of church leaders v have said that they are strugg to capture God's vision for th ministries. It will help reader build a bridge between their strategies and God's ideal pla for the future. Includes Bible studies on vision for church involvement.

Paperback • 300p
ISBN 08307.16017

Regal
A Division of Gospel Light

Discover What the Bible is All About.

What the Bible Is All About™ is one of the all-time favorite Bible handbooks. This classic 4-million copy best-seller and its family of resources will help you stamp out biblical illiteracy.

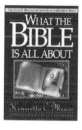

What the Bible Is All About

Henrietta C. Mears

The classic 4-million copy best-seller takes the reader on a personal journey through the entire Bible, covering the basics in a simple, understandable way.

Hardcover • ISBN 08307.16084
Paperback • ISBN 08307.16076

What the Bible Is All About Quick-Reference Edition

This easy-to-use Bible handbook gives a brief overview of the people, events and meaning of every book of the Bible. Includes over 1,000 illustrations, charts and time lines.

Hardcover • ISBN 08307.13905
Paperback • ISBN 08307.18486

What the Bible Is All About Group Study Guide

Wes Haystead

A teaching companion for the best-selling classic. In 5 to 10 weeks you will give your students an overview of the Bible with concrete illustrations and clear commentary. Includes reproducible study sheets.

Group Study Guide • ISBN 08307.16009

What the Bible Is All About for Young Explorers

Frances Blankenbaker

The basics of What the Bible Is All About in a graphic visual format designed to make the Bible more approachable for youth.

Hardcover • ISBN 08307.11791
Paperback • ISBN 08307.11627

What the Bible Is All About Video Seminar

Elmer L. Towns

Here, in just three hours, Dr. Elmer Towns presents an outline of God's plan for the ages. He shows how this plan is established on six key "turning points" in history. Armed with a clear understanding of these foundation points, students can turn to the Bible with a deeper understanding of its content.

Video Seminar • SPCN 85116.00906 (Package includes book, reproducible syllabus and 2 video-tapes.)
Audio tapes • UPC 607135000815

Gospel Light

These resources are available at your local Christian bookstore.

What the Bible Is All About 101 Group Study Guide Old Testament: Genesis–Esther

Henrietta Mears

Here's a 13-session study that takes your class through some of the most important–and yet least-understood–books of the Bible. Students will also get a clear picture of Jesus as He is revealed throughout the Old Testament.

Manual • ISBN 08307.17951

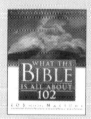

What the Bible Is All About 102 Group Study Guide Old Testament: Job––Malachi

Henrietta Mears

Introduce your students to the poetry and prophecy of the Old Testament–and what it teaches us about God's plan for all time–fulfilled in Jesus Christ.

Manual • ISBN 08307.17978

What the Bible Is All About 201 Group Study Guide New Testament: Matthew–Philippians

Henrietta Mears

Here are the foundational parts of the New Testament from the birth of Christ to Paul's letter to the Philippian church–encouraging students in their walk and challenging them in their faith.

Manual • ISBN 08307.17986

What the Bible Is All About 202 Group Study Guide New Testament: Colossians–Revelation

Henrietta Mears

As you take your class through the last 16 books of the Bible they'll see how all of the Scriptures are woven together by God into a beautiful tapestry that tells about His plan for all time.

Manual • ISBN 08307.17994

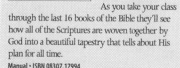